"A number of criticisms of Christianity loom large in our day, hindering many people from participating in the Good News. Paul Copan offers a powerful, wonderfully lucid antidote. He manifests the conceptual skills of a fine philosopher and theologian as well as the heart of a sincere Christian. This combination is potent indeed, illuminating a wide range of pressing issues about the Christian faith. Attentive readers will benefit immensely from Copan's outstanding work."

—PAUL MOSER, PROFESSOR AND CHAIR OF PHILOSOPHY
AT LOYOLA UNIVERSITY OF CHICAGO

"*'That's Just Your Interpretation'* has something for everyone. The topics are wide ranging, important, and relevant; the presentation is powerful and clear; and the conversational style is engaging. The book is accessible to non-specialists, yet Copan clearly brings to each subject careful research and scholarly reflection, and the notes provide a rich resource for graduate students and professors. The chapter summaries are worth the price of the book. The book is a must-read for those in campus ministry, and I cannot think of another book that covers so many topics while maintaining a high degree of quality."

—J. P. MORELAND, PROFESSOR OF PHILOSOPHY,
TALBOT SCHOOL OF THEOLOGY, BIOLA UNIVERSITY

"Paul Copan is a reliable, engaging, philosophically astute critic of contemporary philosophy and theology. He writes with clarity, force, and insight about the credibility of Christianity. He is as at home with challenging popular cultural misperceptions and critiques of Christianity as he is with addressing some of the most sophisticated and subtle scholarly debates."

—CHARLES TALIAFERRO, PROFESSOR OF PHILOSOPHY,
ST. OLAF COLLEGE

"Beneath the clichés of our culture lie some unsettling questions about God. Paul Copan, with genius and simplicity, uncovers the struggle and constructs his answers on a firm foundation."

—RAVI ZACHARIAS, AUTHOR AND SPEAKER

Paul Copan holds graduate degrees from Trinity Evangelical Divinity School (M.A. and M.Div.) and Marquette University (Ph.D.). He is on staff with Ravi Zacharias International Ministries and is visiting associate professor at Trinity International University. His books include *"True for You, but Not for Me"* and *Will the Real Jesus Please Stand Up?*

"THAT'S JUST

YOUR

INTERPRETATION"

RESPONDING TO SKEPTICS
WHO CHALLENGE YOUR FAITH

PAUL COPAN

Baker Books
A Division of Baker Book House Co
Grand Rapids, Michigan 49516

Published by Baker Books
a division of Baker Book House Company
P.O. Box 6287, Grand Rapids, MI 49516-6287

Third printing, August 2003

Printed in the United States of America

Library of Congress Cataloging-in-Publication Data

Copan, Paul.
   "That's just your interpretation" : responding to skeptics who challenge your faith / Paul Copan.
       p.   cm.
   Includes bibliographical references.
   ISBN 0-8010-6383-3 (pbk.)
   1. Apologetics. 2. Skepticism. I. Title.
BT1212.C67 2001
239—dc21   2001037381

For current information about all releases from Baker Book House, visit our web site:
http://www.bakerbooks.com

To
Jacqueline,
my excellent wife and sign of the Lord's favor,
and our five children—Johanna, Peter, Valerie,
Erica, and Jonathan:
May you prove yourselves to be blameless and innocent,
children of God above reproach, shining as lights in the world.

CONTENTS

CONTENTS

INTRODUCTION

When my earlier book *"True for You, but Not for Me"* was published,[1] I was gratified to hear that it had met an important need of, among others, high school and university students (and their parents) who were regularly bombarded with relativistic and pluralistic challenges: "Who are *you* to impose your morality on others?" or, "It doesn't matter what you believe as long as you're sincere." As far as I could see, there were plenty of analyses of relativism and its harmful effects on society, but there was no step-by-step guide that unpacked and responded to specific criticisms that might dumbfound Christians. Since then, other books have come along to offer similar practical assistance, although varied in approach.[2]

Whether at work, in the university, around the neighborhood, or at a party, believers are confronted with one-liners or criticisms attacking truth, morality, or belief in God. My previous book was intended to be a kind of handbook for this general Christian audience with short, easy-to-read chapters centered around commonly heard challenges. In that book, I tried to get behind the criticisms to discern their underlying assumptions. This follow-up volume is similar in format and offers responses to a new—and wide-ranging—set of commonly heard challenges by skeptics and critics of belief in God and Christianity in particular. It is my hope and prayer that this book will be an accessible tool to help Christians deal with these criticisms in the context of caring relationships—although I trust the serious-minded non-Christian will also read this book with profit.

This introduction serves as both (1) an introduction to the themes in this book as well as (2) a response to the question of whether we can even *find* truth. But here we must be careful: "Finding truth" is not just about getting a hold on "facts out there." Getting to the truth—and especially truth about God—is an internal and deeply personal matter. God—that "Hound of

Heaven"—seeks us lovingly and sufferingly that we might become his children. But such a God doesn't let us get off easily with belief *that* he exists; he wants us to know and love him personally. Such a love demands a radical reorientation of our lives around the reality of God; it demands relating to him on his terms. So we can expect defenses and smoke screens to go up when we talk about God—but also earnest, searching questions from seekers intrigued about the idea of God's love in Christ.

But that's not all. As Christians, we attest to the truth not merely by the coherence or the explanatory power of the biblical faith. We also *show* the truth through an authentic, loving community of believers and the integrity of individual Christians. Truth about the God who has lovingly revealed himself in Christ *can* indeed be found.

First, a three-tiered approach to apologetics can serve as a useful grid when defending the Christian faith in the marketplace of ideas.

In the final chapter of *"True for You,"* I suggested a simple guide for believers seeking to persuade their non-Christian friends about the credibility of the Christian faith. Such a strategy involves three areas of emphasis:

1. truth
2. worldviews
3. Christian apologetics

Why use this strategy? It creates a simple, logical progression. (1) We begin with the bare minimum necessary for a coherent intelligent conversation—namely, truth—guided by unavoidable logical laws and everyday experiences and observations. If a person doesn't believe in truths that apply to all people, then we can't meaningfully communicate the significance of God's love in Christ for him. What I believe is seen as just "true for me" but not for him! But once we show that objective truth is inescapable (to deny it is to affirm the truth that it doesn't exist), then we can move to the next area: (2) Which worldview is true? Although many worldviews exist, we can reduce them to three:

1. *naturalism* (all that exists is nature; there is no God or supernatural realm)
2. *monism/pantheism* (all reality is ultimately One—as in many Eastern philosophies and religions)
3. *theism* (a personal Creator exists and is distinct from the created order; we have been made in the image or likeness of this Creator, thus resembling him in certain important ways)[3]

Perhaps the serious-minded skeptic or seeker will come to see—by God's grace and through our loving concern—practical inconsistencies and intellectual flaws in naturalism and monism and that theism does a better job answering questions regarding:

- where we came from (origins)
- who we are (identity)
- what life is about (meaning) and why we are here (purpose)
- and what is our end (destiny)

If such a seeker sees theism as a more plausible alternative, then he or she can explore (3) what *kind* of theism is most likely—Judaism, Christianity, or Islam. This is where Christian apologetics serves an important purpose: Arguments for the Bible's general historical reliability; the historicity, deity, and bodily resurrection of Jesus; the logic of the incarnation and the Trinity; and the like can be used to show the greater likelihood of the truth of Christianity than alternative views.

Given the nature of discussions about these issues and the role of personal relationships, the progression from (1) seeing the inescapability of truth to (2) choosing between various worldviews to (3) acknowledging the truth of the Christian worldview is not strictly linear or mechanically step-by-step. A defense of the faith involves much give-and-take and the revisiting of issues previously discussed in the context of earnest discussions with the unbeliever. In addition, authenticity and personal warmth on the part of the Christian and the opportunity for the unbeliever to witness regularly an authentic Christian community (John 13:35) make for a holistic demonstration of the truth.

Still, this three-tiered approach offers a good model to follow.

Second, when we present our case for the Christian faith, we should do this by "inference to the best explanation."[4]

Since the Enlightenment of the seventeenth and eighteenth centuries, the question has repeatedly surfaced, Is there such a thing as *Christian* philosophy? Ancient or medieval theologian-philosophers such as Augustine or Aquinas would have thought this a very odd question. The Christian faith has made an important contribution to the field of philosophy. The philosopher Alvin Plantinga reminds us that theism—or more specifically, the Christian worldview—"offers suggestions for answers to a wide range of otherwise intractable questions."[5] In other words, the Christian faith has a remarkable range of intellectual resources that utilize the available evidence to answer many questions that would otherwise be "just-so" stories—conundrums or brute facts—and nothing more. For example, take the noted antagonist of religion, Bertrand Russell. When asked in a BBC radio debate by Christian F. C. Copleston how the universe came into being, he asserted, "I should say that the universe is just there, and that's all."[6]

I will argue in the substance of this book that the Christian faith more adequately answers a wide range of questions than do its competitors. I will not address much of what standard apologetics texts already do—present arguments for God's existence, proof of the Bible's textual reliability, evidence for Jesus' resurrection, and so on—as important as these tasks are.[7] Rather, I will deal with objections that such texts generally do not cover given space (or other) limitations.

Let me present some important indicators of God's existence to illustrate what it means to infer to the best explanation. There are certain relevant features of the world worth considering:

- the universe's origin out of nothing
- the universe's delicately balanced conditions that make human life not only possible but actual
- consciousness
- objective moral values
- human dignity, value, and purpose

What worldview *best* accounts for these elements? It seems that the Judeo-Christian explanation for these features is simpler, more powerful, and more familiar than its rivals.[8] How so?

The origin of the universe: Resources within the Christian faith enable us to go beyond Russell's "that's just the way it is" mentality regarding the origin of the universe. The universe came into being roughly fifteen billion years ago, prior to which no space, matter, energy, or physical time existed. Belief that the universe is expanding and cooling is "the essence of the big bang theory,"[9] and today the big bang theory is "no longer seriously questioned; it fits together too well."[10] What caused the big bang? The Christian maintains that the universe could not have come into existence uncaused out of nothing. This is metaphysically impossible. Out of nothing, nothing comes. Being cannot come from nonbeing. But if a powerful, personal Creator exists, this conundrum evaporates: "In the beginning God created the heavens and the earth" (Gen. 1:1).[11]

The universe's delicately balanced conditions for life: If you had to bet on whether a Designer created the universe in all its complexities or the universe somehow came about either by necessity or by chance, where would you place your bet? Physicist Freeman Dyson notes, "As we look out into the Universe and identify the many accidents of physics and astronomy that have worked together for our benefit, it almost seems as if the Universe must in some sense have known that we were coming."[12] The cosmic condition in which we find ourselves has been called the "Goldilocks effect"—everything is "just right" for human existence. Not only were the initial conditions of the big bang just right, but fifteen billion years of cosmic history needed to be *continually* "just right" to bring about the necessary conditions for human/biological life on earth. The slightest alteration in any of the dozens of required conditions would render biological life impossible. For example, a .01 percent increase in the early stages of the universe's expansion would have yielded a present-day expansion thousands of times faster than what we find. An equivalent decrease would have led to a recollapse when the cosmos was a millionth its present size. Or if the gravitational pull of the big bang were to increase as little as 2 percent in strength, hydrogen atoms could not exist, making life impossible. (All hydrogen would become helium.)[13] Bernard Carr and Martin Rees maintain, "Nature does exhibit remarkable coincidences and these do warrant some explanation."[14]

These fine-tuning features of the universe could have been different; in other words, they are not necessary. They could have been otherwise. Belief that this delicate balance came about by chance or necessity is staggeringly improbable. As a result, some of the naturalistic theories that eliminate design from consideration do so on the basis of philosophical bias rather than scientific scrutiny. Ironically, non-design theories tend to be speculative and are not based on concrete scientific evidence (e.g., the existence of other worlds to which we have no access). And no matter how complex the universe appears to be, there is no point at which these naturalistic thinkers would concede design. All they would say is, "It just *appears* to be designed, and that's all." But are such theorists open to the evidence? If an intelligent Mind exists, then we can ask the Pauline question, "Why should any of you consider it incredible that the universe appears designed?"[15]

The existence of consciousness: Matter and consciousness are entirely distinct, and this presents a deep problem in the philosophy of mind: How could consciousness emerge from purely material processes?[16] The naturalistic philosopher Ned Block forcefully notes the bankruptcy of his own system to account for this:

> We have no conception of our physical or functional nature that allows us to understand how it could explain our subjective experience. . . . [I]n the case of consciousness we have nothing—zilch—worthy of being called a research programme, nor are there any substantive proposals about how to go about starting one. . . . Researchers are *stumped.*[17]

Another naturalist, John Searle, notes that "the leading problem in the biological sciences is the problem of explaining how neurobiological processes cause conscious experiences."[18] Yet within the Judeo-Christian framework, in which a supremely aware Being exists, we have a plausible context in which to affirm the existence of consciousness. Consciousness is not "just there, and that's all." Creaturely consciousness is natural given a perfectly aware Creator. We could easily make sense of its existence given theism.

The existence of objective moral values and the intrinsic value of human beings: Objective moral values exist. Acts such as rape or murder or stealing would be wrong even if everyone on earth were a relativist. If people don't recognize that the difference between Adolf Hitler and Mother Teresa is not simply cultural or biological, then their subjective morality becomes difficult to sustain in the face of life's realities. Such persons are just *selective* moral relativists. "Everything's relative" when it comes to sexual morality or cheating on income taxes. But when their "rights" are violated or when their property is stolen, such people act very much as though objective right and wrong exist. What then is the more likely context for affirming objective moral values and human dignity? The existence and character of God make the best sense of objective moral values (God's character being the source of goodness) and of human dignity (since we have been made in God's image).

Ironically, some atheists argue for objective moral values, saying that right and wrong would exist even if God didn't.[19] But I consider this to be without foundation. Why consider human beings of any moral worth and under any moral obligation at all given their nonmoral, valueless, impersonal origins and development? No wonder atheists and skeptics such as Bertrand Russell, Aldous Huxley, J. L. Mackie, William Provine, Daniel Dennett, and Richard Dawkins have rejected the existence of such values as completely incompatible with atheism.

Again, we make an inference to the best explanation: In which context would we more likely have a universe that came into existence without any previously existing matter, that develops such an intricate fine-tuning for life, in which consciousness, objective moral values, and human dignity exist? Is it a *naturalistic* one, in which literally nothing exists prior to the big bang, nothing guides the relevant life-permitting features of the universe, and no consciousness, personality, morality, and so on exist? Is it a *monistic* one that calls the external world, other minds, and distinct entities an illusion and rejects any difference between good and evil? Or is it a *theistic* one in which a powerful, nonmaterial, self-aware, intelligent, personal, good Being exists? I have no trouble seeing that human beings have dignity because they have been made in God's image—the image of the supremely valuable, morally excellent, personal Being. Here theism offers resources where atheism and monism leave us foundationless.

Some people will ask, "But don't Christians have a just-so story—namely, God? After all, Christians believe that 'God is just there, and that's all.'" Christians acknowledge that a sufficient stopping-point is called for, that there is a place where explanations must finally end. But this pertains to *all* worldviews, not just the Christian one. The question then becomes, Which worldview provides the best context in which to account for the universe's origin from nothing, its fitness for life, the emergence of consciousness, the existence of objective moral values, and the dignity of human beings? The Christian worldview can readily accommodate these features and provide the needed context, whereas a nontheistic one is ill-equipped to do so. The reasons for embracing Christian theism are more plausible than the reasons for its denial.[20]

Third, there is not just one way to defend the integrity of the Christian faith. The gospel needs a "plausibility structure" so that truth can be defended in the context of personal relationships and a vibrant Christian community.

In John 13:35, Jesus told his followers that the world would recognize them as his disciples by their love for one another. Yet we seem to have forgotten that for the Christian community, word and life are intimately bound up with each other. To make this point, Francis of Assisi astutely admonished, "Go everywhere and preach the gospel. When necessary, use words!"

Christians may readily give intelligent answers to philosophical questions and articulate the profound ideals of Christian theology. But when there is no loving community in which these truths are lived out, our message sounds like a Platonic world of ideas that seems detached from everyday life. We need a flesh-and-blood *plausibility structure* in which the truth and coherence of the gospel are incarnated and lived out.

In the second-century *Epistle to Diognetus*, the author describes the Christian community as something attractive and remarkable. In the very mundaneness of life, the beauty of Christians pointed the watching world to something—Someone—grander and majestic. The following section is worth quoting at length:

> For the Christians are distinguished from other men neither by country, nor language, nor the customs which they observe. For they neither inhabit cities of their own, nor employ a peculiar form of speech, nor lead a life which is marked out by any singularity. . . . But, inhabiting Greek as well as barbarian cities, according as the lot of each of them has determined, and following the customs of the natives in respect to clothing, food, and the rest of their ordinary conduct, they display to us their wonderful and confessedly striking method of life. They dwell in their own countries, but simply as sojourners. As citizens, they share in all things with others, and yet endure all things as if foreigners. Every foreign land is to them as their native country, and every land of their birth as a land of strangers. They marry, as do all [others]; they beget children; but they do not destroy their offspring. They have a common table, but not a common bed. They are in the flesh, but they do not live after the flesh. They pass their days on earth, but they are citizens of heaven. They obey the prescribed laws, and at the same time surpass the laws by their lives. They love all men, and are persecuted by all. They are unknown and condemned; they are put to death, and restored to life. They are poor, yet make many rich; they are in lack of all things, and yet abound in all; they are dishonored, and yet in their very dishonor are glorified. They are evilly spoken of, and yet are justified; they are reviled, and bless; they are insulted, and repay the insult with honor; they do good, yet are punished as evildoers. When punished, they rejoice as if quickened into life.[21]

Undoubtedly, more people would sit up and take notice of our message if our lifestyle spoke so powerfully![22]

Fourth, the character and demeanor of an individual Christian will often speak more powerfully than the words or arguments he or she uses.

A Pakistani couple—Muslims—moved to Ohio, where the wife came into contact with Christians and eventually became a follower of Christ. She began attending a women's Bible study at the home of a pastor and his wife. Her husband would grudgingly drive her to the study and wait outside in the car until it finished. While the pastor's wife led the study, the pastor came out to the Muslim man with some lunch. This act of kindness got him thinking: "What if the situation were reversed? What if I were a Christian man with a Muslim wife attending a mosque? No one would dream of bringing out lunch for me." Through the pastor's loving and practical initiative, the Muslim man eventually became a Christian.[23]

Writing a book centered around particular challenges has its dangers. The reader might think that defending the Christian faith is nothing more than winning intellectual debates: "The one with the most conversation-stopping quips wins!" But this is hardly my intention.

The snappy-answers-to-silly-slogans mentality is not new. St. Augustine was all too familiar with intellectual put-downs in North Africa.[24] In his own Catholic environment, he witnessed frivolous and mocking answers by Christians in response to the serious and reasonable question, What did God do before he made heaven and earth? Unlike those around him, Augustine refused to evade "by a joke the force of the objection" by saying, "He was preparing hell . . . for those prying into such deep subjects." Augustine continues:

> It is one thing to see the objection; it is another to make a joke of it. I do not answer in this way. I would rather respond, "I do not know," concerning what I do not know rather than say something for which a man inquiring about such profound matters is laughed at while the one giving a false answer is praised.[25]

We have all met Christian "bloodhounds" who can sniff out theological blood trails and pick a good fight with anyone who disagrees. Unfortunately, the watching world may develop the impression that Christians are angry fighters rather than gracious and humble friends. Argument has its place, but we will not get very far without humility, charity, and kindness. After all, if our "chief end" is to "glorify God and enjoy him forever," then we must use our apologetic arguments as humble tools that God's Spirit can use to bring people into right relationship with a loving God. Truly, it is "God's kindness [that] leads you toward repentance" (Rom. 2:4), and it is this kind—though bold and firm—witness of the believer that speaks powerfully and "adorns the teaching about God our Savior" (Titus 2:10). As with Augustine, a humble "I don't know" is often a far more powerful testimony than an arsenal of one-line zingers. Without humility and grace, we may do more damage to the truth by "winning" arguments than by acknowledging ignorance. When good reasons for faith are simply shrugged off, an authentic lived-out faith and personal friendship may lead to open doors for the gospel.

This kind of authentic Christianity is all the more necessary to reach the next generation. The mind-set of Gen-Xers has been characterized by such features as:

- anti-institutionalism ("Jesus is fine; it's the church and 'religiosity' that are the problem.")
- experience ("I'm not really interested in abstractions and theories; what you tell me has to connect with my own experience.")
- suffering ("Our generation lives with much inner pain and familial dysfunction.")
- ambiguity ("You see everything in black-and-white, which strikes me as dogmatic and condescending.")

Tom Beaudoin—a Gen-Xer himself—has incisively discussed these character traits in his book *Virtual Faith.*[26] We would be wiser witnesses if we studied such books and adapted our strategy to make it more personal, realistic, authentic, community-oriented, relational, humble, and gracious.

Fifth, because the gospel message is one of hope in the face of death and goes beyond the satisfaction of any fleeting earthly pleasures, the Christian faith presents a powerfully practical response to the deepest human desires and fears.

In *The Weight of Glory,* C. S. Lewis tells of "a desire for something that has never actually happened."[27] When we desire fulfillment in winning a tennis tournament, taking an exotic vacation, having a sexual experience, or enjoying a gourmet meal, we find ourselves left yearning for something more, something beyond our earthly experience. We are left *not fully* satisfied. Lewis goes on to talk about seeking the fulfillment of desire in books and music:

> The books or the music in which we thought the beauty was located will betray us if we trust in them; it was not *in* them, it only came *through* them, and what came through them was longing. These things—the beauty, the memory of our own past— are good images of what we really desire; but if they are mistaken for the thing itself they turn into dumb idols, breaking the hearts of their worshippers.[28]

The natural gifts that God provides us through creation and common grace—food, drink, sex, culture, music, the arts, and literature—are not ends in themselves. Rather, they point beyond themselves to something transcendent and grand. Jesus' message of the kingdom—with its emphasis on the already and the not-yet—tells us that while we can begin to taste *some* blessings of the life to come in the present (the already), we cannot fix our hopes on these; even as Christians there is a not-yet to our existence. We are in-betweeners, living in two overlapping eras—this age and the age to come.

Perhaps our deep unfulfilled desires can help show us that we were made for something no earthly thing can satisfy. Just as children tire of their Christmas toys shortly after they've received them, so as adults our latest purchases or home renovations or business deals leave us looking for that elusive something. If we live in a fallen world, alienated from God, this is no wonder. God has "set eternity in the hearts" of us all (Eccles. 3:11) so that we will be satisfied with nothing less than God alone. In the psalmist's words:

> Whom have I in heaven but you?
>> And earth has nothing I desire besides you.
> My flesh and my heart may fail,
>> but God is the strength of my heart
>> and my portion forever.
>
> PSALM 73:25–26

Again, I pose the question, Which worldview provides the richest resources to account for such deep desires that cannot be met by any earthly thing? As I will argue later, simply because we have deep needs and desires does not mean that they are illegitimate. (Think of the legitimacy of meeting the needs of our physical hunger and thirst.) Perhaps our deepest desires have been placed within us by God because we are meant for a loving relationship with him. The secular pursuit of the "ultimate experience" will disappoint us because all our desires are properly ordered when God is central in our lives.

In the *Times Literary Supplement* in August 1997, Eric Korn spoke forthrightly of his *timor mortis*—his fear of death: "I need to register an interest. I'll be dying shortly, in the next few decades. And another interest. I'm scared of it. . . . Death and dying, process and product, scare the life out of me."[29] Just as our unfulfilled desires may be pointers toward God, perhaps also is our fear of death. Maybe God has placed within us the awareness of our mortality to prompt us to cast ourselves upon the ever-living God. The Heidelberg Catechism of 1563 begins with the question, What is your only comfort in life and death? The answer, so beautifully put, is:

That I with body and soul, both in life and death, am not my own, but belong to my faithful Savior Jesus Christ, who, with his precious blood, has fully paid for all my sins, and delivered me from the power of the devil; and so preserves me that without the will of my heavenly Father, not a hair can fall from my head; indeed, that everything must fit his purpose for my salvation.

Death issues a call each of us must answer, and in the gospel we have not only resources for our earthly pilgrimage but a confidence of a stunningly bright future in the new heavens and new earth. Perhaps the desperation and panic that overtake so many in the hour of death were intended to be a reminder to call upon God, whose control over our lives we each must ultimately acknowledge.

Finally, in defending their faith, Christians must not ignore the personal and moral factors that prevent persons from embracing God and that prompt people to obscure important evidences for his existence.

When my family lived in Oconomowoc, Wisconsin, my son Peter and I went to a sidewalk sale on a sunny Saturday morning. I got into a conversation with a gentleman who happened to be an atheist. He asserted that there "just isn't any evidence for God's existence." I replied, "Take the beginning of the universe. If the universe came into existence a finite time ago, what caused its beginning?" The atheist replied, "I don't know, but it wasn't God." I responded, "It sounds more like you're not open to God being the cause." Being new to such discussions, my six-year-old son was struck by the fact that this man didn't even *allow* that God might be a possible explanation.

This kind of spiritually resistant mind-set may also lurk behind the demand that God show himself more clearly than he does. Many people make demands of God. They say, "Why doesn't God show himself more clearly? Why isn't he more obvious?"[30] The atheist Friedrich Nietzsche wrote, "A god who is all-knowing and all powerful and who does not even make sure his creatures understand his intention" could not be a "god of goodness." Nietzsche asks, "Would he not be a cruel god if he possessed the truth and could behold mankind miserably tormenting itself over the truth?" The religions of the world "take *lightly* the duty to tell the truth: they as yet know nothing of a *Duty of God* to be truthful towards mankind and clear in the manner of his communications."[31]

What should God do then? Atheist N. R. Hanson proposed the following scenario to dismiss all his doubts. Suppose that one morning just after breakfast everyone in the world is knocked to his or her knees with an ear-shattering thunderclap. Snow swirls, leaves drop from trees, and the earth heaves and buckles, toppling buildings. Then the skies open and a huge, radiant Zeus-like figure appears. This figure points to Hanson and says, "I have had quite enough of your too-clever logic-chopping and word-watching in matters of theology. Be assured, N. R. Hanson, that I most certainly do exist."[32] Does this demand sound reasonable? Maybe there is more behind this demand than we realize.

First of all, couldn't even this scenario be explained away by a skeptic? Perhaps it is the result of extraterrestrials or an optical illusion or a hallucination. Any skeptic worthy of the name could no doubt manage to come up with a way to deny the reality of the encounter.

Second, God desires for us to respond freely to his kindness; divine, wooing love gives us space and doesn't create theological claustrophobia. What if God went beyond such signs and wonders (which one could weasel out of) and made himself *perfectly* obvious—perhaps as our very bodies are to us? This raises another problem: What if we still did not *want* to acknowledge God's existence and thus his claim over our lives but felt that we would look ridiculous if we didn't? This would be a kind of intellectual rape that allowed for no loopholes. The unbeliever would have to acknowledge God to avoid being rationally humiliated.

But third (and most important), this kind of demand that God make himself more obvious is misguided since it doesn't produce the kind of loving relationship God desires with us. Rather than humbling ourselves before God and seeking him earnestly, we set requirements God must meet. What if God did do what we demanded? Would his act produce the kind of reconciled relationship of love God desires? There's no reason to think so. We see plenty of examples in the Bible of people who saw divinely wrought miracles (e.g., the Israelites in the wilderness, religious leaders in Jesus' day) but persisted in their unbelief. No wonder that Jesus repeatedly warned against a sign-seeking mind-set (Matt. 12:39; 16:4), which pursues entertainment rather than commitment, which prefers keeping God at arm's length rather than embracing him. No wonder Jesus proclaimed that some will not believe even if they see someone come back from the dead and that God's scriptural revelation is sufficient for people to turn to him; they don't need to look further (Luke 16:31).

We see plenty of examples all around us of people who *know,* for instance, that they should exercise and avoid a steady diet of Big Macs and fries—not to mention chain-smoking—for the sake of their health. Yet they *choose* to continue in their self-destructive path. At the moral and spiritual level, some people simply don't *want* God to alter their lifestyle. So they find loopholes and excuses to rationalize away the evidence for God's existence.

Out of his kindness, God does indeed show himself in creation and conscience. Truly, "He is not far from each one of us" (Acts 17:27). Perhaps you've met skeptics whose critical questions you've adequately answered, but when you ask them if they want to take the Christian faith seriously, they say, "No thanks. I'm not ready to make any commitments." Despite the ample evidence for God's existence, not all are willing to pursue a loving relationship with the God who shows himself.

I like to think of humans' relationship to the abundant evidence for God's existence in terms of tuning a radio dial. A person might turn on a radio and say, "All I hear is static. There's nothing intelligible out there." Because the dial is not tuned to a clear frequency, no message comes through. Similarly, God has placed us in an environment in which we can tune out the evidence. People can point to the "static" of evil in the world or the problem of God's apparent hiddenness ("Why doesn't God just dazzle us all with a celestial fireworks display?"). Far too often such complaints may stem from deep hurts in one's past that make it difficult to see God as loving, and these must be worked through with a reshaped perspective of God. Or they may stem from a simple unwillingness to acknowledge God's authority over human lives. After all, if God exists, then talking about evidence for his existence turns out to be more than an intellectual exercise, for God is a threat to unfettered human autonomy.

Aldous Huxley frankly admits this:

I had motives for not wanting the world to have meaning, consequently assumed that it had none, and was able without any difficulty to find satisfying reasons for this assumption. . . . For myself, as, no doubt, for most contemporaries, the philosophy of meaninglessness was essentially an instrument of liberation. The liberation we desired was simultaneously liberation from a certain political and economic system and liberation from a certain system of morality. *We objected to the morality because it interfered with our sexual freedom.*[33]

Or listen to the words of New York University philosopher Thomas Nagel:

I speak from experience, being strongly subject to this fear [of religion] myself: *I want atheism to be true* and am made uneasy by the fact that some of the most intelligent and well-informed people I know are religious believers. It isn't just that I don't believe in God and, naturally, hope that I'm right in my belief. It's that *I hope there is no God! I don't want there to be a God; I don't want the universe to be like that.*[34]

Discussing God's existence is no spectator sport. God's existence demands a radical reorientation of our lives. As we speak with non-Christians, therefore, we can expect resistance stemming from what Thomas Nagel calls a "cosmic authority problem." God threatens the self-centered existence of every one of us! If he truly exists and thus has a claim upon our lives, then he can't be ignored.

How then is truth to be found? The gospel demands more than just intellectual reasons for following Christ. There must be existential—lived-out—reasons for doing so as well: The credibility and character of individual Christians and the genuineness of love in the Christian community testify to the fact that there is good news worth embracing. But we can't forget that personal factors figure in to the God-question. Some people simply don't *want* God in their lives, and no amount of rigorous argumentation will alter their course.

◆ Summary

- A three-tiered approach to apologetics is useful when defending the Christian faith in the marketplace of ideas: (1) truth, (2) worldviews (monism, naturalism, theism), (3) Christian apologetics.
- When we present our case for the Christian faith, we should do so by "inference to the best explanation." Which worldview does the best job of explaining the available evidence (such as the universe's beginning and fine-tuning, human dignity and objective moral values, and consciousness)?

- The reasons for embracing Christian theism are more plausible than reasons for its denial.
- There is not just one way to defend the integrity of the Christian faith. The gospel needs a "plausibility structure" so that truth can be defended in the context of personal relationships and a vibrant Christian community.
- The character and demeanor of an individual Christian will often speak more powerfully than the words or arguments he or she uses.
- Because the gospel message is one of hope in the face of death and goes beyond the satisfaction of any fleeting earthly pleasures, the Christian faith presents a powerfully practical response to the deepest human desires and fears.
- In defending their faith, Christians must not ignore the personal and moral factors that prevent people from embracing God and that prompt people to obscure important evidences for his existence. Some people simply don't want God in their lives.
- Even if God were to dazzle everyone with divine fireworks and other signs and wonders, these could still be explained away by the skilled skeptic.
- If God went beyond the divine fireworks and made himself as obvious to us as our own bodies are, it would be a kind of intellectual rape that allowed for no loopholes. The unbeliever would have to acknowledge God to avoid being rationally humiliated.
- Such manifestations of divine power don't guarantee a response of love and faith on the part of the observer.

◆ Further Reading

Budziszewski, J. *How to Stay Christian in College*. Colorado Springs: Navpress, 1999.

Copan, Paul. *"True for You, but Not for Me": Deflating the Slogans That Leave Christians Speechless*. Minneapolis: Bethany House, 1998.

Monroe, Kelly, ed. *Finding God at Harvard*. Grand Rapids: Zondervan, 1996.

Moser, Paul K. *Why Isn't God More Obvious?* RZIM Critical Questions Booklet Series. Norcross, Ga.: Ravi Zacharias International Ministries, 2000.

PART ONE

CHALLENGES RELATED TO TRUTH AND REALITY

IT'S ALL RELATIVE

What is true? What is real? Can we really know?

These days, stating that we can *know* what is *true*—especially in academic settings—can at times bring a shower of insults on our heads: "Arrogant! Narrow-minded! Bigot!" It's ironic that institutions of "higher learning" frequently graduate students who believe they haven't learned anything they can call true. Higher learning for these students is a means to higher *earning*—and nothing more.

As I mentioned in my previous book, *"True for You, but Not for Me,"* relativism is on the increase in the United States—even among those who call themselves "born again" or "evangelical" Christians. Because ideas have consequences, it should not be surprising that, according to a Barna poll taken in 1997, 40 percent of those who call themselves evangelicals assert that there are no moral absolutes.[1] There is an increasing disparity between what Christians *say* they believe and how they actually *live*.

I have observed this firsthand. A couple years ago, our family became members of a nearby church. As I like to do, I began teaching an adult Sunday school class. I would at times hear comments such as, "That's just your interpretation" or (less frequently), "I just don't believe what the Bible says about that issue." As biblical illiteracy increases in our churches and as authority of any kind—including biblical authority—is more frequently called into question, we will continue to see relativism, skepticism, and smorgasbord religion appear in various "Christian" settings.

Genuine knowledge is possible. Truth and reality are not something we invent. There are truths that pertain to all of us, and there is a reality that cannot be wished away. Truth and reality are inescapable. To deny them will ultimately result in an affirmation that they exist. For example, the relativist will inadvertently affirm that objective truth exists (e.g., he believes in the *truth* of relativism), and the anti-realist will affirm that some objective reality exists (e.g., it is an objective *reality* that humans shape all reality).

Before we discuss these matters in detail in the chapters immediately following, let me review and elaborate on certain points about truth and relativism.

First, relativism—the belief that something can be true for one person but not for another—is an example of a self-contradictory viewpoint; it should therefore be rejected as false. If I tell you, "I can't speak a word of English" or, "No sentence is longer than six words" or, "I don't exist," then you can conclude that what I have just said is false. It is quite apparent to you that I can speak English, that there are sentences longer than six words, and that I must exist in order to speak! Because I have contradicted myself in these sentences, my statements should be rejected. They are false.[2] The relativist believes that relativism is true not just for him but for everyone. If we ask the relativist, "Is relativism *absolutely* true for everyone?" he finds himself in a difficult position. Obviously, if he says yes, then he contradicts himself by holding to an absolute relativism. So it should be rejected as false.

Second, relativism is not as individualistic as it's cracked up to be. The relativist frequently claims that relativism pertains to more than just herself. What if the relativist says, "This is just *my* view; it's just true for *me*, and you don't have to believe it"? If this is indeed the relativist's position, then what she is saying is on the same level as asserting, "Vanilla ice cream tastes better to you, but chocolate tastes better to me." The relativist, therefore, is saying *nothing* that is worthy of being believed by another; she is just giving her opinion. But usually relativists believe they are giving more than their opinion. In fact, the classic relativist slogan—"That's true for *you* but not for *me*"—presupposes that relativism applies to at least *two* people! The relativist believes that relativism is true for *both* parties, not just herself. And no doubt the relativist has used this line on quite a few people at various times, presuming that relativism applies to *all* of them.

This casual relativism, which maintains that every belief is as good as every other belief, is in deep intellectual trouble: There is no reason to take it seriously (since this belief itself is no better than any other), and if one does take it seriously, it becomes self-refuting (because it claims to be the one belief everyone should hold to).

Relativists certainly give the impression that they believe their view is true for everyone, and they often try to persuade others to accept their perspective. In fact, they are often willing to give objective reasons—that is, reasons that are *true,* independent of anyone's viewpoint—as to why relativism is true and belief in absolutes is false. And why do relativists get angry with nonrelativists if everything is relative? An angry relativist seems to be a contradiction in terms!

Third, paradoxically, the very basis for relativism—namely, wildly differing views—is invoked as the obvious basis for relativism. One of the slogans I mentioned in my previous book is, "So many people disagree; therefore, relativism *must* be true." This claim of immense disagreement is often exaggerated, but let's leave that aside. The person who believes in objective truth can point out *two truths* that emerge from this relativist's observation. The relativist believes that:

1. Her basis for holding to relativism (i.e., the clear, obvious fact that so many people disagree) is true—not false.
2. Her conclusion that relativism is based on differences is also true—not false.

The very *basis* assumed by the relativist and the very *conclusion* drawn by the relativist are taken to be undeniably true by that very relativist! The relativist believes that she has good reasons to hold to relativism, and these reasons are assumed to be true and not false. Relativists believe their positions are nonarbitrary and objectively justifiable.

Fourth, any claim the relativist makes can be turned into an objective truth claim that is obviously true for all people. All we need to do is introduce a relativistic statement with, "It is true that . . ." or, "It is absolutely true that . . ." or, "It is true and not false that . . ." to show that the statement is not relative after all. For example, if the relativist says, "My view is just true for me," we can say to him, "It is absolutely true that your view is just true for you." If the relativist makes the assertion that "all cultures have their own values," we can say, "It is objectively true and not false that all cultures have their own values." If the relativist says, "This is just what I happen to believe," we can respond, "It is incontestably true that this is what you happen to believe."

It should be clear by now that no matter what position we take when it comes to the truth, we will constantly be making truth statements or pre-supposing certain truths to defend or justify our positions. So let's lay to rest once and for all the question of whether objective truth exists. Since no one can escape objective truth, we (even though we may disagree about which particular view is true) can advance the discussion to the next level—namely, the issue of which worldview best reflects or corresponds to objective reality and why.

As we interact with relativistically minded persons, however, we must remember that they may state, "Who are you to judge others" or, "You're being intolerant" because our manner has been too hard-edged and lacking graciousness or respect.[3] A harsh and unloving spirit is out of place in this discussion. The Christian must recognize that he is not superior to the non-Christian because he follows Christ and the non-Christian does not. Every right-thinking Christian knows that God's gift of salvation through Jesus is nothing for which we can take credit. As Martin Luther put it, telling people about the good news of Jesus is like one beggar telling another beggar where to find bread. Just as beggars can't be choosers, neither can they be braggarts! There is no place for Christian smugness. All we can brag about is God's kindness to us, and so we can tell others, "Taste and see that the Lord is good."

◆ Summary

- Truth and reality are inescapable. To deny them means to affirm some objective truth and reality.
- Relativism is self-contradictory because it claims to be absolutely true for everyone.
- The person who says that something can be "true for you but not for me" believes that relativism pertains to at least *two* people. Therefore, relativism isn't just true for the relativist; he believes it is objectively or absolutely true for others.
- Even the basis for relativism is assumed to be objectively true by the relativist, and the relativistic conclusion based on differences is also taken to be true and not false.
- To show the self-contradictory nature of relativism, we can simply reword a relativistic assertion by inserting, "It is absolutely true that . . ." or, "It is objectively true and not false that . . ."
- We can affirm that it's all right to hold to objective truth—especially because it's inescapable.
- We should tell people about Jesus with grace and kindness, knowing that we have no reason to boast or feel superior.

• Words such as *truth, objectivity,* and *absolutes* are frequently weighted with associations of power and oppression. Therefore, we must clarify and explore misunderstandings rather than engage in emotionally charged word battles.

◆ Further Reading

Beilby, Jim, and David K. Clark. *Why Bother with Truth? Finding Knowledge in a Skeptical Society.* RZIM Critical Questions Booklet Series. Norcross, Ga.: Ravi Zacharias International Ministries, 2000.

Copan, Paul. *"True for You, but Not for Me": Deflating the Slogans That Leave Christians Speechless.* Minneapolis: Bethany House, 1998.

2

THAT'S JUST
YOUR INTERPRETATION

I n September 2000, Indiana University's basketball coach Bobby Knight was fired because of his short fuse, angry outbursts, and refusal to cooperate with the school administration's zero-tolerance policy. In an ESPN interview with Jeremy Schaap,[1] when asked about the charges against him, Knight claimed that people interpret words differently: "What we're talking about here is interpretation"; "that's their interpretation"; "that's his interpretation." Outside the controversy itself, what is striking is Knight's appeal to interpretation to get off the hook.

While I was in college, I attended a nearby Muslim mosque each Friday. As a curious Christian, I found it beneficial to learn about Muslim beliefs and practices and to make friends with members of another religious community. After one Friday gathering, I was speaking with a gentleman I will call Shabaz. I had interacted with him only once or twice before, but he threw this line at me: "What you Christians believe about Jesus being the 'only way'—that's just your interpretation." I went to get my Bible from my car and turned to Acts 4, where a man had just been healed in the name of Jesus of Nazareth. I asked Shabaz to read verse 12 for me, which he did: "There is no other name under heaven given to men by which we must be saved." I then said, "I understand that verse to mean that Jesus is the one by whom we must be saved. How do you understand it?" Shabaz squirmed a bit. Realizing that his case wasn't a very good one, he got up and left.

We have all heard the saying, "That's just your interpretation" (or, "That's just your opinion"). We hear it on TV talk shows and news interviews. Perhaps we have heard it in the midst of a conversation about moral issues such as abortion or homosexuality as they relate to the Bible. Those taking the traditional biblical view on these issues might be told by the pro-abortionist or by those who condone homosexuality, "That's just your interpretation of the Bible." All too often Christians are left wondering, *What do I say now?*—when, in fact, there is a great deal to be said!

I have been engaged in theological discussions in which I've gone through the trouble of explaining a biblical text and offering reasons for believing it only to be casually dismissed with, "That's just your interpretation." This criticism, however, is actually an invitation for further discussion. But we must be able to articulate our position and give reasons as to why we believe it— even if we can readily agree that we as humans are not always as clearheaded as we would like to be and that we can and do misinterpret passages. Also, we must keep in mind that we may have a perspective that another does not share.

First, gently ask, "Do you mean that your interpretation should be preferred over mine? If so, I'd like to know why you have chosen your interpretation over mine. You must have a good reason." In my experience, those who say, "That's just *your* interpretation" have not thought through their position, and they are not able to offer valid reasons for their viewpoint. If they *do* have reasons, however, you can talk freely about the basis for accepting or rejecting those beliefs.

Second, point out that you are willing to give reasons for your position and that you are not simply taking a particular viewpoint arbitrarily. In one adult Sunday class, I was giving reasons for interpreting a biblical passage in a particular way—discussing grammatical and contextual issues to justify my point. One man in the class said, "That's just *your* interpretation." Responding to this casual dismissal and sensing that this man just didn't *like* what I was saying, I again clarified my basis for interpretation. I then said, "I have laid out reasons for my position. I'm willing to hear yours and correct my own position if I'm wrong, but all you've done is dismiss my viewpoint without any basis."

Third, since people often toss out this criticism because they don't like *your interpretation, ask for clarification: "Do you mean that you don't like my interpretation?"* If a person doesn't like what the Bible says about hell or sin or

God's holiness but appears to cloak his dislike of these doctrines by calling them "your interpretation" or "your opinion," then explore the matter further. You can also add, "There are many truths that I myself don't like or find difficult to accept, but not liking them doesn't give me the freedom to reject them. I have to accept that they are true."

The philosopher John Searle, though an atheist, put his finger on the heart of the matter of the slogan, "That's just your interpretation":

> I have to confess . . . that I think there is a much deeper reason for the persistent appeal of all forms of anti-realism [in which we create our own reality and everything anyone believes is a matter of personal preference, interpretation, and spin], and this has become obvious in the twentieth century: it satisfies a basic urge to power. It just seems too disgusting, somehow, that we should have to be at the mercy of the "real world." It seems too awful that our representations should have to be answerable to anything but us.[2]

We have to admit that there *are* abiding truths and historical facts that we cannot simply wish away or pass off as interpretation and opinion. We may want to remain in control, but this attitude does not change the way things are.

Fourth, if a person doesn't believe there are any legitimate interpretations, playfully say, "That's just your interpretation of my interpretation!" In other words, if everything is a matter of interpretation, opinion, and spin, then why should the person with whom you're speaking believe he has correctly interpreted *your* words? Doesn't that person assume he has done so? Doesn't he believe that the differences between the views are not a matter of interpretation, that there are real and obvious differences between them? Perhaps you could carry this matter further: "I think our interpretations are identical. You are just using different language to express yours." Of course, your friend will likely resist your point, arguing that you really do disagree. And this is just the point: It's not *all* a matter of interpretation; there are conflicting interpretations, and not all of them can be true.

Fifth, some interpretations are better than others, and to see this is simply not a matter of interpretation. Some have claimed that in Jewish talmudic belief, each passage of the Torah (the law of Moses) contains forty-nine different interpretations. In one story, a student comes to his rabbi and offers an interpretation of a passage. The rabbi says, "No, you're quite wrong." Shocked, the student asks, "But aren't there forty-nine meanings for each passage?" The rabbi replies, "Yes, but yours isn't one of them."[3] Similarly, some people conclude that because there are so many spin doctors and wordsmiths around, twisting words and ideas to fit their agendas, *any* suggested interpretation is therefore legitimate. But we recognize that some interpretations are better or more plausible than others. And if this is so, then we assume that one interpretation—or at least a range of interpretations—better conforms to the truth than others.

Lawyers in America don't have the greatest reputation. Here's one lawyer joke I heard: Why are lawyers buried twelve feet under rather than six feet under? Answer: Because deep down, they're really good people! During the November 2000 presidential elections, we witnessed how lawyers could bypass established election laws in Florida, go to court, and have the laws rewritten or refitted by judges to secure more votes. While there are certainly many fine lawyers around, a general impression is that they are masters of spin and interpretation. No matter what a lawyer's earlier position or argument, he can ably twist words later on to wriggle out of the hole in which he has gotten himself! But we have to ask, "Is there ever a point at which one of these spin meisters will admit that he's wrong? Is it realistic for us to think that one will always be right in his interpretation?" It is not difficult to conclude that a personal or moral agenda is driving the discussion rather than honesty and fairness. We thus have reason to raise a skeptical eyebrow at such maneuverings. No matter how much some people claim that all truth claims are a matter of interpretation, at some point glaring inconsistencies will surface.

The Christian philosopher J. P. Moreland tells the story of an illuminating encounter with a student at the University of Vermont. Moreland was speaking in a dorm room, and a student who lived there said to him, "Whatever is true for you is true for you, and whatever is true for me is true for me. If something works for you because you believe it, that's great. But no one should force his or her views on other people since everything is relative."[4] As Moreland left the room, he unplugged the student's stereo and started out the door with it.

The student protested, "Hey, what are you doing? You can't do that!"

Moreland replied, "You're not going to *force* on me the belief that it is wrong to steal your stereo, are you?"

Moreland went on to point out that when it's convenient, people will say they don't care about sexual morality or cheating on exams, but they become moral absolutists in a hurry when someone steals their things or violates their rights. They drop the "that's just your interpretation" mentality rather quickly. They *do* believe that certain rights or the claim to ownership is not a matter of "your interpretation" versus "my interpretation." The matter of morality is not merely a matter of interpretation or opinion.

Sixth, those who resort to "that's just your interpretation" implicitly believe that they are right and that those who disagree with them are wrong. The German philosopher Friedrich Nietzsche declared, "There are no facts—only interpretations." Many today take up this citation and quote it freely to endorse a kind of relativism. However, the question remains, Is this statement itself a fact—or just an interpretation? If it is a fact, then this statement must be altered: "There are no facts—except one: that there are no facts!" Thus, it is self-refuting. On the other hand, if this statement is merely an interpretation, then why take it seriously? In all likelihood, the person quoting this line believes his statement is factual, not merely another interpretation.

Although there are many perspectives about many things, this doesn't mean we can't draw true conclusions about certain matters; we are not merely stuck in the mire of interpretation. Even if we see things from different perspectives, this doesn't mean we can't agree to the truth of many things.

When confronted with "that's just *your* interpretation," ask the person:

- Is there ever a *wrong* perspective?
- Can one's perspective ever be *correct?*
- Why would you ever *disagree* with another interpretation? What does it matter if everything is interpretation and there's no truth?
- Is it *universally true* that everything is a matter of interpretation?

Asking such questions can help draw out some of the implausibilities and inconsistencies of this position.

◆ Summary

- Gently ask, "Do you mean that your interpretation should be preferred over mine? If so, I'd like to know why you have chosen your interpretation over mine. You must have a good reason."
- Remind your friend that you are willing to give reasons for your position and that you are not simply taking a particular viewpoint arbitrarily.
- Try to discern if people toss out this slogan because they don't like your interpretation. Remind them that there are many truths we have to accept even if we don't like them.
- If someone doesn't believe there are any legitimate interpretations, say, "That's just your interpretation of my interpretation!" He assumes that he has correctly interpreted your view and that it differs from his.
- Some interpretations are better than others, and to see this is simply not a matter of interpretation.
- "There are no facts, only interpretations" is a statement that is presented as a fact. If it's just an interpretation, then there is no reason to take it seriously.

◆ Further Reading

Copan, Paul. *Is Everything Really Relative?* Norcross, Ga.: Ravi Zacharias International Ministries, 1999.

———. *"True for You, but Not for Me": Deflating the Slogans That Leave Christians Speechless.* Minneapolis: Bethany House, 1998.

Nagel, Thomas. *The Last Word.* New York: Oxford University Press, 1997.

THAT'S JUST YOUR REALITY

n September 1998, I wrote a letter to the editor of *The Wheel,* the student newspaper at Emory University in Atlanta. A student had written an essay about the nature of reality.[1] He claimed that reality is like a piece of wet clay—we can mold it any way we want to. Therefore, my reality can be completely different—and just as legitimate—as your reality. But in this same article, he contradicted himself by making the very opposite point—namely, that reality is shaped by powerful forces beyond our control. He asserted that anyone who has seen *The Truman Show* or any student of sociology knows that social forces determine the reality in which we find ourselves.

Not surprisingly, the two opposing points offered by this student are popular in our day:

1. We all can shape reality any way we choose.
2. Reality is shaped for us by factors independent of us (e.g., genetics,

history, culture, language); therefore, all that each of us can claim is, "This is my perspective." We cannot say, "This is true."

Both (1) and (2) cannot be true. This chapter examines the question of creating reality. In the next chapter, we will look at the question of forces beyond our control that ultimately shape reality.[2]

First, reality is that which is, that which exists. The church father Augustine wrote in his *Confessions,* "What, then, is time? If no one asks me, I know; if I want to explain it to someone who does ask me, I do not know."[3] Maybe some of us think the same way about reality—we know what it is until someone asks us! While in a toy store, my wife pointed to a bag of gold-colored rocks. The label read: "Authentic gold nugget replicas." That's like saying "a genuine imitation" or "a true fake"! It rings rather hollow, doesn't it?

What then *is* reality? Is cyberspace real? Do newspapers report what really happened? Is reality confined to things that can be perceived or sensed? Although we will indirectly address these sorts of issues below, let's simply say that reality is that which is, that which exists. Therefore, a unicorn is not real since it does not exist. But reality does include physical things such as tables, chairs, trees, and stones, and it also includes spiritual entities such as God, angels, and human souls. And if something is true, it will correspond to what is, to what exists. As a result, mathematical truths such as 2+2=4 can be said to be real. Propositions such as "kindness is a virtue" or propositions about past, present, or future states of affairs truly exist.[4]

Second, while we have the ability to bring about certain realities through our choices and actions, we must acknowledge certain unchangeable realities over which we have no control. Deepak Chopra, a medical doctor from New Delhi, India, has been involved in promoting a mix of New Age ideas (including transcendental meditation) and medicine. He sent out a promotional letter for his book *The Higher Self,* which read:

Dear Friend:

You *are* your own reality.

You create it; you carry it around with you; and, most importantly, you project it onto everyone else and everything else you encounter.

But the traditional Western notion of reality is much too limiting for a true realization of life. If you are to understand yourself and the world around you properly, you need to expand the boundaries of reality—of time, space and matter.

Once you've done this, you can align the energy of your physical body with the energy of the universe. In doing this, you tap into an infinite reservoir of intelligence.

This is the Higher Self. The "you" inside of you. The living force that knows why you are here on earth, what you need and how to get it.[5]

Chopra claims that we can create reality, but is this obvious or clear? It seems foolish to deny our ability to bring about certain events that would not have existed had we not acted. Had I not decided to write a book, then a book by me would not exist. A couple may choose to eat out rather than prepare dinner at home; they have the ability to produce real changes by carrying out their decisions.

Or take movies such as *The Wizard of Oz, The Matrix,* and *What Dreams May Come,* which are "created realities." Such films bring together background artwork, special effects, superimposed computer-generated images, and the like. In some sense we have the power to "create" what might otherwise not have been.[6] But that is not at issue. Clearly, there are images that are merely *virtual.* They are real only in *effect* rather than in *actual fact.* We know that once the movie is over, we can return to "normal life"—even if with gratitude that a *Matrix*-like world does not exist. As we will explore more fully below, however, there are certain realities we must acknowledge rather than wish away.

Third, the person who believes reality is like a wet lump of clay says something self-contradictory or just trivial. He either believes his view is a universal reality, or it is just something he himself has created, which means it does not apply to others. Gary Zukav, a best-selling author, begins his book *Soul Stories* with the sentence, "This is a book of true stories."[7] But what exactly does he mean? Sometimes the stories are about events that actually happened; other times they are not (or they are a combination of the two).

He tells about a reporter who spoke to an elder from the Lakota, a Native American tribe. The tribe tells a story about the white buffalo calf woman who gave them their sacred pipe. Asked whether this story is true, the elder replied, "I don't know whether it actually happened that way or not, but you can see for yourself that it's true."[8] Of course, stories can be told that *communicate* truths. Aesop's fables and the parables of Jesus do not describe actual events, but they teach important truths. But this isn't what Zukav means. He goes on: "You may find that something that is true for someone else is not true for you. You might also find that something that is true for you is not true for someone else. . . . You have to decide.[9] Zukav claims that we *create* what is true and real.

You've been told, "That's just *your* reality." Or maybe you've heard, "It's real if it's real for you." How do we respond? Let's ask the person who says that each of us can custom make our own reality whether he *actually* believes this. If he says yes, we can tell him, "Then you believe that there is at least *one* thing that cannot be shaped by human beings—that is, the incontestable reality that everyone can shape his own reality." In other words, if something is real for him but not for me, then he believes the following statement is undeniable: It is absolutely the case that something can be real for one person but not for another. If that is true, then there is at least *one* thing that applies universally to all people, and this would contradict what he originally affirmed.

Or we can ask him, "Is your idea—that each of us can shape our own reality—nothing more than a reality you yourself created? Is this wet-lump-of-clay idea something you invented? If so, why do you think it applies to me at all?" Of course, our friend certainly appears to be saying that his view *does* apply to everyone. In that case, he has contradicted himself. He ultimately believes that not *all* reality can be created. Some things are real or exist, about which we can do absolutely nothing.

There is at least *some* objective reality that applies to everyone and that cannot be altered by us. We are not being "arrogant" or "imperialistic," therefore, if we assert that *some* aspect of reality cannot be manipulated by human thought or action. If a person strongly disagrees with us, he will presumably do so on the basis of a reality he thinks applies to both parties! So even if a person is incorrect about what is actually real, everyone inescapably believes that some kind of objective reality exists. This being so, the discussion can move beyond the question, "Does objective reality exist?" to, "Given that objective reality is unavoidable, how do I justify or support my understanding of objective reality?"

Fourth, how far do we want to go in our reality-creation—to the point of denying evil and suffering in the world? Such a view is implausible on the face of it. As I type these words, I am in southern India—a land of breathtaking landscapes, magnificent architecture, hospitable people, as well as the finest dishes I've ever eaten. Despite this, much of India's population lives in squalor and poverty. When I visited Calcutta in 1984, I was struck by the fact that so many people—literally hundreds and hundreds of thousands—were homeless and slept on sidewalks and in rail stations. The thought hit me: "I'm going back to the States, and these impoverished people will continue to live as they are." But isn't our reality-creating friend claiming that poverty, diseases such as AIDS, pollution, and other problems can be eradicated simply by fabricating his own reality? Perhaps a visit to places such as Calcutta would bring some realism to such anti-realistic talk! The poorest of Calcuttans do not have the luxury of fabricating a problem-free reality. This hollow "solution" to cure the world's ills is literally unbelievable.

Fifth, to believe something sincerely does not make it real. Some things cannot be made real or true no matter how sincere our belief. Also, this conviction ("sincere belief makes it real") is itself believed to be a universal reality apart from anyone sincerely believing it. According to some, reality is what you sincerely believe it to be. Sincerity, they believe, makes something real. For example, if I sincerely believe that Marxism or some form of Eastern philosophy is true, then it somehow *becomes* true. But I can think of a number of things that are false or wrong no matter how sincerely one might believe they are true or good: sincere serial killing, sincere rape, sincere torture of innocent victims, sincere random shootings, sincere Fascism, sincere Satanism. Sincerity does not make 2+2=5, nor does it alter the law of gravity. Sincere belief will not bring a lost loved one back from the dead. Sincerity won't change the fact that my favorite baseball team, the Cleveland Indians, lost the World Series to the Atlanta Braves in 1995 and then to the Florida Marlins in 1997.

You may have seen the bumper sticker that reads, "God said it! I believe it! That settles it!" But let's ask ourselves, "If God exists and communicates with human beings, then how does my believing it (or not) settle anything at all?" A more accurate rendering of this slogan would be, "God said it! That settles it whether I believe it or not!" We have to differentiate between the truth of a particular belief and the belief (or the act of believing) itself. For example, it's true that 2+2=4. But this or that person may not believe that 2+2=4. How does my sincerely believing something make it true? Had it been false before and then it became true? Why not, instead, accept the commonsense intuition we share and live by each day—that things are true or false whether we believe them or not? After all, sincerely believing won't make rush hour traffic or mounting utility bills go away! If we're honest, we have to admit that many things are not under our control.

Furthermore, this "sincere belief" criterion for truth is itself a fixed and absolute rule of those who proclaim it. In essence, they say, "You are wrong and mistaken if you disagree with my view that sincere belief makes something true." The person who believes that reality is not created by sincerity can reply, "What if I sincerely believe that believing something sincerely *does not* make something true?" This question reveals the self-contradictory nature of the notion that truth is created by sincere belief. If it were, *both* of these sincere believers would be correct—though holding to contradictory points of view. The sincere-belief person believes that her criterion is true and that those who disagree—even sincerely—are wrong.

As I said earlier, our present choices *do* make a difference and give shape to certain realities. But the crucial point is this: Once we have made a choice, it is an unalterable reality that the choice cannot be un-chosen. That is, it is metaphysically (or in reality) impossible to change the past—whether by humans or by God. (Remember that God's power does not extend to self-contradictory or nonsensical notions such as making square circles or making a stone so big that he can't lift it. No power can bring about these states of affairs. Similarly, this also pertains to "unfixing" the necessarily fixed past.) The past has a certain "hardness" to it that the future does not have. No amount of human manipulation can alter what has already taken place. Therefore, the past—history—is a reality we have to acknowledge; it is not a wet lump of clay to mold any way we want. We see, therefore, that all reality cannot be shaped by our choosing or by our sincerely believing, and we must come to grips with this fact.

We must also remember what John Searle said about anti-realism: It satisfies a basic urge to have power. People don't like being at the mercy of the real world, to live in accordance with it, to acknowledge certain constraints.[10] Anti-realism is in large part motivated by a desire to control. Of course, this motivation factor doesn't *disprove* anti-realism. (That's why we looked at *reasons* to reject it.)

But it is important to keep this factor in mind when talking with anti-realists. Perhaps gracious conversation and friendship will expose some of these motivations as well as provide ample reasons as to why we don't have to give up on a serious-minded realism that acknowledges human limitations and is willing to face life's harsh realities.

◆ Summary

- That which is real exists (whether it is physical, spiritual, propositional, and so on).
- We have the capability to bring about certain events or states of affairs by our choices and actions.
- But there are many things that are not simply "real for you but not for me." Many things exist that are real for both of us and that we have no power to change (e.g., the past, gravity, mathematical truths, the harsh realities of life).
- The person who believes that reality is like a wet lump of clay that we can shape any way we like believes that this is a universal reality—not just for him.
- Respond to the anti-realist by asking, "If something is real for you but not for me, don't you believe the following truth: It is absolutely the case that something can be real for one person but not for another"? If this is true, then there is at least one thing that applies universally to all people.
- If a person believes that the wet-lump-of-clay idea is just something she has created and nothing more, then you can ask, "Why do you think it applies to me at all?"
- If sincere belief makes something real, then is this viewpoint universal and absolute? What if I sincerely believe that sincere belief does *not* make something real? Both views obviously cannot be true.
- We must not forget that the motivation for power or control is behind much anti-realism today. While this point itself is not an argument against anti-realism, it is important to take into account.

◆ Further Reading

Copan, Paul. *Is Everything Really Relative?* Norcross, Ga.: Ravi Zacharias International Ministries, 1999.

———. *"True for You, but Not for Me": Deflating the Slogans That Leave Christians Speechless.* Minneapolis: Bethany House, 1998.

Groothuis, Douglas. *Truth Decay.* Downers Grove, Ill.: InterVarsity Press, 2000.

Nagel, Thomas. *The Last Word.* New York: Oxford University Press, 1997.

REALITY IS SHAPED
BY FORCES
BEYOND OUR CONTROL

Earlier I made passing mention of *The Truman Show,* a movie about a man named Truman Burbank whose life is literally a TV show in a sheltered environment called Seahaven. Everyone in his life is an actor, and this "world within a world" is equipped with five thousand cameras that monitor Truman's every move. He thinks that his world is reality. In the movie, Christof is the producer of *The Truman Show* and the manipulator of Truman's life. He says, "While the world [Truman] inhabits is somewhat counterfeit, Truman is genuine." Marlon, an artificial "friend" of Truman's, says about the show, "It's all true. It's all real. Nothing here is fake.... It's merely controlled." This movie and others, such as *The Matrix,* raise interesting questions about reality.

In the last chapter we saw that reality is not a wet lump of clay to be shaped any way we want. In this chapter we will look at the view that reality is shaped by certain sociological or biological forces beyond our control. This second view about reality is a kind of determinism. That is, whatever we happen to think or do or say can ultimately be traced to a preceding series of causes and effects. The present has been determined by the past. The conclusion people draw from this assumption is, No matter how hard we try to gain objectivity or arrive at the truth about a matter, our historical and cultural context or our genetic makeup ultimately overpowers us. Thus, all we can say is, "This is just *my* perspective"—and no more.

In the scenario under consideration, people claim that we don't have *any* power to create our own reality. Rather, it has been determined for us by forces beyond our control.

First, although we must acknowledge our limitations, biases, and perspectives, we are not doomed by our environment to mere "perspective." Some measure of objectivity is possible. Before examining this issue, however, we should recognize the humbling truth about ourselves: We are limited and never as objective as we'd like to be. Our cultural environment, family background, place in history, and a host of other factors can and often do distort our perceptions. We are not 100 percent bias-free, purely objective individuals. That's the downside. On a more positive note, we can still achieve objectivity despite an array of influences that shape us. To deny the possibility of *any* truth statements or *any* objectivity is to declare the following a true and objective fact: It is *objectively true* that we cannot know something as objectively true! Again, truth is inescapable.

Second, those who claim that we are determined purely by certain forces or by nothing more than genetics don't really believe this. Those who say we have been determined by social or genetic forces do not believe they themselves have been. When someone says, "We're just the products of our environment or our genes," she does not believe that this statement is nothing more than the product of her environment or her genes. She believes that there is good reason to hold such a view, that such a view has been reflected on and rationally concluded; therefore, she makes herself an exception to her own rule. Furthermore, if this determinist really believed her own statement, then she would have to affirm another contradiction: She would have to say that both (1) her views on anything and (2) all opposing views would be on the same level, since both parties are the products of culture or genes or whatever. If our environment or culture or genetic makeup is responsible for what we think and do, then there seems to be no rational way to tell *which* view (if any) is true.

The geneticist and Nobel Prize winner, Francis Crick, writes in his book *The Astonishing Hypothesis:*

The Astonishing Hypothesis is that "You," your joys and your sorrows, your memories and your ambitions, your sense of personal identity and free will, are in fact no more than the behavior of a vast assembly of nerve cells and their associated molecules. . . . This hypothesis is so alien to the ideas of most people today that it can truly be called "astonishing."[1]

On the contrary, what is *truly* astonishing is what Crick fails to see: If Crick is right, then his book is "no more than the behavior of a vast assembly of nerve cells and their associated molecules"! Crick gives the impression that he, unlike the rest of us, has somehow been able to evade the physiological forces that determine what the rest of us think. (This is called the "self-excepting fallacy.") He gives the impression that *his* particular nerve cells and their associated molecules had absolutely nothing to do with his "rational" conclusions.

A couple years ago, on a plane to Boston I sat next to a rather hard-nosed atheist. He spoke to me in a rather condescending tone, as though belief in God were old-fashioned and quaint—though intriguing. When I talked with him about objective moral values, he maintained that they do not exist. He said, "What we call morality is no more than an attempt to survive and reproduce. In fact, *all* that we do is nothing more than our struggle to survive and reproduce."

I replied, "Does this mean that your own atheistic beliefs are nothing more than an attempt to survive and reproduce? If you take this route, then you'll have to admit that both your atheism and my theism spring from the same underlying instinct to survive and reproduce, and there's no way to tell which of us is correct—or if we're both wrong."

In a similar vein, the behaviorist makes this claim: Human beings are nothing more than the product of their personal background; freedom is an illusion, and our choices are simply the predictable outcome of a series of pre-existing conditions. The famous behaviorist and author of *Walden Two*, B. F. Skinner, declared, "If I am right about human behavior, I have written the autobiography of a nonperson. . . . So far as I know, my behavior at any given moment has been nothing more than the product of my genetic endowment, my personal history, and the current setting."[2] But again, Skinner's very statement should not be taken as an assertion of an objective truth. Rather, what he said was itself "nothing more than the product of [his] genetic endowment, [his] personal history, and the current setting." Thus, there is no good reason to believe what he claimed. If Skinner was correct, it was purely by accident.

The pragmatist thinker Richard Rorty's perspective bears a family resemblance to that of Skinner. Rorty claims that nothing can be said about truth or rationality apart from one's own society's descriptions.[3] The problem here is that Rorty is being ethnocentric and therefore arbitrary. Why should we take *our* society as the boundary-setter for truth or knowledge? Why should we think *our* society—as opposed to anyone else's—has a monopoly on this question? And why think that we cannot learn from other societies and adopt some of their practices or skills for knowing?[4] Furthermore, it sounds as though what Rorty asserts would cut across cultures and societies.

The study of history bears out another illuminating example. Keith Windschuttle, an Australian historian, has documented in his book *The Killing of History* the decline of serious historical study. Until recently, knowledge about history was presumed to be accessible:

> For most of the last 2,400 years, the essence of history has continued to be that it should try to tell the truth, to describe as best as possible what really happened. Over this time, of course, many historians have been exposed as mistaken, opinionated and often completely wrong, but their critics have usually felt obliged to show they were wrong about real things, that their claims about the past were different from the things that actually happened. In other words, the critics still operated on the assumption that the truth was within the historian's grasp.[5]

Since the beginning of the 1990s, however, historians have increasingly disbelieved that there is any distinction between myth and fact, between fiction and nonfiction: "The newly dominant theorists within the humanities and social sciences assert that it is impossible to tell the truth about the past or to use history to produce knowledge in any objective sense at all."[6] The writing of history is virtually no different from propaganda. Or it can be seen as the attempt of one racial, social, or political group to assert power over another. Literary critics and social theorists are now writing their own versions of history.

This leads us to ask, "And what of these very historians themselves who claim that writing history is nothing more than asserting power or nothing more than a reflection of ever changing cultural ideas? What should we make of the claim that we cannot distinguish between fiction and nonfiction?" As you probably concluded, such assertions end up either being mired in self-contradiction, or they say nothing at all. On the one hand, the "expert" who maintains that we cannot distinguish between fiction and nonfiction in history doesn't *really* believe this. After all, he believes that at least his statement is not fictitious! He expects his audience to take what he is saying to be factual rather than mythical. He certainly does not want them wondering, "Is this scholar giving me fact or fiction?" Thus, the relativistic historian contradicts himself by making his own views the exception to the rule. On the other hand, if all history writing is an assertion of power or the product of one's social environment, then the person making this claim is doing nothing more than exerting power or expressing what his social environment has determined for him to believe. In other words, he says nothing meaningful. His view is no different from the next person's. Both views have been shaped by external factors.

As we noted earlier, the slogan "There are no facts, only interpretations" (which springs from the belief that we are completely context-bound) falls prey to this problem: The person asserting this statement makes himself an exception to it. Clearly, the one saying this believes that his statement is factual, not merely interpretive.

Here is another slogan related to the alleged inability to speak about objective reality due to the fact that we have been shaped by forces beyond our control: "There is no reality, only appearances." Woody Allen once mused, "What if everything is an illusion and nothing exists? In that case I definitely overpaid for my carpet." However, the person who declares this only-appearances view believes that at least this viewpoint properly reflects reality. And, furthermore, if there is no reality, aren't the appearances themselves still real?

The following slogan is quite common in many academic circles: "The truth (or a text) is just an assertion of power." The atmosphere of many American universities is politically charged, and the bashing of "dead white males" has become something of a cottage industry of late.[7] The Western canon of "great books" by Plato, Shakespeare, and Milton has been seriously challenged by radical professors and politicized campus groups. They assert that any claim to truth or to authority in a text is merely ideological—an attempt to assert individual or group power over others. Rather, we can make texts say what we want them to; there is no "authorial intent" to discover. And what is in a text that gives it objectivity anyway? We are all culture-bound and socially limited. Why should one ethnic group or interest group be preferred over another? How can we speak about objective reality or truth?

The problem with the truth-as-power or text-as-power mentality is that (1) it is not always true, and (2) so what? There are plenty of truths that have zero power attached to them. "It's cold at the North Pole" and "My shirt is green" are true statements, but uttering them is hardly a matter of pushing one's propositional weight around. Truth does not necessarily connote power. But even if it is the case that truth or texts assert power, so what? The (presumably true) statement that truth or texts assert power also asserts power. That is, if every truth statement is an assertion of power, then to say so is also an assertion of power. And if texts are attempts to exert power, then so are the texts that try to tell us this. Thus, such assertions do not get us very far. Why not? As we have repeatedly seen, the person either contradicts himself (by acting as though *his* statement *is not* an assertion of power) or says nothing at all (since his statement is one among many assertions of power and nothing more).

A final slogan to note is this: "Question authority!" Although there is undoubtedly a tendency for, say, political authorities to overstep their bounds (just as there *are* some texts that can oppress), there is something fundamentally flawed in the assumption of this quip. This slogan presupposes an authority of its own. It essentially says, "Question all authority, but don't question *my* authority!" Some kind of objective (or, dare we say, authoritative) standpoint will be inevitable; objectivity is inescapable. Those who deny objectivity in the name of cultural limitations and multiple perspectives will make themselves exceptions to their own rule, asserting that their words *are not* culture-bound, that their perspective about perspective *is* correct.

Again, those who reduce all that we think and do to genetics, environment, reproduction and survival, or the workings of language do one of two things: (1) They contradict themselves by acting as though they have escaped the influences to which everyone else is subject (the self-excepting fallacy), or (2) they say nothing at all since what they express is nothing more than the product of those influences. Again, we are confronted with inescapable, objective reality.

◆ Summary

- We should recognize the humbling truth about ourselves: We are limited and never as objective as we would like to be.
- Despite our limitations, we are not doomed by our environment to mere perspective. Some measure of objectivity is possible.
- Those who claim that we are determined by certain forces or nothing more than genetics do not really believe this. Either (1) they too are determined by the same forces that determine what the rest of us think, or (2) they are just giving their perspective, which has been shaped by the very same forces that have shaped everyone else's.
- Slogans such as "There is no reality, only appearances" or, "Question authority" presume a certain reality and authority.
- To claim that the truth (or a text) is merely an assertion of power is (1) not always true and (2) not very interesting. In the first place, certain truths ("My shirt is green") assert no power. Second, if every truth statement is an assertion of power, then to say so is an assertion of power; if texts are attempts to exert power, then so are the texts that say so.

◆ Further Reading

Beckwith, Francis, and Greg Koukl. *Relativism: Feet Firmly Planted in Midair.* Grand Rapids: Baker, 1999.

Beilby, Jim, and David Clark. *Why Bother with Truth? Finding Knowledge in a Skeptical Society.* RZIM Critical Questions Booklet Series. Norcross, Ga.: Ravi Zacharias International Ministries, 2000.

Nagel, Thomas. *The Last Word.* New York: Oxford University Press, 1997.

PART TWO

CHALLENGES RELATED TO WORLDVIEWS

5

Everything Is One with the Divine; All Else Is an Illusion

n her book *Out on a Limb,* Shirley MacLaine said that the "tragedy of the human race was that we had forgotten that we were each Divine." She then added, "*You* are everything. Everything you want to know is inside of you. You are the universe."[1]

Such a view is typical in certain Eastern philosophies, such as the Advaita Vedanta school of Hinduism. One collection of Hindu scriptures, the Upanishads, speaks of the undifferentiated unity of reality (called monism). Some types of Eastern monism—though not all—are referred to as pantheism (from the Greek *pan*—"everything"— and *theos*—"God"): Everything that exists is ultimately reduced to the Reality that Hindus call Brahman. The Upanishads declare that the self *(atman)* is identical with Brahman.

- "All this is Atman."[2]
- "Atman is being known. . . . Everything is known."[3]
- "This self is the Brahman."[4]
- "I am Brahman."[5]

Within this school of thinking, there is no dualism (an actual distinction between two things, such as subject and object, or between persons) or plurality of things. Any apparent difference between you and me or between you and the Ultimate Reality can be compared to a wrinkle in a carpet. The wrinkle is not ultimately distinct from the carpet, as, say, my desk is different from the computer on which I am typing.

As the Hindu philosopher Sankara held, the ultimate reality of Brahman, with which each of us is identical, is pure consciousness without any distinctions whatsoever. Although this notion is difficult to grasp, we can compare it to our own consciousness—but without any thought, reason, or emotion. Brahman is

> what your own consciousness would be like if you were able to completely blank your mind of all internal differentiation and distinctions—that is, if through meditation you eliminated all sense impressions, feelings, and thoughts and simply experienced a state of pure awareness.[6]

This reality—Brahman—alone exists; it is the sole reality, and there are no distinctions. Everything else is illusory.[7] This Ultimate Reality has no personality; it is impersonal and beyond description.

The cosmic amnesia that Shirley MacLaine speaks of is resolved by a kind of mystical illumination or intuitive insight. We do not reason our way to this insight, since this pure consciousness is beyond reason. New Age thinkers tell us that we must look within ourselves to find our true identity.

This kind of thinking is reflected in Neale Donald Walsch's *Conversations with God*, in which he claims that God "told" him that "words are the least reliable purveyor of truth."[8] (This raises the obvious question, Isn't Walsch's "God" using words, which are an unreliable means of communication?) Look at Walsch's alleged conversation with God:

> [God:] I cannot tell you My Truth until you stop telling Me yours.
> [Walsch:] But my truth about God comes from *You.*
> [God:] Who said so?
> [Walsch:] Leaders. Ministers. Rabbis. Priests. Books. The *Bible,* for heaven's sake!
> [God:] Those are not authoritative sources.
> [Walsch:] They *aren't?*
> [God:] No.
> [Walsch:] Then what *is?*
> [God:] Listen to your *feelings.*[9]

The West's embrace of such Eastern ideas is not by accident. The cold rationalism of the Enlightenment, modern technology's depersonalizing influence on society, and the ecological ruination of the earth by human beings have helped make Eastern monism more appealing. New Age thinking—a kind of souped-up Hinduism—holds that humans are evolving toward the recognition of their godhood or union with "God." This unified global spirituality will lead to a unified humanity (a kind of social utopia) and harmony with nature.

Yet ironically, Eastern monism actually *undermines* the divinely given gifts of rationality, personality, and creation. And those who have leaned toward the East overlook the resources within the Christian tradition to affirm the importance (though not the deification) of reason, personality and relationships, and care for creation. But we are getting ahead of ourselves.

There are philosophical problems with Eastern monism, and I want to suggest some points that might be useful in helping to *dis-orient* our Eastern-minded friends and assisting them in seeing the greater plausibility of theism. Theism emphasizes the Creator-creature distinction. Human beings, though not divine, are made in God's image and reflect certain characteristics of the Creator in important ways: God is relational, self-aware, rational, personal, volitional, and moral; we have been made with these characteristics, though in limited measure. Below, therefore, are reasons for preferring theism over monism/pantheism.

First, the universal amnesia regarding our divinity is difficult to account for. If the human self is really divine—if there is no difference between God and humans—then doesn't it seem strange that so many human beings have forgotten this? How do we account for this cosmic amnesia?[10]

Second, perhaps it is the monist who is misperceiving reality. The Eastern-minded person claims that the traditional Westerner, who takes as real the world external to her mind, is caught in the grip of illusion and does not see things clearly. But if we are deceived about our consciousness of our own individual existence and about our being distinct from other persons or from physical entities around us, perhaps we could argue that the monist or pantheist is also being deceived in maintaining that reality is ultimately one.[11] After all, the monist has drawn his conclusions based on his own individual experience as well. Further, why should we take the Eastern monistic view seriously when it seems to be so contrary to our experience?

Third, how does the pantheist distinguish between fact and fantasy? The burden of proof is on the monist to tell us why the common ability to distinguish between these two is a mistake. Monism has some serious practical consequences. If the world is illusory, how can we distinguish between imagination or fantasy and what is real? Lao-Tzu, the purported founder of Taoism, asked, "If, when I was asleep I was a man dreaming I was a butterfly, how do I know when I am awake, I am not a butterfly dreaming that I am a man?"

It seems that for the most part (unless we're habitually on mind-altering drugs or under alcohol's influence), we humans can differentiate between a dream state and an awareness of a real world outside our minds. This seems quite obvious to us, and the burden of proof falls to the one who rejects what is apparent to so many. As philosopher Peter van Inwagen puts it, the question arises why anyone would accept this Eastern view of reality. The best procedure is to believe what is apparently true unless there is some known reason to believe that it is not. For example, many centuries ago, belief that the earth was flat seemed true, but this thinking needed to change when the earth was shown to be spherical. The best we can do as humans is to believe what seems to be true unless we have good reasons to reject it. But to believe what does not even *seem* to be true when we have no good reason to accept it is profoundly counter-intuitive.[12] Why think that our senses are regularly deceiving us? Aristotle was right when he said that the rejection of sense perception is a rejection of common sense: "To disregard sense perception . . . would be an instance of intellectual weakness."[13]

The monistic Indian guru Sathya Sai Baba has said:

> Rebuked by his wife
> For not shedding even a tear
> Over the death of their only child,
> The man explained
> "I dreamed last night
> That I was blessed with seven sons;
> They all vanished when I woke up.
> Whom shall I weep for?
> The seven that are vapour
> Or the one that is dust?
> The seven are a dream
> And the one a day-dream."[14]

Yet monism does not allow us to distinguish between dream and non-dream. It compels us to reject the everyday-ness and matter-of-factness of life. Even gurus such as Baba must eat, sneeze, relieve themselves, look both ways before crossing streets, and comply with the law of gravity. If monists truly practiced what they preached, would any of them be left?[15]

If monism is true, then another bizarre result follows. Say you are holding a pen in front of you. You press your eyeball a certain way so that you see double. But you know by other means of perception (such as your sense of touch) and by memory that the pen is not double. If monism were true, however, then the object would be both double and non-double in the same manner! We would be left with an utterly impossible state of affairs.

Fourth, if the external world does not exist and everything is ultimately one, why does the monist try to explain away the external world in the first place?

If the external world is illusory, how did it ever come into people's thinking that it is real? What motivates the monist to try to convince distinction-making persons that those differences do not really exist? Shouldn't the very attempt to do so make us slightly suspicious—like the older child who volunteers "I didn't do it" to his mother when his toddler sibling is wailing and has a red welt on her cheek? If the monist tries to convince those who disagree with his view, isn't he assuming that he knows precisely what his friend appears to be experiencing? Wouldn't that perhaps be an argument in favor of an external world, at least on the face of it? Furthermore, the very fact that the monist disagrees with his detractor assumes that their views are really different. Otherwise, why try to change another person's mind?

In any event, there is no satisfactory experiential basis for believing in this illusionistic philosophy.[16] Everyday experience and observation are completely at odds with this claim. Should we really give up on the validation and verification of certain scientific discoveries? This monistic approach is out of touch with life as we live it each day. The wisest and commonsense course to take is this: Our sense perception of the physical world should be presumed innocent until proven guilty.

On the other hand, the Christian faith does not call us to abandon a critical realism about the world around us. While we may misperceive (e.g., we see a mirage on the hot pavement making it look wet) or commit errors, we can still get a great deal right. The fact that we can recognize our errors actually presupposes that truth exists; by knowing what is true, we can judge something to be erroneous. The fact that we differentiate between illusions or mirages and true (veridical) perception attests to our ability to differentiate between accurate and inaccurate sensory experience.

Fifth, if the external world is illusory, at least the illusion is real, which creates a serious problem for monism: There are two real entities instead of just one. If I am just a man dreaming I am a butterfly, or vice versa, then can't it be said that at least the dream has a certain reality to it, even if this dream state does not correspond to the external world or to the Ultimate Reality? In other words, at least *two* realities in the universe would exist: (1) the One/Ultimate Reality and (2) the *illusion* of the external world.[17] Thus, everything is not all one.

Sixth, the monist will deny rules of logic, which is self-defeating. The monist can, therefore, give us no reason for believing his view is true. D. T. Suzuki wrote in his *Introduction to Zen Buddhism* that we comprehend life only when we abandon logic.[18] Yet Suzuki uses logic to deny the use of logic. He uses the law of non-contradiction (A cannot be both A and non-A) to make his point. Rejecting the either-or distinction common in Western logic, Suzuki favors the both-and "logic" of monism (Eastern logic). But to do so is actually to utilize Western logic. The Easterner is assuming that he must decide between either Western logic or Eastern logic. If making logical distinctions is not necessary to discern the truth, then the monist cannot hope to explain his view.

A similar blunder was made by Alan Watts, a former Christian minister who became a Buddhist. He maintained that apparent opposites such as good and evil, active and passive, truth and falsehood, yin and yang do not exist in light of a higher unity. He rejected rules of logic since all reality is ultimately one. He rejected Christianity as truth because it was "incorrigibly theistic." But to reject Christianity, he used logic. He believed in the very distinctions he claimed his worldview denied. He believed Christianity was the false or incorrect view and that Buddhism was *true*. The acceptance of monism *and* the rejection of distinctions present us with a clear and obvious distinction.

Since logic presupposes distinctions, the monist cannot even *argue* for the truth of his position since this would entail that non-monistic views are false. He would use Western (either-or) logic to do so. One cannot eliminate another philosophy of life without using the hard edge of logic. And the monist's own position is further undermined because he himself makes distinctions within his own worldview. For instance, he presupposes a distinction between the enlightened person and one who is unenlightened. Again, basic laws of logic are necessary and inescapable. To deny them is to use them.

Seventh, it is difficult to take seriously a worldview that denies the existence of good and evil. In his book *The Lotus and the Robot*, Arthur Koestler tells of an interview he and several others had with a Zen Buddhist scholar at the International House of Tokyo. Writing in 1961, Koestler recounts the conversation:

> "Buddhism lays great stress on truth. Why should a man tell the truth when it may be to his advantage to lie!"
> "Because it is simpler."
> Somebody else tried another tack. "You favor tolerance toward all religions and all political systems. What about Hitler's gas chambers?"
> "That was very silly of him."
> "Just silly, not evil?"
> "Evil is a Christian concept. Good and evil exist only on a relative scale."
> "Should it include those who deny tolerance?"
> "That is thinking in opposite categories, which is alien to our thought."
> And so it went on, round after dreary round.[19]

Koestler offered this assessment of the conversation: "This impartial tolerance towards killer and the killed, a tolerance devoid of charity, makes one sceptical regarding the contribution which Zen Buddhism has to offer the moral recovery of Japan—or any other country."[20]

Eastern monism ultimately yields a moral relativism. Herman Hesse's *Siddhartha* shows us the tragic moral consequences of monism. Siddhartha (or Buddha) states at the closing of his life:

> Everything that exists is good—death as well as life, sin as well as holiness, wisdom as well as folly. Everything is necessary, everything needs only my agree-

ment, my assent, my loving understanding: then all is well with me and nothing can harm me. I learned through my body and soul that it was necessary for me to sin, that I needed to lust, that I had to strive for property and experience nausea and the depths of despair in order to learn not to resist them, in order to love the world, and no longer compare it with some kind of desired imaginary world, some imaginary vision of perfection, but to leave it as it is, to love it and be glad to belong to it.[21]

Also, *if* the Ultimate Reality is beyond good and evil—that is, it is neither good nor evil—and *if* evil is only an illusion, there are ultimately no wrong acts or thoughts: "What difference would it make whether we praise or curse, counsel or rape, love or murder someone? If there is no final moral difference between these actions, then absolute moral responsibilities do not exist."[22] Cruelty and compassion are not ultimately different. Monism obliterates any objective moral order as well as one's personal moral responsibility to do right and reject wrong.[23]

Neal Walsch's *Conversations with God* makes the same kind of relativistic assertions. Claiming to speak God's words, Walsch writes, "You have no obligation. Neither in relationship, nor in all of life. . . . Nor are you bound by any circumstances or situations, nor constrained by any code or law. Nor are you punishable for any offense, nor capable of any—for there is no such thing as being '*offensive*' in the eyes of God."[24] Again, "I have never set down a 'right' or 'wrong,' a 'do' or 'don't.' To do so would be to strip you completely of your greatest gift—the opportunity to do as you please."[25] This prohibition, it is claimed, would deny the reality of who a human person really is. There are no objective moral standards or obligations according to such a view, as these would interfere with one's freedom.

On the other hand, our being made in the image of a personal and good God enables us to affirm objective goodness and reject evil; we can affirm them as truly distinct. In the depths of our being, if our moral faculties are functioning reasonably well, none of us really wants to admit that there is no difference between good and evil.

G. K. Chesterton saw through the kind of affirmations that Eastern monists make: "That Jones shall worship the god within him turns out ultimately to mean that Jones shall worship Jones."[26] There is no moral challenge in the monistic view because "we alter the test instead of trying to pass the test."[27]

Eighth, Eastern monism ultimately obliterates our uniqueness as persons made in the image of a personal God. The Japanese poet Issa (1762–1826), one of the best-loved haiku poets, led a very sad life. All five of his children died before he was thirty. After one of their deaths, he went to a Zen master and asked for some advice to help him make sense of his suffering. The master told him that the world is just like the dew, which evaporates when the sun shines upon it. Life is transient, and to grieve such loss and desire something more is a failure to transcend one's own selfish desires. Despite this philosophical answer, Issa recognized that there is something more than such an impersonal explanation. He wrote this poem:

> This Dewdrop World—
> A dewdrop world [it is],
> And yet,
> And yet. . . .[28]

It seems that a view that completely contradicts the deeply personal dimension of life—which is so fundamental to our human identity—is tragically flawed. And the ultimate goal of much of Eastern thought is the annihilation of the self—the absorption of the self into the Ultimate Reality. We could compare the self to a drop that loses all identity in the ocean of the Ultimate Reality (e.g., Brahman); this takes place at *moksha* (being "snuffed out" as a self), when the cycle of reincarnation finally ends. But the philosophy of Issa's Zen master requires denying the preciousness of our deepest relationships and actually embracing an evil, callous mind-set. (We could also add that the Buddhist doctrine of transience or impermanence is self-contradictory: It affirms the permanent principle of impermanency. Oddly, it demands that we desire the elimination of desire, which is the source of suffering.)

In the Christian worldview, evil, suffering, and loss are to be faced with realism. They are not to be disowned since this would ultimately devalue us as human beings created with dignity and made for relationship with the living God. Death and suffering are actually *reminders* of our limitations and that we are not divine after all. They show us that all is not right in the world and that we must cast ourselves on the God who loves us, suffers with us, and has dealt decisively with evil in the death of Jesus on the cross. His death and resurrection paved the way for a glorious renewed existence in the new heavens and the new earth, where we'll enjoy unmediated access to God and where there will be no more sorrow and suffering—all this without obliterating our distinctive identities.

Many interreligious dialogues emphasize ritual or ethical commonalities between religions. One fundamental difference that is frequently ignored is what happens to the self in the future. Theism stresses the ongoing existence of individual humans; according to many Eastern views, the self is annihilated or extinguished.

Finally, when dealing with the Eastern mind-set in general, we must be careful to build bridges and contextualize the gospel for Eastern cultures whenever we can. As Christians, we must look for rays of truth within these cultures in order to tailor-make the gospel for them. As many from the East move to and take up residence in the West (e.g., Indian Hindus in London or Chinese in Vancouver), Christians will discover tremendous opportunities to build bridges.

Take Hinduism, for instance.[29] E. Stanley Jones, the famous missionary to India, noted that philosophical Hinduism affirms tenets that Christians can (to varying degrees) uphold and use as openings in their discussions with Hinduism's adherents:

- The Ultimate Reality is spirit(ual).
- There is unity to the whole universe.
- There is justice at the heart of the universe.
- There is a passion for freedom/liberation of the soul from death.
- There is a tremendous cost (discipleship) to living for religious devotees.[30]

Since all truth is God's truth, such topics can serve as the basis for respectful dialogue between Hindus and Christians.

But it is not only *what* we affirm that is important; it is also important *how* we do so. For instance, history is cyclical for the Hindu, not linear as Westerners commonly understand it. Obviously, this presents a problem for Christians when attempting to connect with Hindus, for the Christian faith is a historical one. For the Hindu, to say that our faith is historical implies that it had a beginning and may have an ending; on the other hand, Hinduism is an eternal and enduring religion. Many prominent Hindu thinkers believe the Hindu god Krishna of the Bhagavad Gita is merely legendary and not historical. It is not essential to the devotee of Krishna that he was incarnated (as an avatar) in history.

Where then does the Christian make a connection with the Hindu? First, the Christian should read the Bhagavad Gita, which summarizes the heart of Hindu thought. She can then say, "Hindu scholars claim that Krishna is legendary rather than historical, but what if divine truth was manifested in a historical person?" She should strongly emphasize that Christ is an eternal cosmic Person, the second member of the Trinity, and that he existed prior to the creation of the world and since creation has continued to sustain the being of everything (Col. 1:15–20). But she should also stress God's manifestation *(saguna)* in history. Christ is first cosmic and second has appeared in history. The Hindu finds this kind of message relevant and important. This connects with the Hindu. The Word was eternal before he became incarnate. He was with God and was God (John 1:1) before he became flesh (John 1:14). The Hindu ideal of hearing *(shruti)* is fulfilled in the good news of God made flesh that has been *announced* to us: "Faith comes from hearing" (Rom. 10:17).

Even the earliest Christian apologists attempted to show that their religion was not an innovation but was enduring. They plundered the writings of ancient classical literature such as that of Virgil and Homer to find themes that resembled or appeared to foreshadow or even predict God's revelation in Christ (e.g., Virgil's mention of an anticipated golden age in which a virgin would give birth to a glorious son).[31] In the same way, perhaps we can find truths within Hindu books that can provide a bridge for the gospel. Even if other religions do not possess the divine revelation found in Scripture and in Christ, they may affirm certain truths, which must be understood as God's truth. These truths should be harnessed for building bridges and cultivating relationships. At Athens, Paul cited two pagan thinkers in Acts 17:28: "In him we live and move and have our being" (Epimenides), and "we also are his off-spring" (Aratus). He quotes the pagan poet Menander in 1 Corinthians 15:33 ("Bad company corrupts good character") and Epimenides again in Titus 1:12 ("Cretans are always liars, evil brutes, lazy gluttons"). Note that he quoted these writers without affirming their particular understanding of God or the divine inspiration of their texts. Yet he used truths within classical literature to point to Christ or reinforce his moral teaching.

Therefore, we can cite other religious scriptures, not because we accept them as divinely revealed nor because we fully accept the worldviews of these religions, but because these religious books often contain longings and important spiritual themes fulfilled in the gospel of Jesus Christ.[32] Rather than criticizing their culture and holy books, we can build bridges with those from the East. We can, as Paul did, proclaim to them whom they worship in ignorance (Acts 17:23).

Even though we can have good philosophical reasons for not accepting the core of Hinduism, some of its truths may provide an open door for talking about the full revelation of God in Christ and themes of grace, sacrifice, and forgiveness.

◆ Summary

- Eastern monism maintains that all reality is ultimately one. Any apparent differences are the result of illusion *(maya)*. There is no difference between the self and this Ultimate Reality.
- The universal amnesia regarding our divinity claimed by the monist is difficult to account for.
- How does the pantheist distinguish between fact and fantasy? The burden of proof is on the monist to tell us why the common ability to distinguish between these two is a mistake.
- If the external world does not exist and everything is ultimately one, why does the monist try to explain away the external world in the first place?
- If the external world is illusory, at least the illusion is real, which creates a serious problem for monism: There are two real entities instead of just one. Ultimate Reality, therefore, cannot be one.
- The monist denies rules of logic, which is self-defeating. The monist, therefore, can give us no reason for believing his view is true.

- It is difficult to take seriously a worldview that denies the existence of good and evil.
- Eastern monism ultimately obliterates our uniqueness as persons made in the image of a personal God.
- Regarding Buddhism, its doctrine of transience or impermanence is self-contradictory: It affirms the permanent principle of impermanency.
- Buddhism makes the odd demand that we desire the elimination of desire, which is the source of suffering.
- When dealing with the Eastern mind-set in general, we must be careful to build bridges and contextualize the gospel for Eastern cultures whenever we can, picking up on their yearnings and longings that coincide with what the gospel offers.
- With Paul, we can use the literature of other worldviews to build bridges without affirming their particular understanding of God or the divine inspiration of their texts.

◆ Further Reading

Collins, Robin. "Eastern Religions." In *Reason for the Hope Within,* edited by Michael Murray. Grand Rapids: Eerdmans, 1999.

Maharaji, Rabindranath. *Death of a Guru.* Eugene, Ore.: Harvest House, 1986.

Mangalwadi, Vishal. *The World of Gurus.* 2d ed. New Delhi: Vikas, 1987.

Newport, John P. *The New Age Movement and the Biblical Worldview: Conflict and Dialogue.* Grand Rapids: Eerdmans, 1998.

WHY NOT BELIEVE IN REINCARNATION?

L ucy M. Montgomery, author of the famed Anne of Green Gables series and wife of a Presbyterian minister, adhered to some rather unorthodox views regarding the afterlife. She wrote in her journal:

I believe that if we range ourselves on the side of good the result will be of benefit to ourselves in this life and, if our spirit survives bodily death, as in some for I feel sure it will, in all succeeding lives; conversely, if we yield to or do evil the results will be disastrous to us. . . .

But I believe that *life* goes on and on endlessly in incarnation after incarnation, co-existent with God, and Anti-God, rejoicing, suffering, as good or evil wins the upper hand. To me, such an anticipation is infinitely more attractive than the dull effortless, savorless existence [!] pictured to us as the heaven of rest and reward.[1]

The idea of reincarnation (sometimes called transmigration or metempsychosis) is an integral part of Eastern philosophy. One lives and dies and is reborn many times. The actual status a person/soul has in any given life is based on his behavior in a previous life; this retribution or reward is called karma.

Montgomery's viewpoint on reincarnation is far too lighthearted when compared to much of Eastern philosophy. In the East, reincarnation reveals the failure to achieve the ultimate goal of the self, whereas in the West the identity of the self is secure. In the optimistic Westernized styling of reincarnation, rebirth offers another chance for self-improvement.[2]

The Bhagavad Gita is often quoted in connection with this doctrine. In it, the god Krishna (who is one of the incarnations of the god Vishnu) says to Arjuna, a soldier, "Both I and thou have passed through many births. Mine are known to me, but thou knowest not of thine." Krishna adds, "As a man throweth away old garments and putteth on new, even so the dweller in the body, having quitted its old mortal frame, entereth into others which are new."[3]

Because so few in the West have any awareness of purported previous-life experiences, this idea may seem farfetched to us. There is some surface evidence, though, for reincarnation. Medical doctor Ian Stevenson is probably considered the world's leading expert on reincarnation.[4] He wrote of a four-year-old Indian boy named Prakesh, who believed that his real name was Nirmal and that his real home was in another village. He wanted to go to his village, but his parents scolded him for his behavior. Five years later, however, a connection with Nirmal's family was made. Nirmal's father came to Prakesh's village, and Prakesh recognized him. As it turned out, Nirmal was the name of the man's son who had died prior to Prakesh's birth! Prakesh wanted to—and did—go to the man's village, where he identified Nirmal's former relatives and provided precise details of furnishings in Nirmal's home. Stevenson listed thirty-four items that Prakesh "remembered" and then verified these details.[5]

That said, the Eastern doctrine of reincarnation is not without its problems. Let's look at some of them.

First, reincarnation could be just as easily explained by demonization or demonic invasion. Dr. Stevenson recognized one rival option to explain the data for reincarnation: demonic intrusion.[6] When we read the Gospels, we see Jesus encountering demonic spirits regularly.[7] The apostle Paul confronts demonic powers that furnish a young girl with fortune-telling powers (Acts 16:16–18). There are ample theological reasons to believe that a demonic spirit could have furnished Prakesh with the information about his supposed relatives, village, and home.

Or take Rabi Maharaji, who grew up in a Hindu home in Trinidad and whose life was eventually transformed by an encounter with Jesus Christ. He testifies to demonic activity in his youth: "My world was filled with spirits and gods and occult powers, and my obligation from childhood was to give each its due."[8] The point here is simple: Before the doctrine of reincarnation is embraced, one must seriously consider the possibility of demonic intrusion as an explanation of alleged knowledge of a previous life.

Second, simply because someone has access to information about someone from another life does not imply that this was his own life. If a person recounts details of a past life, must it therefore be *that* person's life? This simply does not follow. What may be shown from this "recollection" is that a person possesses some knowledge of another person who once lived.[9] The reincarnationist must demonstrate that the person who possesses knowledge of another's life is indeed one and the same.

To illustrate, take the noted psychic Peter Hurkos. He provided detailed and precise information to help solve crimes, furnishing the time of certain thefts, the getaway course of the thieves (including street names), and their final destination. He had an accuracy rate of 87 to 99 percent. But Hurkos's detailed awareness of another's life is not evidence that Hurkos was the thief![10] Similarly, Prakesh's detailed knowledge of Nirmal's relatives and surroundings does not necessarily mean that Prakesh was Nirmal in a previous life.

Third, why embrace reincarnation when the biblical doctrine of a bodily resurrection has historical warrant and intellectual plausibility? How did the early church begin in Jerusalem so suddenly? Why did early Christians have such a lofty view of Jesus as early as A.D. 50? Why would good Jews switch their weekly holy day from Saturday (the Sabbath) to Sunday (the Lord's day)? What accounts for the post-resurrection appearances of Jesus to his followers? What transformed a band of frightened and cowardly disciples, who felt deeply disappointed when their hoped-for Messiah was crucified, into bold witnesses for Jesus—even to the point of persecution and martyrdom? Since much literature defending the historical plausibility of the resurrection exists,[11] I point out only that there is good reason for embracing the Christian doctrine of the bodily resurrection. This doctrine has historically opposed the (Eastern) doctrine of reincarnation. If the *Easter* faith is true, then the *Eastern* doctrine of reincarnation is not.[12]

Fourth, the doctrine of reincarnation with its cycle of births conflicts with the notion of reality's oneness and the illusory nature of the external world. In the last chapter, we noted some of the problems with Eastern monism ("everything is one"), which rejects the material world and any distinctions as illusory. According to this view, human souls and the Ultimate Reality ("God") are identical. Any difference between them, then, is purely illusory. While not all who believe in reincarnation are monists, the adherence to reincarnation by Eastern religious or philosophical monists is standard fare.

But here we run into a problem that comes with holding to both reincarnation and monism: How can one maintain both (1) that all souls are really the one Reality and (2) that distinct, individual souls can undergo successive reincarnations? The assumption of a distinct self, which is different from other selves, conflicts with the doctrine that souls are identical to Brahman, the one Ultimate Reality. So if each of us is one with this Reality, what does it mean to say that, for example, Socrates' soul rather than Plato's has been reincarnated in some present-day person?[13]

If everything is undifferentiated oneness (monism), how can one believe in the reincarnation of distinct individuals at all? Who is being reincarnated if not different individuals who are distinct from those who have already broken out of the cycle of reincarnation? Further, those who defend reincarnation speak about a real difference between those who have reached enlightenment (they realized they are one with the Ultimate Reality) and those who have not and are therefore reincarnated. In fact, the very idea of reincarnation, which is distinct from the Ultimate Reality, would have to be an illusion. Philosopher Stuart Hackett remarks that it is "not surprising that [Hindu philosopher] Sankara dismisses these problems with the supposition that the whole notion of rebirth is a part of the grand illusion."[14] If the world is an illusion, why appeal to something grounded in the external world (such as the cycle of births) to explain away the illusion?

Reincarnation, therefore, presupposes the following distinctions:

- The distinction between individual souls (Socrates and Plato).
- The distinction between the karmas of individual souls who have not yet reached enlightenment.
- The distinction between the enlightened and the unenlightened.
- The distinction between individual souls and the Ultimate Reality.

It seems that the distinctions presupposed by the doctrine of reincarnation undermine the notion of undifferentiated oneness of Reality—and vice versa.

Fifth, reincarnation does not solve the problem of evil as some claim; it only infinitely postpones it. Despite the claim that reincarnation deals with the problem of evil, it is far from obvious that it succeeds. The doctrine of karma—what you receive in this life is payback for your past life—continually postpones any explanation. How does this work—or fail to work? First, to explain away the evil in my present life, I must refer to my previous life. But to explain the evil in my past life, I must explain it away on the basis of the life before that one, and so on. "This method results in an infinite regression which only eternalizes the problem of evil without solving it."[15] If we try to account for the suffering of individuals, the root problem of evil still remains.

Sixth, if we forget our past lives, what purpose does reincarnation serve for improvement? New Age guru Shirley MacLaine wrote that the "tragedy of the human race was that we had forgotten that we were each Divine."[16] But if reincarnation is true, most people are, oddly, completely unaware of it. If this is the case, then it follows that people have no idea *why* they are being punished.

Therefore, they seem bound to repeat the evil of previous lives since they cannot remember enough to learn from them:

> It's very interesting that the reincarnationist tells us we go through cyclic rebirth and we suffer in various lives to atone for our sins. But it's very puzzling that nobody remembers his past life enough in detail to profit from it! So we don't know what we're being punished for. And if we don't know what we're being punished for, we're likely to repeat the offense. If reincarnation is really karma, or the law of justice ("as you sow, so shall you reap"), why not protect the person? Why not give him a full vision of what he had been before, with all his flaws, so that the necessary corrections could be made?[17]

People who "remember" a past life most likely live where reincarnation is believed and accepted. When investigations are made into the backgrounds of the subjects and their parents, in every case of Ian Stevenson's study, "the subjects were surrounded by a cultural and religious milieu that encouraged belief in reincarnation."[18] According to Stevenson, Americans are much weaker in details of an alleged previous life than those in non-Western countries, where reincarnation is commonly believed (e.g., Asia). At the very least, we should take into serious consideration this cultural and religious backdrop.

Seventh, if reincarnation were true and the series of rebirths were infinite, we should all have reached perfection by now. Many Eastern-minded persons believe all human beings will eventually achieve perfection and ultimately attain this enlightened state of *nirvana* (Buddhism) or *moksha* (Hinduism)— the "snuffing out" of personal existence.[19] We run into a major philosophical problem here, which is also probably the most serious objection to reincarnation: "Since most Indian views believe that everyone will achieve release from the cycle of births, it is difficult for me to see why, in an infinite series of chances, this release has not already been achieved by all."[20] Such a problem is examined more closely in the next point.

Eighth, an actual infinite series of past events is, in actuality, incoherent. Tied to the question of evil's origin is the matter of accounting for the manner in which the cycle of births came about in the first place. If we cannot account for this, then reincarnation makes little sense.[21] We have two options: (1) The cycle of rebirths is infinite, or (2) there was a first birth for each individual. The problem with reincarnation is that an actual infinite series of past events is logically impossible. As we will see, this idea is simply incoherent.

Let's begin by saying that time is the succession of events. Without any "happenings," time does not exist. Time depends on events—whether physical or mental—for its existence. So we ask, "Could past time be infinite? Could the series of past events be beginningless?"

If we subtract a number from an infinite series $\{1, 2, 3, \ldots\}$ so that we then have $\{2, 3, 4, \ldots\}$, we *still* have the same amount of events (viz., an infinite number). This becomes a problem if we apply it to the world in which we live. Or what if we removed all odd numbers from an infinite series so that we had {2, 4, 6, ...}? Would this new set be any smaller than the set of all natural numbers {1, 2, 3, ...}? No. Strangely, both would be equal, mathematically speaking, but this is absurd when we talk about the everyday world.

Furthermore, if the past is infinite and we assign to each past event a negative natural number {...−3, −2, −1, 0}, with 0 representing the present, then all of the negative numbers would have been enumerated, which is absurd. We can always add one more event yet still have the same outcome.

Let us again assign to every event in the past a series of corresponding numbers {...−3, −2, −1}.[22] If we assume that the series of past events is beginningless and therefore an infinite time had elapsed by the time of, say, Socrates, then would not *more than an infinite number* of events have been added by the present time? We would naturally think so, but an infinite number cannot be added to. At any point in the past, an infinite series of events has already elapsed. But how could this be since we have arrived at today?

Therefore, while the idea of an actual infinite is not a problem in the world of mathematics, it becomes a serious problem when applied to the goings-on of the world in which we live.

Ninth, besides the philosophical problems with karma and reincarnation, these Eastern ideas, practically speaking, can be quite oppressive. Take the caste system in India. Those who are born into a low caste or as "untouchables" are, in the minds of many Hindus, receiving payment for a previous life. In speaking with Indian friends (or American friends who have worked there) and having been to India several times myself, I have come to know that a deep-seated fatalism dominates the mind of many in the caste system and that those from higher castes actually have qualms about helping, as Mother Teresa did, "the poor of the poor." Why? Because those in the lower castes are just reaping what they sowed in a previous life. It would be unwise—or even immoral—to work against their karma and assist them. In doing so, one's own karmic status in the next life is lowered rather than elevated. The same would apply to a person in a low caste: Why should he try to improve his lot in life if his undesired status is the result of karmic law? It is indeed ironic that the East has been exporting to the West this fatalistic system, which has been such a burden to those living under it. To many Westerners enamored with the East, reincarnation gives them the sporting chance they need to reach perfection! But many in the East know the enslaving tyranny of this doctrine.

By contrast, the Christian gospel offers, literally, karmic relief! Rather than the oppressive burden of payback from a previous life, Jesus offers rest for the soul to those who would come after him (Matt. 11:28–30). After listing immoral past practices of the Corinthians—sexual immorality, stealing, drunkenness— the apostle Paul writes the good news: "And that is what some of you were. But you were washed, you were sanctified, you were justified in the name of the Lord Jesus Christ and by the Spirit of our God" (1 Cor. 6:11). The gospel offers hope from the burden of the cosmic law of cause and effect. God's kindness and grace bring forgiveness from the guilt and shame of sin because Jesus has borne the weight of our sins on the cross. It is a glorious *dis-orientation* to be freed from this Eastern doctrine and to be rescued by Christ's death!

Take Krister Sairsingh, for example. Krister, who received his Ph.D. in religion from Harvard, grew up in a Hindu home in Trinidad. Although he firmly believed that "all religions are valid paths to the spiritual life,"[23] he made a pact with a friend to devote their lives to a defense of the Hindu way of life. In fact, his entire family was devoted to this task. Despite his religious zeal, however, Krister lived a life of terror and dread. And although he believed in his own divinity, he did not treat beggars kindly and disliked "uncultured" Hindus from lower castes. The more he realized his failings and self-centeredness, the more desperate he began to feel. As a Hindu, he recognized that he would have to pay for such evil attitudes in the next life. Although he had a Christian friend who told him about the person of Jesus, Krister thought it arrogant to think there was something unique about him. But he began to read about Jesus in the Bible. He asked himself, "Could this Jesus possibly rescue me from the terror and dread which had enveloped my soul?"[24]

Krister writes about his pilgrimage:

> I began to read the gospel accounts of Jesus to learn more about him. He struck me as utterly unique, different from anyone I had known or read about. . . . What astounded me most was Jesus' claim to have the power to forgive sins. . . . Who was this Jesus who could break the bondage of karma, who said he had the power to forgive sins? I had to know. I delved deeper into the Gospels. Over the next six weeks, I went into the sugarcane fields to pray, hoping that something of God's truth would be revealed to me. More than anything else, I wanted the truth.[25]

But how could this Jesus, who lived so long ago, make a difference in the life of a twentieth-century Harvard student? His mother, a prominent Hindu, noticed.

> My mother . . . admitted that she was baffled by the sudden transformation of my life. She noticed that I was no longer fearful. . . . She could not understand how such joy could have filled my life in just a few weeks. . . . She later told me [that] she would prostrate herself on the floor of the puja room [with the images of various Hindu gods], crying out for the truth. Within three weeks she too had become convinced by the teachings of Jesus.[26]

Embracing Christ and the hope of his resurrection has not only more solid philosophical and historical footing than does reincarnation, but the outworking of these radically different beliefs also has bearing on the way we live our lives each day.

◆ Summary

- Reincarnation could just as readily be explained by demonization or demonic invasion.
- Simply because someone has access to information about someone from another life does not imply that this was his own life.
- Why believe in reincarnation when the Christian doctrine of resurrection has good intellectual and historical warrant?
- The doctrine of reincarnation with its cycle of births conflicts with the notion that the external world is an illusion. How can one maintain *both* that all souls are really the one Reality *and* that distinct, individual souls (e.g., Socrates and Plato) can undergo successive reincarnations?
- The very idea of reincarnation, which is distinct from the Ultimate Reality, would have to be an illusion anyway, which is what the Hindu philosopher Sankara thought.
- Reincarnation renders the oneness doctrine (monism) incoherent because of the distinctions it presupposes: (1) between individual souls, (2) between the karmas of individual souls who have not yet reached enlightenment, (3) between the enlightened and the unenlightened, and (4) between individual souls and the Ultimate Reality.
- Vice versa, the doctrine of monism undermines the intelligibility of reincarnation.
- Reincarnation does not solve the problem of evil as some claim; it only infinitely postpones it.
- If we forget our past lives, what purpose does reincarnation serve for improvement? In most cases, those who have purported experiences of previous lives have grown up in an environment that endorses reincarnation.
- If reincarnation were true and the series of rebirths were infinite, then we all should have reached perfection by now.
- An actual infinite series of past events is, in reality, incoherent. Therefore, reincarnation seems highly unlikely.
- The doctrine of reincarnation has practical consequences: Why seek to improve my lot in life or help others when I might be working against my or another's karma?
- The Christian doctrine of forgiveness in Christ brings relief for those weighed down by reincarnation's oppressiveness.

◆ Further Reading

Albrecht, Mark. *Reincarnation: A Christian Appraisal.* Downers Grove, Ill.: InterVarsity Press, 1982.

Geisler, Norman, and J. Yutaka Amano. *The Reincarnation Sensation.* Wheaton: Tyndale, 1986.

Gudel, Joseph, Robert Bowman, and Dan Schlesinger. "Reincarnation: Did the Church Suppress It?" *Christian Research Journal* (summer 1987): 8–10, 12.

Hackett, Stuart C. *Oriental Philosophy.* Madison: University of Wisconsin Press, 1979.

IF GOD MADE
THE UNIVERSE,
WHO MADE GOD?

The famous atheist Bertrand Russell wrote about God and the universe in his essay "Why I Am Not a Christian." Having read the philosopher John Stuart Mill's autobiography, Russell was struck by what Mill wrote: "My father taught me that the question 'Who made me?' cannot be answered, since it immediately suggests the further question, 'Who made God?'"[1] Reading this, Russell concluded, "If everything must have a cause, then God must have a cause."[2]

Although Russell wrote this essay in 1927—before the big bang theory became well established—it is still startling to hear Russell make such a jump. But much more recently, even the noted Cambridge physicist Stephen Hawking does so in his best-seller, *A Brief History of Time*. He asks questions about what started the universe and what makes the universe continue to exist. What theory exists to unify everything? "Or does it need a creator, and, if so, does he have any other effect on the universe? And who created him?"[3]

Although we commonly hear children ask, "Who made God?" or, "Where did God come from?" it is surprising to hear sophisticated philosophers and scientists ask the same questions! When we examine the concept of God and the history of the universe, we begin to see that these questions are less diffi-cult to answer than we had perhaps imagined—most obviously because they are ill conceived.

The big bang theory states that the universe—physical time, space, mat-ter, and energy—came into existence cataclysmically roughly fifteen billion years ago. This discovery is based on observations such as the expanding uni-verse and the tendency of energy to spread out or dissipate; the fact that the universe is "winding down" (based on the second law of thermodynamics) implies that the universe will eventually die a "heat death" and thus meet its demise. Such discoveries have remarkably confirmed the biblical doctrine of creation out of nothing: "In the beginning God created the heavens and the earth" (Gen. 1:1). Even naturalistic scientists acknowledge this scenario. According to the astrophysicists John Barrow and Joseph Silk, "Our new pic-ture is more akin to the traditional metaphysical picture of creation out of nothing, for it predicts a definite beginning to events in time, indeed a defi-nite beginning to time itself."[4] In fact, Nobel Prize–winning physicist Stephen Weinberg once remarked that the now rejected "steady state theory [which views the universe as eternally existent] is philosophically the most attractive theory because it *least* resembles the account given in Genesis."[5] But, of course, the universe did begin, much to Weinberg's dismay, and the physical state prior[6] to the big bang was literally nothing.[7]

Some people would claim that the universe came into existence uncaused out of nothing. One atheist, Michael Martin, says that "this beginning [of the universe] may be uncaused" and that such theories are in fact "being taken seriously by scientists."[8] But clearly something cannot come into existence uncaused out of nothing since being cannot come from nonbeing. This is a basic truth about reality itself (i.e., metaphysics); it isn't, as Martin believes,[9] some culture-bound conviction that will be overturned in some future scien-tific revolution (comparable to what Newton or Einstein introduced). Think about it: How can something be produced when absolutely no potentiality exists for its emergence? (By "nothing," I do not mean subatomic particles or other unobservable entities.) The chances of something coming from absolute nothingness are zero, since there is not even the potentiality for a universe to come into existence. It seems that such claims about something-from-noth-ing may be rooted in an underlying attempt to avoid the implications of God's existence. That is, the principle "from nothing, nothing comes" *(ex nihilo, nihil fit)* would likely be universally assumed by skeptics were it not for the fact that the universe's beginning greatly resembles the account in Genesis 1:1.

This something-from-nothing idea was called "absurd" even by the Scottish skeptic David Hume.[10] The atheist philosopher Kai Nielsen acknowledges how misplaced is the notion of something coming from nothing: "Suppose you hear a loud bang . . . and you ask me, 'What made that bang?' and I reply, 'Nothing, it just happened.' You would not accept that. In fact you would find my reply quite unintelligible."[11] If this is true of a little bang, then why not the big bang as well?

Having given a bit of context to our discussion, let's go back to the question, "Who made God?" How do we respond? *First, the theist does not claim that whatever exists must have a cause, but whatever* begins *to exist must have a cause.* No right-thinking theist argues that everything must have a cause; if this were the case, then God would need a cause too! Rather, we begin with the fundamental principle about reality that anything that begins to exist has a cause. The universe clearly began and therefore has a cause. On the other hand, the eternal and self-existent God by definition does not need a cause; he is uncaused.

When talking to a skeptic, you might be told, "Everything—even the cause of the universe—must itself have a cause." But the skeptic is making a questionable assumption, one that has no room for a being like God. This is question-begging or assuming what one wants to prove. It's like saying, "All reality is physical; therefore God can't exist." Clearly, all reality is not physical. For example, laws of logic or moral truths (e.g., "torturing babies for fun is wrong") are not physical but are still obviously real. Similarly, it is not self-evident that *everything* must have a cause (as we will see shortly).

Furthermore, to say that "everything that begins to exist has a cause" does not automatically entail that *God* created the universe. (For example, the question to explore is whether the cause is personal or impersonal.)[12] *Our second response to the skeptic is this: "We must begin with a non-question-begging starting point, and 'everything that begins to exist has a cause' does just that."*

Let me elaborate on this by making a third point: Thinkers in the past such as Plato and Aristotle assumed that the universe was eternal and needed no caused explanation for its origin. Two hundred years ago atheists assumed the universe's eternality and that it needed no cause or explanation. *If the universe can hypothetically be self-explanatory, then why can't the same be true for God?* But no one could reasonably accept that something could pop into existence uncaused, out of nothing. Now that contemporary science has revealed that the universe began, many nontheists are squirming at the possible theistic implications of this fact. What I'm saying is that our principle does not rule out the possibility of something being self-existent—whether God or the universe. And we should ask those who persist in arguing that the universe came from literally nothing, "Why should this be any more likely than its having come from God?" As the philosopher Dallas Willard rightly states,

"An eternally self-subsistent being is no more improbable than a self-subsistent event emerging from no cause."[13]

Fourth, certain realities—such as logical laws or mathematical truths—are clearly uncaused, as they are eternal and necessary; therefore, it cannot be true that everything must have a cause. Even if the world did not exist, would the statement 2+2=4 still be true? Of course! Would the law of non-contradiction (A cannot equal non-A) still be true? Yes. Such truths are *real* (even though they are not physical), but there is no good reason to think that they have been caused. If this is true, why couldn't we say the same about God himself? The point, again, is that not everything must have a cause.

Fifth, the question "Who made God?" commits the "category fallacy." It is another form of begging the question. In other words, it eliminates from the outset any possibility of God being the explanatory cause of the universe. How so? The question assumes that everything must be a contingent (dependent) entity and that there can be no such thing as a self-existent and uncaused entity like God. But God is in a different category than caused entities; to put them in the same category is unfair. It's like asking, "How does the color green taste?" or, "What flavor is middle C?" God, by definition, is an uncaused, necessary (non-contingent) being. God must not be blamed for not being finite and contingent! If we reframe the question "Who made God?" to clarify our categories, we will find that the question answers itself. Let's rephrase the question in this way: *"What caused the self-existent, uncaused Cause, who is by definition unmakeable, to exist?"* Any further questions?

I remember when I was ten years old, lying in bed at night and wondering about how God could always have existed. I reasoned that if the universe began, then something must have existed prior to it to bring it into being. Even though it was mind-boggling to me—and still is today!—to think about how God could *always* have existed, I concluded, "At some point I'll have to reach a stopping place beyond which I cannot go. *Something* had to exist before the universe began. Why not God?" Although my thinking was considerably less refined as a ten-year-old than it is today, the conclusion still seems quite reasonable.

◆ Summary

- The state prior to the big bang was literally nothing—which implies not even the potential for something—and nothing can begin to exist without a cause. To claim that something can come from literally nothing is metaphysical nonsense.
- The theist does not claim that whatever exists must have a cause but whatever *begins* to exist must have a cause.

- To claim that everything must have a cause assumes from the start that God cannot exist (which is question-begging). The theist offers a non-question-begging starting point since it is not immediately apparent whether the universe's cause is personal or impersonal.
- Plato and Aristotle (and later thinkers) assumed that the universe was eternal and did not need an originating cause. Now that we know the universe began, why can't we allow for God as an uncaused Cause?
- We can ask those who persist in arguing that the universe came from literally nothing, "Why should this be any more likely than its having come from God?"
- Logical and mathematical truths (e.g., 2+2=4) are uncaused even though they are real; therefore, not everything must be caused. Why can't this be true of God?
- To ask, "Who made God?" commits a category fallacy: It assumes that God is a contingent (dependent), caused entity. God by definition is uncaused and eternally existent.

◆ Further Reading

Craig, William Lane. *God, Are You There?* RZIM Critical Questions Booklet Series. Norcross, Ga.: Ravi Zacharias International Ministries, 1999.

———. *Reasonable Faith.* Wheaton, Ill.: Crossway Books, 1994.

Moreland, J. P., and Kai Nielsen. *Does God Exist?* Amherst, N.Y.: Prometheus, 1993.

IF GOD KNOWS WHAT WE'RE GOING TO DO, THEN WE DON'T HAVE FREE WILL

The poet Robert Frost penned these memorable lines:

> I shall be telling this with a sigh
> Somewhere ages and ages
>   hence:
> Two roads diverged in a wood,
>   and I—
> I took the one less traveled by,
> And that has made all the difference.[1]

Unfortunately, some have confused freedom with license to do whatever one wants. The poet Walt Whitman wrote about choosing any road he wanted:

> Afoot and light-hearted I take to the
>   open road,
> Healthy, free, the world before me,
> The long brown path before me,
>   leading wherever I choose.[2]

Although freedom can be abused, there is something very important about it. Without a genuine freedom or self-determination to choose between alternatives, we find we are stripped of true moral responsibility. If I say, "Tobacco companies are responsible for my lung cancer" (despite decades of warning from the Surgeon General), I am ignoring personal responsibility for my actions. If everything we do is determined simply by our genes, culture, or Madison Avenue advertisers, then how can we be personally responsible for the actions we take? How can a criminal be justifiably punished if his social environment alone made him what he is? Moral responsibility makes sense if we can choose between alternatives and are not determined by previous states and events.

But think about this: What if my choices are known in advance, for example, by God? Do I then have genuine freedom in everyday choices? If God knows my future, then there's absolutely nothing I can do to change it. Am I really free? Some skeptics find such a scenario troubling and consider the idea of God tyrannical and limiting. But are human freedom and God's foreknowledge really contradictory?

Let me make three initial points—one about God's knowledge in the Bible, one about God's initiating grace in salvation, and the third about human freedom. Then we will move on to the foreknowledge-freedom question.

Point 1: The Bible clearly affirms God's knowledge of future human choices and actions. Before a word is on our tongue, God knows it (Ps. 139:4). Indeed, God knows the end from the beginning (Isa. 46:10). Jesus knew that his disciple Peter would deny him three times (Mark 14:30) and that another disciple, Judas Iscariot, would betray him (John 6:64). Jesus predicted the circumstances surrounding his crucifixion (Mark 10:33–34) and knew even minute details about future human actions (Mark 14:13–14). Some people—including Christian theologians and philosophers[3]—have concluded that if the future is known in the mind of God, then we are like the cartoon character Popeye: "I am what I am; that's all that I am—I'm Popeye the sailor man!" We cannot do anything about who we are nor take significant action since God already knows everything. The future is fixed and determined. To escape this locked-in future, these thinkers deny that God knows what human beings will do in the future; they overturn the traditional Christian belief that God knows future choices of human beings. Can we be truly free even if God knows what we will do? I believe the answer is yes (more on this below).

Point 2: Regarding our ability to accept God's free offer of salvation, we must admit that on our own we are powerless to do so. We do not pull ourselves up by our bootstraps and say, "I have decided to follow Jesus." Left to ourselves, none of us seeks God (Rom. 3:11).[4] Such empowering comes through God's initiating grace and the assistance of the Holy Spirit, which are available to all. The influence of God's Spirit and the availability of God's assistance—what John Wesley called "prevenient grace"—enable a person to respond to God.

But this influence and availability can be rejected, as in Acts 7:51: "You . . . always resist the Holy Spirit." Yet in choices not related to salvation, we have the power of self-determination.

Point 3: What is freedom? By freedom, I do not mean simply doing whatever one wants. A drug addict, chain smoker, or alcoholic can do whatever he wants—namely, take drugs, smoke, or drink. But because of a long series of choices, he may be a slave to his habit without much hope for change.[5] A person under hypnosis or someone who has been brainwashed may do what she wants, but this does not strike us as genuine freedom. Furthermore, a person might be in a rut of bad habits (constantly eating chocolate, say) that enslaves her so that at present she cannot break out of the pattern. But that in no way means that the chocoholic does not have the freedom of will to develop the ability to refrain from indulging certain negative impulses and engaging in positive ones in the future. We have the capacity both to grow in our freedom and to diminish it.[6]

Simply put, the freedom of which I am speaking[7] means that the buck stops with the human agent, and there is no reason to look further for the cause of human decisions. As agents or self-movers, we have the capacity to bring about certain potentialities. By creative—or even not-so-creative—choices, we can make a difference and set new events in motion. Just because our character, inner motives or desires,[8] ingrained habits, and family upbringing shape and deeply influence our choices, this does not mean that such things determine them. In fact, we can argue that our character is shaped by our choices rather than our choices by our character.

Free will means my choices are not determined by prior causes ("causal necessity"), and I am able to be a self-mover or self-determiner. *I*—and not my character or inner states—decide. Certain traits, therefore, such as stubbornness (or being easy-going) and feelings such as depression (or cheerfulness) are not the sum total of who I am. It is my soul or my very self—the I— that *has* certain character traits, feelings, and states. As a self-mover, I have the capacity to choose. It is the I that experiences various events and undergoes the changes of life, but these should not be equated with the I. All of these "influencing factors" (motives, character qualities) may be sufficient to account for my choices, but they do not necessitate them.[9]

At the infamous Auschwitz concentration camp, prisoner Viktor Frankl discovered that people with similar backgrounds and education responded in opposite ways to hardship and suffering. Some struggled intensely to survive whereas others gave up and lost the will to live. Often the latter, having given up all hope of surviving, ran to the wire and invited machine gun fire to bring an end to their misery and despair. Frankl concluded that "the sort of person the prisoner became was the result of an inner decision, and not the result of camp influences alone."[10] Even though everything could be taken away in such a camp, "the last of the human freedoms"—namely, to "choose one's attitude in any given set of circumstances"—could not be taken away.[11]

If we understand the nature of human choices as the outcome of previous causes and effects,[12] then we will tend to think of our own choices as the product of these preceding causes.[13] But if we, like Frankl, believe our choices are goal oriented ("I'm eating this food in order to survive") or reason oriented ("I choose not to run to the wire for the reason of a hopeful future"),[14] we will have a more robust understanding of human choice. I am free in that I act for a reason or a goal, not because of preceding causes or states.[15] Though we do not ignore our past or our environment, these factors need not override genuinely free choices.

Another matter involves the question, How does God know what we will do in the future? The simple answer is this: God knows truths about the future because it is essential for God to know all truths. Two models have been used to understand this concept. The philosopher Thomas Aquinas illustrates the first model. He assumed that God is "outside time" and sees the entire sequence of historical events at once. He used the analogy of one who sits on a mountaintop or a high watchtower and sees travelers walking along a long stretch of road.[16] This person better anticipates what travelers can expect because a wider vista is available to him than to the travelers.[17] Aquinas spoke about God's "glance" or "the divine sight."[18] We can call this model the *perceptual* model.

This kind of model, however, does not show how God can have a "vision" of the entire sweep of events—past, present, and future—since the past and future do not *now* exist.[19] God is reduced to making inferences about future states that do not yet exist based on awareness of past and present states. For example, based on information about past patterns, we make general calculations about how far the earth's tectonic plates will shift in twenty-five years; what the phase of the moon or the location of particular planets will be at a certain time; what the life expectancy of the sun is. But this method seems somewhat uncertain and can appear to be more like guesswork when it comes to the less predictable area of human choices. If God inferred future choices on the basis of present knowledge or causes, then a great deal of guesswork—however divinely educated—would still be involved.

I think there is a better model for understanding God's foreknowledge: the *rational* or *conceptual* model. To grasp this model, let's first ask ourselves, What makes God what he is? He has a certain nature that makes him the maximally great Being he is.[20] He is all-powerful, all-good, all-knowing, and the like. Without any of these attributes, he would not be God. These attributes are essential to God—they make him what he is. If some great being were all-powerful but not all-good, then this being could not be considered God and thus would not be worthy of worship. When it comes to God's knowledge, it is *essential* and *innate* to God to know all truths—whether past, present, or future.[21] If he did not know future events, he could not be God. Why not? God is the kind of being who necessarily knows all truth statements—including truth statements about the future.[22] Knowledge of future events and human choices is intrinsic to God—just as being all-powerful and all-good are intrinsic to him. God cannot help but know truth statements about the future. Therefore, even if we cannot explain *how* God knows future events—just as we cannot explain *how* God is all-powerful—this does not mean that God cannot *have* perfect foreknowledge.[23]

Now that we have taken the time to do some explaining and defining, let's look at the question of the coexistence of human freedom and divine foreknowledge.

First, God's knowledge of future actions does not by itself hinder human freedom since knowledge does not actually cause *anything.* For the sake of argument, let's assume that a psychic has an intuition that a murder will take place tomorrow in a house down the street. Tomorrow turns into today and . . . the butler did it! But what did the psychic's knowledge actually *do?* Certainly, the psychic's awareness of this pending murder did not necessitate the murder taking place or cause the butler to do it. Even if we can truly say that this psychic *knew* that a murder would take place, we do not conclude that the butler did not freely commit murder. It would seem strange to claim that simply to *know* something will take place is virtually to cause it to happen. So why should things change if God is the knower? Knowing that a future event (such as a murder) will occur is distinct from its actual cause (the free actions of the butler).

Or take this example: As a Christian, I believe that Jesus Christ will one day return. Based on the revelation of God in the Bible, I can make the stronger claim: I *know* that Jesus will return in the future. My knowing that Jesus will return, however, has nothing to do with bringing it about. Knowing and bringing about are distinct. Someone might ask, "But don't we know that Jesus is coming because God himself has made this known to us?" Yes. But my point here is that (fore)knowledge by itself does nothing. The fact that God knows ahead of time that the second coming will occur is beside the point. The real question is, Does foreknowledge itself *cause* anything? The answer is no. (We could add that divine foreknowledge of the timing of the second coming does not demand that Jesus return at a particular moment and not a moment sooner or later. This is up to the free choice of God.)

In the same manner, God can have foreknowledge of free human choices without that foreknowledge causing anything. Something else—namely, human choice—must be added to the equation to cause human actions that God foreknows. In this sense, my foreknowledge is no different from God's since by itself foreknowledge does nothing. Even the predestinarian theologian John Calvin admitted that "mere prescience [foreknowledge] lays no necessity on the creatures" even though some have thought that it itself is the "cause of things."[24]

For the moment, however, let's forget about human knowers altogether. Let's talk about the supreme Knower—God himself. God knows not only what *we* will do in the future, he also knows what *he* will do in the future. Christian theologians have assumed that God is not hemmed in by entities or forces external to himself; he is entirely free. God freely chose to create the world. He did not have to. He freely chose to populate the world with humans, and he selected this particular world over another. Again, he did not have to. He freely chose to come to earth in the person of Jesus and to rescue us from our estrangement with God, our fellow human beings, and the rest of creation. God was not compelled to act so lovingly as though we deserved to be created. But if God foreknows what he is going to do (e.g., to answer my prayer tomorrow), is he also determined to do it simply because he knows his own future actions? Of course not! God's foreknowledge of his own actions does not cause him to do them; rather, he does them freely. In the same way, God's foreknowledge of what I'll do in the future need not cause me to do something either. St. Augustine got it right when he said, "Don't you see that you will have to be careful lest someone say to you that, if all things of which God has foreknowledge are done by necessity and not voluntarily, his own future acts will be done not voluntarily but by necessity?"[25]

To reinforce the point, let's set aside all knowers from consideration—whether divine or human. Borrowing from a notable example from Aristotle,[26] we will assume that it is true that a sea battle will take place next Saturday. That is, the statement "A sea battle will take place next Saturday" is true if and only if a sea battle will take place next Saturday.[27] Next Saturday comes, and there is a sea battle. Even though this future event does not exist now, the truth that it will take place exists, without anyone existing to know it. Remember that there is absolutely no knower of this future human action in our thought experiment; no divine or human knower is necessary for this event to come about.[28] If this sea battle will truly take place next Saturday, then it is up to humans to bring it about. Obviously, no one *knows* that the event will happen; therefore, knowledge is not doing the causing.

Or take this statement: "It is true that Paul Copan is typing at his computer on 18 January 2001." Because of my free choice to type today (18 January 2001), a statement expressing the truth that I would type on 18 January 2001 was true a thousand (or million) years ago.

Some people will say that if God knows past and future truths, then both sets of truths are logically the same in that they are "locked in place." The future is just as unpreventable as the past.[29] But besides being counter-intuitive, such a fatalistic position is simply not true. By definition, we cannot act on or cause anything in the past (backward causation). We simply have no power over it, whereas we can act in the present to bring about future events.[30]

The point is this: God's foreknowledge of free human choices is no different from (possible) human foreknowledge in that this *knowledge* does not actually *cause* anything to happen. Furthermore, truth statements about the future could be made *without* appeal to God as the knower. Thus, God's knowledge about a future event sidesteps the issue. When it comes to causing a human event to take place, it is up to humans to bring these events about. If it was true last year that a sea battle would take place next Saturday, then (in one sense) it does not matter if God (or any human) knew that it would take place in order for it to come about. Just because this event is known to God does not mean that human beings have not freely made the choice to engage in a sea battle. Knowing and causing are separate matters.

Second, we must distinguish between certainty and necessity—between what will *happen and what* must *happen.* Over the years, my wife and I have enjoyed reading aloud to each other classics such as *Silas Marner, The Scarlet Letter,* and *A Tale of Two Cities.* Let's say that tonight my wife and I want to read Jane Austen's *Sense and Sensibility.* If God foreknows that we will read *Sense and Sensibility* tonight, then we *will* read it tonight. Does that mean that we *must* read it? No. We could choose to read *Pride and Prejudice* instead. In that case, God's foreknowledge would be different. Our free choices give content to a portion of God's foreknowledge. God's foreknowledge of our choices means only that we *will* choose what he foreknows; it does not mean we *must* choose what we do. In other words, while it is *certain* that my wife and I will read *Sense and Sensibility* tonight (and God foreknows this), this does not mean that it is *necessary.* Certainty does not entail necessity.

The skeptical argument—that God's foreknowledge nullifies human freedom—results from the confusion between certainty and necessity. Look at the following two statements:

A. If God knows in advance that I will do x, x will necessarily come about.
B. Necessarily, if God knows in advance that I will do x, x will come about.

What is the difference between A and B?[31] Statement A implies that the action God foreknows *had to* come about (that it *must* happen); because God foreknows it, it is necessarily so and could not have been otherwise. Statement B implies that my action that God foreknows *may* have been different (e.g., if I had chosen differently), but it *will* happen.[32] Therefore, *if* God knows that my wife and I will read *Sense and Sensibility* tonight, then we *will,* but, logically speaking, this does not mean that we *have to.* While our reading this particular novel is *certain,* it is not *necessary,* We must be careful not to confuse these two different ideas, as is so often done. While something that is necessary is also certain, what is certain may not be necessary.[33]

Some people will ask: "If our free choices become the basis or ground for part of God's foreknowledge, doesn't that make God subject to the whims of human choices? Doesn't this minimize God's actual rule of the universe?" Let's briefly tackle this question.[34]

Third, God, knowing what we would do in all possible worlds, brought about a world that utilizes free human choices to accomplish his purposes in history. What we would freely do in possible worlds and what we *will* freely do in the *actual* world are known to God because he is God. Thus, the fact that humans will, say, make the free choice to fight at sea in the actual world is the basis for God's foreknowledge about this event. But lest I be misunderstood, this does not mean that God is no longer sovereign over history. Far from it.

As we have seen, in order to be God, God must be not only all-knowing regarding future human choices, but he must also know all possible worlds and any free human choices that would take place in them.[35]

Based on knowing what we would do in certain worlds, God arranges the details of the actual world without eliminating our freedom. (Again, God is not merely inferring what we would do. God, by virtue of who he is, knows what we will do in the actual world.) Obviously, God himself also freely *acts* in the world—not to mention preserves it from nonexistence; he freely and graciously sent Jesus into the world to rescue us from our plight. God decrees or orders that certain things come about, but such decrees do not violate genuine human freedom.

Therefore, when we say that our freely made choices are the basis of part of God's foreknowledge ("If I had chosen this instead of that, God's foreknowledge would have been different"), we are not minimizing God's sovereignty. Rather, God's precise foreknowledge of all truths—possible and actual—takes into full account what we would choose in various possible worlds. Based on this knowledge, he brings about the *actual* world in which we find ourselves and knows what we *will* choose. We freely choose what God—who, because of who he is by nature—knew we would choose in this actual world.[36] Thus, God plans a world in which his purposes are, in significant part, brought about through his innate knowledge of what free creatures would freely do in all the possible worlds in which they might have existed, down to the minute details. Therefore, there are no surprises for God in the free choices that I make, and God's own action, providential care, and ruling of history are not undermined.[37] As we will see in a later chapter, God creates a world in which as many persons as possible are saved and as few persons as possible are lost.[38] Thus, anyone who is lost would have been lost in all possible worlds in which he existed, suffering from "transworld depravity."

Someone might ask, "But aren't events and human choices rigged by God since he chose this particular world over another possible world?" No, they are not rigged because the basis of God's choosing this world over others is his knowledge of what we would freely do in this world. For example, in Scripture God is portrayed as knowing contrary-to-fact (counterfactual) circumstances. God tells David that *if* he remains at Keilah, *then* Saul will come after him. David flees, and what would have been true *if* David had stayed does not come to pass (1 Sam. 23:6–13). God, through the prophets, gives warnings of what will happen *if* people act in one way rather than another (Amos 7:1–6; Jonah 3). Jesus knows that *if* his disciples obey his commands, *then* they will find things just as he predicted (Matt. 17:27; John 21:6). From these examples of freely chosen human actions and contrary-to-fact scenarios, it becomes apparent that God is not rigging human choices. Rather, he takes human choices into account in his foreknowledge and acts on that knowledge in creating this world. This is far from determinism (or compatibilism), in which the basis for my acting is ultimately rooted in God's decree rather than in my choosing.

Therefore, God's foreknowledge is obviously chronologically prior to my actual choices (i.e., God knew from eternity what my choices would be in the actual world—not to mention any possible worlds in which I may have existed). But my actual choices are logically prior to God's foreknowledge. In other words, what I *will* freely choose (or what I *would have* freely chosen in various possible worlds) becomes the basis or ground on which God decides which world to create (and which to leave uncreated). God's foreknowledge is the logical *consequent* or outcome, and our future actions in this world are the *reason* why God foreknows what we will do.[39]

As a result, we are able to preserve human freedom and divine foreknowledge and sovereignty. By keeping certain distinctions in mind—between knowing and causing, between certainty and necessity, between will choose and must choose—we can steer clear of the mistaken belief that divine foreknowledge eliminates human freedom. Humans are free, and God is knowledgeable of all that they will do.[40]

◆ Summary

- Free will implies that the buck stops with the agent (the self-mover or self-starter), and there is no need to look for some cause beyond the agent (such as inner states, character, or environment). While such factors are sufficient for making choices, they do not necessitate the choices.

- Because I (my self or soul—not my inner states or my character traits) act with a goal or reason in mind, my choices are not determined by prior causes and states.

- God knows truths about the future because it is essential for God to know all truths. Just as being all-powerful and all-good are essential to God (i.e., God could not be God without these traits), so is his knowledge of the future.

- The *rational* model—"God intrinsically knows the future"—is preferred over the more hazy *perceptual* model, in which God somehow "sees" the future.

- God's knowledge of future actions does not by itself hinder human freedom since knowledge does not actually cause anything.

- Simply because I know, say, that Jesus will return does not mean that my knowing it has anything to do with bringing it about. Knowing and bringing about are clearly distinct.
- Further, if God knows what he will do in the future, this does not mean that he is therefore compelled or determined to do it—only that he *will* (freely) do it.
- With or without God, truth statements can be made about the future (e.g., a thousand years ago, it was true that I would be typing at my computer today), but this is no reason to believe humans are determined to act the way they do.
- God's foreknowledge of free human choices is no different from (possible) human foreknowledge in that this knowledge itself does not actually cause anything to happen.
- We must distinguish between certainty and necessity—between what *will* happen and what *must* happen.
- God, knowing what we would do in all possible worlds, brought about a world that utilizes free human choices to accomplish God's purposes in history.
- While God's foreknowledge of what I will do is obviously chronologically prior to my actual choices, my actual choices are logically prior, serving as the basis on which God decides which world to create and which to leave uncreated.

◆ Further Reading

Beilby, James, and Paul Eddy, ed. *Divine Foreknowledge: Four Views.* Downers Grove, Ill.: InterVarsity Press, 2001.

Craig, William Lane. *The Only Wise God.* Grand Rapids: Baker, 1987; Eugene, Ore.: Wipf and Stock, 2000.

Plantinga, Alvin. *God, Freedom, and Evil.* Grand Rapids: Eerdmans, 1977.

If God Predestines Some to Be Saved, What Choice Do I Really Have?

once knew an elderly Austrian gentleman who would reply to my question, *"Wie geht's?"* ("How's it going?") with a glum, *"Wie Gott will"* ("As God wills"). Behind his thinking lurked a fatalistic attitude: "If God wills something, then I can't do a thing about it." After all, the Bible says, "For who resists his will?" (Rom. 9:19).[1]

The previous chapter addressed the harmony between God's foreknowledge and human freedom. This chapter deals not with God's foreknowledge but with his power to decree, order, or determine certain things. The primary issue in question is the predetermined salvation (or lack thereof) of individuals *as* individuals.

Biblical references to predestination, election, calling, choosing, or foreordaining have caused believer and unbeliever alike to be baffled and even troubled. Not a few have wondered if the doctrine of predestination, associated with Augustine and John Calvin, makes God appear arbitrary. Does God choose some for salvation (and they cannot resist it) and the rest, ultimately, have no hope of belonging to God's family?

Plenty of Bible verses are marshaled in defense of this position: God "works out everything in conformity with the purpose of his will" (Eph. 1:11); "No one can come to me unless the Father who sent me draws him" (John 6:44); "All that the Father gives me will come to me" (John 6:37); "No one knows the Son except the Father, and no one knows the Father except the Son and those to whom the Son chooses to reveal him" (Matt. 11:27); "When the Gentiles heard this, they were glad and honored the word of the Lord; and all who were appointed for eternal life believed" (Acts 13:48).[2] The list could go on.

But let's get back to the question of God's apparent capriciousness in election. John Calvin writes that "God of his mere good pleasure" elects some and "passes by others."[3] By God's decree, "some are preordained to eternal life, others to eternal damnation."[4] However, does God, as a professor of mine once asked, "pick people to be saved like one picks peanuts out of a bag?" Is God being arbitrary in selecting certain persons for salvation (which is a view commonly associated with Allah in Islam)[5] and allowing the rest to be rejected? Is the ultimate explanation as to why some do not embrace Christ the fact that God has chosen to leave them in sin?[6]

The assumptions and arguments swirling around this topic are complex, and many respected theologians and scholars have articulated a defense of both sides of this position. I, however, would like to set forth a view that I have found not only intellectually satisfying and refreshing but (most importantly) biblically accurate as well. While some from the Reformed/Calvinistic persuasion may consider my view *De-formed,* I think it has much to commend it.

A major reason for addressing this topic is that it emerges frequently in conversations with Christians and non-Christians alike. One far more seasoned than I—Norman Geisler—dedicated his book *Chosen but Free* to "all my students who for the past thirty-five years have asked more questions about this than any other topic."[7] I want to sketch, therefore, a biblical response to the charge of divine arbitrariness regarding those who are saved and those who are not. I will do so by arguing for a *corporate* rather than an *individual* understanding of God's election to salvation—something more readily appreciated by the Mediterranean or Middle Eastern mind than the Western mind.[8] According to biblical scholar William Klein, "God has chosen the church as a body rather than specific individuals who populate that body."[9] Instead of saying, "God, chose *me,*" I should say, "God, chose *us.*"[10]

One point of clarification, which I mentioned earlier: God's prevenient or initiating grace is necessary for any of us to be in the position to choose freely to respond to God's love. In other words, salvation begins with God and not us. None of us is righteous or seeks after God (Rom. 3:10–11); God's Spirit must first awaken us to our need to be reconciled to God. He must make us aware of our deep moral failures, of our pride and self-centeredness. He must prepare the soil of our hearts so that we might freely accept—or reject—his love. Let us not make the mistake that salvation originates with us or that we meritoriously choose God. Rather, God initiates and influences, but we have the opportunity to embrace this God of love—or resist his loving call.

First, whoever responds to God in faith becomes part of God's chosen people. As we read the Old Testament, we see that ethnic Israel, which traces its line to Abraham, Isaac, and Jacob, is "God's chosen people" (Ps. 105:6; Isa. 44:1; 45:4; Amos 3:2). Israel was chosen to be a "light of the nations" so that God's salvation would "reach to the end of the earth" (Isa. 49:6 NASB). If a foreigner or "Gentile" (such as Ruth or Rahab) wanted to become part of God's chosen people, she would have to embrace as her own the God of Israel and the law he revealed to Moses for national Israel at Mount Sinai. Through their choice or decision, therefore, these foreigners would then *become* part of the people of God. These converts were not considered "chosen" or "elect" before this point.

Similarly, in the New Testament, the person who becomes a Christian by making a faith decision *at that point* becomes part of God's chosen people, the community of the elect. Through God's initiating influence and opening of hearts[11] (or prevenient grace), the choice is graciously made available to us to *become* elect or not, to *join* God's chosen people on the basis of Christ's work. As a hymn writer put it, "I sought the Lord, and afterward I knew, he moved my heart to seek him, seeking me." Yet God's enabling influence to believe can be resisted (Acts 7:51), his persistent wooing ignored. And it is noteworthy that the New Testament never states that the reason some individuals are not saved is simply because they were not elect or predestined.

Second, individuals are never called "chosen" or "elect" unless it is for a task or function.[12] Jesus tells his disciples, "You did not choose me, but I chose you and appointed you to go and bear fruit" (John 15:16). Here he is speaking of the fruit-bearing task or mission of the twelve disciples rather than their salvation.[13] In fact, John 6:70 makes this clear: "Have I not chosen you, the Twelve? Yet one of you is a devil!" Judas Iscariot, the betrayer of Jesus, was "chosen"— but clearly not for salvation. Jesus chose these twelve individuals to perform a specific task. And then, in similar language, a successor to Judas as one of the Twelve is "chosen" by God to carry out a specific task (Acts 1:24). Later Paul becomes a "chosen instrument" to bring the name of Jesus throughout the Roman world (Acts 9:15).

It is not particular individuals who are "chosen" or God's "elect" for salvation.[14] Rather, as Klyne Snodgrass notes, "Election is primarily a corporate term."[15] Romans 8:29 (NASB) states, "For whom He foreknew, He also predestined," but the *whom* is plural, not singular. It is general and corporate. Ephesians

1:4 tells us that God "chose *us* in him [Christ]." The very chosen Son Jesus is God's elect par excellence (Mark 1:11; Luke 9:35; 23:35; 1 Peter 1:20).[16] Christ is the head of this new people, a "chosen race" (1 Peter 2:9), and it is only *in* him (Eph. 1:3) and *through* him (Eph. 1:5) that we are chosen. We partake in the election of Christ, as God's chosen Son.[17] We become part of the elect by placing our faith in him: "Individuals are not elected and then put in Christ. They are in Christ and therefore elect."[18] We are elect because we are united with Christ ("in Christ"). When we proclaim the good news of Jesus' life, death, and resurrection, we are calling others to become part of God's elect/chosen people, who are "in" God's chosen Son.[19]

Third, God desires that all people without exception find salvation. Although we are undeserving of God's kindness, Scripture affirms God's love for a rebellious world alienated from him (John 3:16–17) and his desire for humans to be rightly related to him. Two points bear this out.

1. The biblical text expresses God's love for all and his desire that all repent and turn to him (Ezek. 18:23, 32; 33:11; Lam. 3:33; John 3:17; 1 Tim. 2:4; 2 Peter 3:9; 1 John 2:2). Jesus—God incarnate—yearns for the city of Jerusalem: "How often I have longed to gather you . . . but you were not willing" (Matt. 23:37). To Israel "[God] sent prophets . . . to bring [the people] back to him, and though they testified against them, they would not listen" (2 Chron. 24:19). God sent messengers "because he had pity on his people and on his dwelling place." But they "mocked" God's prophets and "despised his words" (2 Chron. 36:15–16). So we see that God's desires for humanity are not always fulfilled. Second Peter 2:1 describes certain false teachers who deny the Lord Jesus and turn away from him, yet it is Jesus "who bought them." That is, Christ's death was *for them,* even though these false teachers rejected the offer of salvation available to them. God is not willing that any perish but that we turn to him and come to a knowledge of the truth (1 Tim. 2:4; 2 Peter 3:9).

2. Jesus died for all people, not simply those who respond by faith to God's offer of salvation. Some scholars claim that Jesus died for a definite number of people, not literally everyone. That is, Jesus died for all *kinds* of people—regardless of their ethnic grouping, skin color, or social class—but according to this view, he did not die for *each and every* person.[20] I disagree. Christ died for *all* humanity, not just for those who find salvation. Jesus did not come to condemn the world but to die for *the world,* which God loves (John 3:16–17). The world for which Jesus died is a bad place—not just a big place. The "whole world"—a phrase used only twice in 1 John—for which Jesus died (1 John 2:2) is the "whole world" that "is under the control of the evil one [Satan]" (1 John 5:19). Jesus is not just the Savior of those who believe; he is the "the Savior of *all* men" (1 Tim. 4:10)—even if his help to rescue from sin is realized only by believers.

Fourth, as God's will is not always achieved, we must distinguish between God's determined will and his desired will. Some scholars have taken Ephesians 1:11 ("God works out everything in conformity with the purpose of his will") as a clear expression of God predestining individuals to salvation.[21] But this raises the question, How are we to understand what "God's will" means? Should we understand that God's will determines every choice that we make, or should we understand "all things" in a less sweeping manner?[22]

Examples in the Bible reveal that what God desires or wills is not always accomplished. For example, Jewish leaders who opposed Jesus "rejected God's purposes for them" (Luke 7:30). We have seen that the influence of God's Spirit can be "resisted" (Acts 7:51) and that God's Spirit can be "quenched" (1 Thess. 5:19). Jesus wept over Jerusalem, lamenting, "How often I have longed to gather your children together . . . but you were not willing" (Matt. 23:37).[23] Paul, citing Isaiah 65:2 in Romans 10:21, writes of God's exasperation at Israel's faithlessness: "All day long I have held out my hands to a disobedient and obstinate people." The problem is not that the Israelites are condemned to unbelief, but that they are a "disobedient and obstinate people."[24]

The fact that God's desires for humanity are not always achieved leads us to distinguish between two aspects of God's will: God's *desired* will (preferred will) and his *determined* will (perfect will). When we speak of God's *desired* will, we mean that which God *wants* to be realized, but it may or may not be. For example, God's desire that all people turn to him (2 Peter 3:9) is a real desire, but it is not achieved because of certain resistant human hearts. The implication here is that God has not determined specific individuals to receive salvation.[25] On the other hand, God's *determined* will cannot be hindered. What he decrees will come about: Jesus' second coming, the defeat of evil, the final state of the new heavens and the new earth, and so on. Human beings cannot hinder or thwart this aspect of his will.

Furthermore, if God predestines literally everything that happens—including acts such as the disobedience of our first ancestors[26]—then he is too closely connected to evil. James 1:13-17 tells us, however, that only what is good comes from God. Some distinction between God's desires and God's decrees is needed, therefore, so that God's sovereign purposes do not closely align him with creaturely sin.[27]

Fifth, the outcome of final salvation or condemnation is to be understood in general terms rather than specific outcomes designated for particular individuals. We read certain verses in the Bible that seem puzzling at first glance: "They [unbelievers] stumble because they disobey the message—which is also what they were destined for" (1 Peter 2:8); "Their condemnation has long been hanging over them" (2 Peter 2:3). Again, we must be careful to distinguish between the general and the specific: God has not picked individuals to be damned or to be saved. Rather, God has generally determined the outcome of those who are saved and those who are damned depending on their response to his kind initiative. That is, the outcome of those who reject God is final separation from him. Notice that the texts just cited do not say that these people cannot turn from their paths and become believers. Rather, the emphasis is that while they are still/presently rebelling, their determined outcome is damnation.[28] After all, we were all "objects of wrath" (Eph. 2:3) before we became Christians. That is, we were *destined* for separation from God had we continued living the way we did.

Rather than embracing the view that God has picked out individuals for salvation and allowed (or destined) others to be damned, we can affirm that God has chosen a body of people in Christ, and they become part of the chosen people as they embrace Christ by faith.[29]

◆ Summary

- God does not choose individuals for salvation; he chooses a body of believers. His election is corporate and general rather than individual and specific.
- If any individuals are called elect or chosen, it is for a function or task that God has for them—not specifically for salvation.
- As a group of believers "in Christ," we are "chosen in him" precisely because Jesus is God's "chosen Son." We are therefore also chosen by virtue of our union with Christ.
- Christians are not called elect or chosen until they have become Christians; this term is never used for prospective Christians (who are unbelievers and not yet part of the chosen people).
- God has graciously initiated salvation, choosing a people for himself, but God enables individuals to respond to him and thus become part of his chosen ones—or, tragically, to reject him (Acts 7:51).
- We must distinguish between what God desires and what God decrees or ordains. God's will that none perish, for example, is something God desires but is not ultimately achieved.
- Jesus' death is for all without exception rather than all without distinction; Jesus died for literally "the whole world" of people.
- While nonbelievers are *presently* rebelling against God, they are predestined to punishment (which is true of all believers who "were by nature objects of wrath" [Eph. 2:3]), but this does not imply that those destined to God's wrath are doomed to *remain* under it.

◆ Further Reading

Geisler, Norman. *Chosen but Free.* Minneapolis: Bethany House, 1999.

Klein, William. *The New Chosen People: A Corporate View of Election.* Grand Rapids: Zondervan, 1990.

THE COEXISTENCE
OF GOD AND EVIL IS A
LOGICAL CONTRADICTION

A young Muslim mother in Bosnia was repeatedly raped in front of her husband and father, with her baby screaming on the floor beside her. When her tormentors seemed finally tired of her, she begged permission to nurse the child. In response, one of the rapists swiftly decapitated the baby and threw the head in the mother's lap.[1]

We are horrified when we read about such atrocities. The Christian philosopher Alvin Plantinga says that the problem of evil is "deeply baffling."[2] Sometimes philosophical arguments seem "cold and abstract comfort" when we are faced with the shocking effects of evil in day-to-day life.[3]

We should keep in mind, however, the following points when examining the charge that God and evil are contradictory notions:

First, all worldviews must deal with the problem of evil, not just the Christian one. The question really is, Which worldview does the *best job* of adequately facing this problem? Which has the *most abundant resources* to handle it? Some atheists will simply deny the obvious by rejecting the idea that evil exists at all. The atheist Oxford zoologist Richard Dawkins declares:

> If the universe were just electrons and selfish genes, meaningless tragedies . . . are exactly what we should expect, along with equally meaningless *good* fortune. Such a universe would be neither evil nor good in intention. . . . In a universe of blind physical forces and genetic replication, some people are going to get hurt, other people are going to get lucky, and you won't find any rhyme or reason in it, nor any justice. The universe we observe has precisely the properties we should expect if there is, at bottom, no design, no purpose, no evil and no good, nothing but blind pitiless indifference.[4]

But atheists who make this move do so at great cost; they deny what is clearly understood by most human beings: an abhorrence of horrific evils, the value of human beings, moral intuitions. The implication behind Dawkins's denial could well be that if evil does exist, such a fact would point us in the direction of God's existence, as we will see.

Again, *each* worldview has to deal with evil. Will evil and suffering be explained away as illusory (as in some Eastern religions) or nonexistent (as with Richard Dawkins)? What should we make of a worldview that counterintuitively denies this universally troubling issue? Or what of an atheistic worldview that affirms objective goodness and evil yet offers no plausible background for affirming their existence?

Second, a number of atheistic (or nontheistic) thinkers flatly deny that evil even needs to be defined, which is telling. Take Edward Madden and Peter Hare: "Defining the notion of evil is irrelevant to the problem of evil we have posed because the problem remains unchanged whatever definition is accepted."[5] Such a move is characteristic of atheists and skeptics. The Christian philosopher Douglas Geivett speaks of the "almost total silence of atheist philosophers of religion on this question."[6]

But this refusal to define evil exposes a hole in the atheistic worldview. As it is, *theists* are the ones offering a definition of evil. For example, the absence, lack, or corruption of goodness is one notable definition.[7] Just as sex within the context of marriage is a good gift from God, it becomes evil and twisted when it is abused or experienced beyond its proper bounds (e.g., adultery). However, if evil presupposes a standard of goodness, then the atheist or skeptic has to deal not only with the problem of evil but with the problem of goodness as well. Where does objective goodness come from in a cosmos of matter, chance, and time? The problem of evil actually points us in the direction of God, whose character is good and the ultimate standard by which we judge something as good or evil. C. S. Lewis found this to be true in his own experience as an atheist:

> My argument against God was that the universe seemed so cruel and unjust. But how had I got this idea of *just* and *unjust?* A man does not call a line crooked unless he has some idea of a straight line. What was I comparing this universe with when I called it unjust? If the whole show was bad and senseless from A to Z, so to speak, why did I, who was supposed to be part of the show, find myself in such violent reaction against it? . . . Thus in the very act of trying to prove that God did not exist—in other words, that the whole of reality was senseless—I found I was forced to assume that one part of reality—namely my idea of justice—was full of sense. Consequently atheism turns out to be too simple. If the whole universe has no meaning, we should never have found out that it has no meaning: just as, if there were no light in the universe and therefore no creatures with eyes, we should never know it was dark. *Dark* would be without meaning.[8]

Rather than serving as an argument *against* God's existence, the reality of evil actually serves as an argument *for* God's existence:

1. If objective moral values exist, then God must exist.
2. Evil exists, and evil is an objective (negative) moral value.
3. Therefore God exists.

Evil presupposes a standard of goodness by which evil is measured.

Or perhaps we could understand evil as a departure from the way things ought to be. Even this minimal definition of evil, however, points in the direction of a design plan—and thus a Designer. If certain features of our world should be one way but are not (e.g., as a result of birth defects or disease), doesn't this presuppose a pattern to which things were designed to conform? It would seem that the failure or refusal of atheists to offer a definition of evil points to philosophical problems within their worldview.[9]

Third, philosophical responses to evil must be placed within the broader theological framework of God's revelation and work in Jesus Christ. While philosophical arguments are important in showing that God's existence does not exclude the possibility of evil, such reasonings are *partial* and must be seen against the fuller theological backdrop of the following doctrines:

- the creation and fall (God created what is good, but his creation has been marred by sin.)
- spiritual warfare involving heavenly powers (There is more to evil than merely the human sphere.)
- the inauguration of the kingdom of God in the person and ministry of Jesus Christ (Satan's kingdom is being set back, and God's is advancing.)
- Jesus' work on the cross (Jesus dealt a death blow to evil powers.)

- the final judgment (Evil acts in this life will not go unpunished.)
- the establishment of the new heavens and earth (Evil will be completely overcome.)

Philosophical arguments deal with evil only in part. Christian theology is needed, therefore, to flesh out a context in which we can make the best sense of evil in the world and to fill important gaps in our knowledge.[10]

Take, for example, the death of Jesus. This event brings insights where philosophical attempts fall short. Alvin Plantinga remarks, "As the Christian sees things, God does not stand idly by, coolly observing the suffering of his creatures. He enters into and shares our suffering. He endures the anguish of seeing his Son, the second Person of the Trinity, consigned to the bitterly cruel and shameful death of the cross."[11] The comforting and heartening news that God is with us in our suffering inspires us to press forward and do what is right in the face of evil, to hope and not despair (1 Peter 2:23–25; Heb. 12:1–2).

Fourth, there are various problems associated with evil—not just one—and there are also appropriate responses that correspond to these particular problems. Books that deal with "the problem of evil" give the impression that there is just one problem. But addressing the problem of evil is a multifaceted task. C. S. Lewis said it well in his preface to *The Problem of Pain:*

> The only purpose of the book is to solve the intellectual problem raised by suffering; for the far higher task of teaching fortitude and patience I was never fool enough to suppose myself qualified, nor have I anything to offer my readers except my conviction that when pain is to be borne, a little courage helps more than much knowledge, a little human sympathy more than much courage, and the least tincture of the love of God more than all.[12]

This quotation identifies two broad aspects of the problem of evil: the philosophical/theoretical and the emotional/practical. Furthermore, even though these problems often overlap, attending to these problems often requires different approaches.[13] In dealing with the emotional/practical problem of evil, pastoral counseling and personal relationships are most important. A person who has suffered sexual abuse as a child or who has just lost a loved one does not need—at least immediately—philosophical answers to emotion-laden problems. On the other hand, dealing with the philosophical/theoretical problem of evil requires the use of evidence and arguments.

Fifth, the logical problem of evil does not prove that God and evil are contradictory because it does not properly factor in human freedom or God's overarching purposes. Is the coexistence of God and evil a contradiction in terms, such as a square circle or a married bachelor? Philosophers have attempted to make this argument, but is it successful?

The late atheist philosopher at Oxford, J. L. Mackie, wrote an essay titled "Evil and Omnipotence,"[14] in which he declared that the following three statements are logically contradictory:

1. God is omnipotent.
2. God is a wholly good God.
3. Evil exists.

Mackie states, "The theologian, it seems, at once *must* adhere and *cannot consistently* adhere to all three."[15] Given that it is obvious that evil exists, God cannot exist.

Mackie wrongly assumed, however, that an all-good, all-powerful being must eliminate evil insofar as he can. God *could* eliminate a great deal of evil, but he would do so only at the expense of other goods (such as human freedom). Perhaps a person suffers from severe migraine headaches. A doctor could eliminate this suffering by simply "eliminating" the person with a lethal dose of morphine. But eradicating one evil would just create a greater evil. It is not obvious that a good person ought to eliminate evil insofar as he can—namely, when other evils come about as a result.

Mackie's assumption does not take into account an important good: human freedom. God created human beings as self-determining agents.[16] We have the capacity to bring about freely one state of affairs or another. Human beings have the ability to bring about great good (as did Mother Teresa), but this capacity also involves being able to do great harm (as did Josef Stalin).

One might ask, "But can't God do *anything?* Can't an all-powerful God make a world in which we freely do what's good all the time? Isn't that what omnipotence is all about?" No. He can't do things that are *logically* or *morally* impossible. Here are some things God cannot do:

- make 2+2=5
- change the past
- make square circles
- cease to exist (as he is necessarily self-existent)
- lie (Titus 1:2)
- break his promises (Heb. 6:17–18)
- violate his moral character and holiness (Hab. 1:13; Mal. 3:6; Heb. 13:8)

The "stone paradox" (if God can do *anything,* then he should be able to make a stone so big that he can't lift it) is a misguided one. No power can accomplish this, since it is nonsensical. C. S. Lewis said:

I know very well that if it is self-contradictory it is absolutely impossible. . . . His Omnipotence means power to do all that is intrinsically possible, not to do the

intrinsically impossible. You may attribute miracles to Him, but not nonsense. . . .
It remains true that all *things* are possible with God: the intrinsic impossibilities
are not things but nonentities. . . . Nonsense remains nonsense even when we
talk it about God.[17]

Just as God cannot do certain things because they are illogical or violate his
moral nature, so too God cannot commit the moral wrong of overriding genuine human freedom and moral responsibility. Perhaps, therefore, God cannot create a world in which human beings never do evil.

*Sixth, we must distinguish between logically possible worlds and feasible
worlds for God to create.* While a sin-free human world is logically possible, it
may not be feasible for God to create it. I have often heard this objection: "Certainly it is *logically* possible that a world could exist in which all people freely
choose to do good all the time. Why didn't God create it?" Admittedly, this
freedom-without-evil scenario is *theoretically* or *logically* possible. But it may
be that such a world is simply uncreatable in *actual fact.* That is, God cannot
feasibly create a world in which human beings always choose good without
compromising other more important goods—namely, human freedom. It may
be the case that no matter "how hard God tried," he simply could not create
a world with persons who always freely choose good, since it is up to humans
to do the choosing.[18] Therefore, while logically possible, it seems that such a
world is not feasible. If God creates free creatures, he cannot feasibly create
some logically possible worlds, at least not one with as much good in it as our
world has. If God were to create a sinless world, this would be a violation of
God's moral nature and the deepest purposes for which we have been made.

*Seventh, if God has a morally justifiable reason for permitting the evils that
he does, then this reasoning also undermines the logical problem of evil.* We
saw that a good person may not and often does not necessarily eliminate all
the evil and suffering that he can.[19] After all, he may eliminate one evil state
of affairs by bringing about a far greater evil.

Suppose your child joins a bizarre cult. In most cases, the wisest alternative is *not* to kidnap your child, confine him, and try to deprogram him. This
often backfires, resulting in far greater alienation of the cultist from family
and friends. It may further harden him against you and anything outside his
cult circle. Trying to eliminate one evil, therefore, could result in a far greater
one. In this case, though suffering or evil can be eliminated, doing so is not
the wisest course to take.

Similarly, God does not eliminate the world's evils, since he has an overriding purpose for allowing them to take place. God has a greater goal in mind.
Even if we do not know all of God's reasons (and there is no reason to think
we should), this does not prove that reasons do not exist. Philosopher Stephen
Evans remarks, "It's perfectly possible to have strong evidence that someone
has a good reason for an action without knowing what that reason might be."[20]

If God has a morally justifiable reason for permitting evil, then the logical problem of evil is overcome. All we have to do is add a fourth proposition to the first three:

1. God is omnipotent.
2. God is a wholly good God.
3. Evil exists.
4. God, therefore, has good reasons for permitting evil.

By adding this fourth proposition, we show that there is no contradiction between the first three. We can then say this: A good being will try to prevent evil as far as he can unless he has a good reason for permitting it.[21]

Eighth, informed philosophers of religion today acknowledge that the logical problem of evil is not a good argument against God's existence. Whether among theists or atheists, there is something of a consensus that the logical problem of evil is not a problem. Let me cite three respected philosophers of religion. Peter van Inwagen writes about the present state of affairs:

> It used to be widely held that evil—which for present purposes we may identify with undeserved pain and suffering—was incompatible with the existence of God; that no possible world contained both God and evil. So far as I am able to tell, this thesis is no longer defended.[22]

Daniel Howard-Snyder, a theist, says that the logical problem of evil "has found its way to the dustbin of philosophical fashions."[23] Even the atheist William Rowe has written, "Some philosophers have contended that the existence of evil is *logically inconsistent* with the existence of the theistic God. No one, I think, has succeeded in establishing such an extravagant claim."[24]

Although this chapter has focused on the logical problem of evil, let me round out the discussion of evil by making the following points.[25]

Ninth, real evil exists because God made us with the capacity for doing not only great good but also great harm. Without these alternatives, true freedom would not exist. As Christians, my wife and I have sought to instill in our children the meaning of being loyal and faithful friends, not only within the family but outside as well. Friends trust one another, give the other the benefit of the doubt, and stand up for one another. In the bumps and scrapes of life, our children have come to realize that schoolmates who have called themselves "friends" often have a shallow idea of friendship and thus can deeply disappoint. By contrast, our children's solid friendships are rewarding because of the trust, love, and loyalty that characterize them. The joy and meaning of friendship are set against the backdrop of having the power to hurt one another deeply. After all, we do not feel betrayed or wounded by strangers but those closest to us.

When it comes to the question of evil, if we had only the power to help others but not to harm them, we would not have a deep or meaningful responsibility for one another.[26] A world in which we cannot have a deep influence on one another—for good or ill—is a world of superficial relationships. If we could never really injure others by our words or actions, we would not have a kind of freedom worth having. Furthermore, if the consequences of our evil choices were blocked, we could not develop and deepen our own characters, which requires self-sacrifice and effort.[27]

Tenth, if God were to eliminate the consequences of evil choices, he would be a deceiver by allowing us to live in an illusory world. In the movie *Groundhog Day,* a TV weather reporter named Phil Conners (played by Bill Murray) goes to Punxsatawney, Pennsylvania, to cover the story of Punxsatawney Phil the groundhog and whether he will see his shadow. Conners is an ungracious, rude, and self-centered man who hates being in this quaint town. After reporting the groundhog's action, a freak snowstorm hits and prevents him and his crew from returning home. Remarkably, the next day when Conners wakes up, events identical to those of the previous day occur: The radio-alarm clock goes off at 6:00 A.M. playing the song "I Got You, Babe"; he encounters an old friend who wants to sell him insurance; the groundhog makes his appearance; the TV crew goes to a local restaurant. No one except Conners is aware that time is stuck in this routine day after day—as though life is rewound every night. So at one point, he figures he will do anything he cares to, taking advantage of people and acting recklessly, but the next day the same thing starts all over again. In these redundant days, Conners kills himself, kills the groundhog, and damages relationships by his foolish remarks, but the consequences of his actions are wiped out when "I Got You, Babe" wakes him up for another day of the same old thing.

What if our lives were like this? What if we could do all kinds of moral damage and experience no destructive consequences for our actions?[28] What if God always intervened to prevent us from seeing the havoc that sin and separation from God can wreak? The negative effects are not difficult to envision. We would live a life of illusion, thinking we are doing just fine in our miserable, sinful state. Unlike the prodigal son in Luke 15 who returned to his father when he finally became desperate enough, we would encounter nothing that would prompt us to move in a Godward direction. We would never be dissatisfied in our state of separation from God. If God is to deliver us from our sin and separation from him, he must make us aware of it. This is done as God permits the natural consequences of sin to be made evident to us so that we see our miserable condition and become dissatisfied with it. God wants us to see a connection between our separation from him and the consequences that follow from it: evil and suffering. As C. S. Lewis famously put it, pain is God's megaphone to rouse a dulled world.

Eleventh, natural evils that occur through tornadoes, earthquakes, and hurricanes presuppose a natural world with uniform laws that not only contribute to the well-being of human beings but also provide a context for carrying out free choices.[29] We have noted the significance of moral evils and the importance of human freedom to do either great good or great evil. But what about natural evils that devastate human lives?

As surprising as it may seem, events such as hurricanes, tornadoes, or earthquakes are actually *necessary* for the benefit of humankind. Planetary scientists affirm that these events *must* occur for the earth to maintain its delicate balances of atmospheric and other environmental conditions necessary for humans to survive. Take hurricanes, for instance.

> [They] counterbalance the ocean's tendency to leach carbon dioxide from the atmosphere. This leaching, if unchecked, would result in a catastrophic cooling of the planet. On the other hand, hurricanes prevent the oceans from trapping too much of the sun's heat by helping to circulate greenhouse gases globally as they shade the ocean locally, preventing heat from building up too dramatically for the safety of certain sea creatures.[30]

What about earthquakes? The shifting of tectonic plates (which results in earthquakes) allows the essential nutrients for life to be recycled back onto the continents. Without earthquakes, "nutrients essential for land life would erode off the continents and accumulate in the oceans. In a relatively brief time, land creatures, at least the advanced species, would starve."[31]

In general, natural laws of cause and effect actually help make human freedom possible. What if we could not predict the outcome of our actions in the world? Or what if our actions had no effect in the world? For human choices to have predictable effects, a certain uniformity in nature is required. If, say, bullets turned to cotton candy every time a criminal fired a gun and general haphazardness replaced cause and effect in the natural world, then there would be no predictable outcome to our actions. Only in a world of general regularities can we perform meaningful actions.

But there is a downside to these natural laws: They not only benefit us but also furnish a context in which harm can occur. The law of gravity is terrific if you want to get exercise by jogging, but not if something goes terribly wrong with a plane's engines in mid-flight. Fire can warm us, but it can burn us too. The laws of thermodynamics enable us to talk using our vocal chords, but they are also the cause of hurricanes and tornadoes. The effects of natural forces are by-products that make the greater good of significant human freedom possible.[32]

Someone might suggest, "Why couldn't God have created different natural laws so that natural evils could be diminished?" Daniel Howard-Snyder notes that this assumes that a stable environment for freedom can exist that does not lead to any natural evil as a side effect. But one wonders *how* such laws could be specified. As it is, the very conditions in the universe that make human life possible, if only slightly different, would not support life at all and thus no free human beings. For all we know, there may not be a more suitable world that is governed by laws that have no natural evil as a by-product.[33]

◆ Summary

- All worldviews must deal with the problem of evil, not just the Christian one.
- A number of atheistic (or nontheistic) thinkers flatly deny that evil even needs to be defined, which is very telling about the lack of explanatory resources in their worldview.
- Evil can be understood as (1) the absence, lack, or corruption of goodness (e.g., the corruption of sex in an adulterous relationship) or (2) a departure from the way things ought to be. But (1) presupposes a standard of goodness, and (2) presupposes a design plan. Both point to God, whose character is the very standard of goodness and who is the Designer of the universe.
- There are various problems associated with evil—not just one—and there are also appropriate responses that correspond to these particular problems.
- The logical problem of evil does not prove that God and evil are contradictory because it does not properly factor in human freedom or God's overarching purposes.
- We must distinguish between *logically possible* worlds and *feasible* worlds for God to create. While a sin-free human world is *logically* possible, it is not *feasible* for God to create it.
- If God has a morally justifiable reason for permitting the evils that he does, then this reasoning also rebuts the logical problem of evil.
- Even if we don't know God's reasons for permitting evil (and there is no basis for thinking we should), this does not prove that such reasons do not exist.
- Informed philosophers of religion today acknowledge that the logical problem of evil is not a good argument against God's existence.
- If we had the power only to help others but not to harm them, we would not have any deep or meaningful responsibility for one another.
- If God were to remove pain and suffering so that the consequences of sin would be hidden from us, we would live in an illusory world, having the impression that we are doing fine without being reconciled to God.

- If we did not experience the consequences of sin, we would never be dissatisfied in our state of separation from God. If God is to deliver us from our sin and separation from him, he must make us aware of our sin.
- Regarding natural evils, phenomena such as tornadoes, hurricanes, and earthquakes actually serve an important function in maintaining livable conditions on earth.
- Natural regularities furnish a context in which human freedom is exercised. For all we know, there may not be a more suitable world that is governed by laws that have no natural evil as a by-product.

◆ **Further Reading**

Geivett, R. Douglas. *Can a Good God Allow Evil?* Norcross, Ga.: Ravi Zacharias International Ministries, forthcoming.

Howard-Snyder, Daniel. "God, Evil, and Suffering." In *Reason for the Hope Within,* edited by Michael Murray. Grand Rapids: Eerdmans, 1999.

Howard-Snyder, Daniel, ed. *The Evidential Argument from Evil.* Indianapolis: Indiana University Press, 1996.

Plantinga, Alvin C. *God, Freedom, and Evil.* Grand Rapids: Eerdmans, 1977.

Van Inwagen, Peter. "The Magnitude, Duration, and Distribution of Evil." In *God, Knowledge, and Mystery: Essays in Philosophical Theology.* Ithaca, N.Y.: Cornell University Press, 1995.

WHY WOULD
A GOOD GOD SEND
PEOPLE TO HELL?

oday the idea of hell is scoffed at and ridiculed as outmoded. It is often a joking matter. For example, in a *Far Side* cartoon, Satan—with stereotypical horns and pitchfork in hand—is in "hell," surrounded by flames and the damned doing hard labor, pushing wheelbarrows and wielding pickaxes. Pointing to a round protrusion on the wall, the devil demands to know, "Hey! Hey! Hey! . . . Who's the wiseguy that just turned down the thermostat?"[1]

But hell is far from being *Far Side*-like, and its existence deeply troubles Christians and non-Christians alike. Before discussing whether the idea of hell counts against God's goodness, we should first define what we mean by hell and then proceed from there.

First, contrary to popular belief, hell is not a place with high thermal output; hell is figuratively described to depict the terrible tragedy of life apart from

God. Hell is *figuratively* characterized in the Bible as a realm of both (1) darkness and (2) flames. Why do I stress the word *figuratively*? Because if these images were literal, they would cancel each other out. How could hell be a physical fire when it is also described as darkness?[2] Taken literally, fire and darkness would be mutually exclusive. In fact, even in extrabiblical Jewish literature (e.g., 2 Enoch 10:2), a figurative understanding of the place of final anguish is assumed, as the author links "black fire" with "cold ice."

The figurative nature of the images of hell is further reinforced by the fact that hell has been prepared for spirit beings—the devil and his angels. How would unbelievers, who will most likely exist as spirit beings in the afterlife, be physically pained by eternal fire?[3] Theologian William Crockett puts it this way: "Physical fire works on physical bodies with physical nerve endings, not on spirit beings."[4]

Therefore, the "fire" in Scripture should not be taken literally—any more than the "worm" that "will not die" (Isa. 66:24) should be literally expected in hell.[5] Fire within Jewish writings around the time of Jesus simply denoted an ordained end to wickedness. Moreover, fire was often nonliteral in Jewish writings as well as the Old Testament. For instance, God is a "consuming fire" (Deut. 4:24), whose throne is "flaming with fire," and a "river of fire" issues from beneath the throne (Dan. 7:9–10). Jesus' eyes are "like blazing fire" (Rev. 1:14). The image of fire in Jewish and early Christian writings was used to create a mood of seriousness or reverence. Hell at its root is the agony and utter hopelessness of separation from God. To be "in hell" is to be "shut out from the presence of the Lord" (2 Thess. 1:9), to be deprived of an intimate union with God (i.e., heaven). "To be in hell is to have no positive contact with God, to not be an object of efficacious divine compassion or a beneficiary of effective divine mercy."[6]

In Dante Alighieri's *Divine Comedy*, the inscription above the entrance to hell reads: "Abandon all hope, all ye who enter here." This, as 2 Thessalonians 1:9 urges, is what hell is—the ultimate, everlasting separation from the source of life and hope: God. This is truly the greatest loss possible. The pain of hell should not be seen in terms of something physical (since one could potentially build up an ascetic resistance to it) but rather as pain within a person's spirit. As Mortimer Adler states, "The damned in hell do not suffer bodily fires or tortures. Their punishment is pain of loss, not of sense."[7]

Even Reformers such as John Calvin and Martin Luther maintained that the "fiery passages" regarding hell should be taken as metaphorical expressions. Calvin said, "We may conclude from many passages of Scripture, that [eternal fire] is a metaphorical expression."[8] Luther said that it is "not very important whether or not one pictures hell as it is commonly portrayed and described."[9] Even today many conservative theologians reject this literal viewpoint of hell. For instance, J. I. Packer states, "Do not try to imagine what it is like to be in hell. . . . The mistake is to take such pictures as physical descriptions, when in fact they are imagery, symbolizing realities . . . far worse than the symbols themselves."[10]

We are not trying to soften the Bible's stance regarding hell by taking a metaphorical view.[11] There really *is* biblical warrant for taking images of hell metaphorically. On the other hand, we must be careful not to make the Bible say more than it intends to say. A high view of Scripture does not necessitate taking every word in the Bible *literally*. For example, Jesus calls himself "the gate" in John 10:7, which is not literally true. Jesus spoke of his followers' "hating" their relatives (Luke 14:26), but again, he did not mean this literally.

Conversely, our final state as believers—first in "heaven" or "paradise" during the intermediate state[12] and then ultimately in "the new heavens and the new earth"[13]—should be understood fundamentally as being present with God, enjoying unmediated access to him and living in deep union with him. In this final state, when all things have been made new, the ancient prophetic promises will finally be fulfilled: "[God] will live with [his people]. They will be his people, and God himself will be with them" (Rev. 21:3). God's people "will see his face" (22:4).

Second, hell is the logical outcome of living one's life away from God. Some people ask, "Isn't it unjust for God to punish people infinitely for sins they committed during a finite period of time on earth?" The punishment seems wildly out of proportion to the crime. But this is just the problem: To focus on discrete, individual, sinful acts rather than a mind-set opposed to God or a life lived away from God is to misunderstand the crux. Heaven and hell[14] are not surprise outcomes.[15] Rather, they logically and naturally flow from how one lived and operated on earth. Just as a believer eagerly anticipates being in perfect harmony and union with his Creator and Savior in heaven, an unbeliever should see hell as a final divorce from God. "The punishment fits the crime because the punishment is the crime. Saying no to God means no God."[16] To put it another way:

> The orthodox Christian need not hold that *every* sin merits hell or has hell as its consequence; rather hell is the final consequence (and even just punishment) for those who irrevocably refuse to seek and accept God's forgiveness of their sins. By refusing God's forgiveness they freely separate themselves from God forever. The issue, then, is whether the necessity of making this fundamental decision is too much to ask of a human being.[17]

Or as Joel Green and Mark Baker put it, God's wrath is directed against ungodliness and unrighteousness (Rom. 1:18); these are identified not with "individual acts of wickedness" but with a general disposition to "refuse to honor God as God and to render him thanks."[18]

Hell is the natural consequence of one's rejection of God. For those who are lovers of God, the natural consequence is to enter the divine presence and enjoy God forever. To force someone into heaven who would hate the presence of God would be like compelling someone who cannot rise above rap music to listen endlessly to the works of Johann Sebastian Bach and Georg Friederich Handel. It would be horrible![19] Hell is both a punishment and the outcome of a mind-set against God. D. A. Carson notes that heaven would surely be hell for those who don't enjoy and desire the blessing of God's presence.[20]

Third, even if one is not fully aware of the immense horrors of hell, this does not mean that this choice is too great a weight for a person to bear—or that God's grace to choose responsibly is unavailable to all. Some people might argue that it is unfair for God to condemn someone to hell since a person does not know the full ramifications of rejecting God. But take marriage. My wife and I, convinced we were meant for each other, recited our wedding vows sincerely and cheerfully. Committed as we were at our wedding, we *later* were struck by the breadth and the immensity of the words we had spoken: "for richer, for poorer" and "in sickness and in health." We had expressed our vows seriously and responsibly, even though we could not have realized their full extent at that moment.

Similarly, the fact that we cannot *fully* comprehend the horrors of hell (or, we should add, the bliss of heaven) does not mean that we cannot choose responsibly between heaven and hell or that this decision is too heavy a responsibility for humans to bear.

Furthermore, God does not leave human beings to make this choice on their own. He offers his prevenient grace through the Holy Spirit, who convicts all people (John 16:8) and is able to draw them to himself (John 6:44). That is, God is ready to equip anyone for salvation.[21] The problem, therefore, is not that people—such as Mahatma Gandhi or Aristotle—are uninformed about Jesus or are not completely aware of the full gravity of their eternal destiny. The issue is much broader—namely, it involves resisting the influence of God's Spirit and not lovingly responding to God's kind initiative.

Fourth, what prevents the salvation of all is the free will of individuals who reject God's initiating grace. As we saw in the last chapter, while it is theoretically or logically possible for a world to exist in which every person would freely choose to do good all the time, it is not *feasible.* No matter how ideal the world God could have created, human beings would have always freely chosen to do wrong. God simply cannot in actual fact create a world in which all people freely choose to respond to his kindness and be saved.

The answer to the question, "Why would a good God send people to hell?" is therefore answered: He does not *send* people to hell; rather, people *freely choose* to ignore and resist God's initiating grace in their lives and as a result condemn themselves. In the song "Who Can Abide?" the Christian singer Michael Card articulates this truth: "This sad separation was their choice . . ."; God "simply speaks the sentence that they have passed upon themselves."[22]

C. S. Lewis, in *The Problem of Pain,* said hell exists for those who refuse to acknowledge their guilt; therefore, they can accept no forgiveness.[23] He goes on to say, "I willingly believe that the damned are, in one sense, successful, rebels to the end; that the doors of hell are locked on the *inside.*"[24]

God has given us freedom of will, which means there is the possibility of "always resisting the Holy Spirit" (Acts 7:51). God desires that all persons come to a knowledge of the truth (2 Peter 3:9). The only obstacle to universal salvation is human free will.[25] Some people just do not want God to rule over them. Philosopher Paul Moser tells of an atheist friend who would rather die than acknowledge God's existence.[26] We noted earlier that Thomas Nagel does not want a universe in which God exists. Nagel himself wants to be the Big Cheese! So why should people fault God for the existence of hell—the absence of God's presence—when all who go there have freely resisted his initiating grace and do not want to draw near to God in love and worship? Would it have been better for God not to have created humans at all for the sake of those who would resist him? Should he have deprived those who would come to experience intimacy with God of such a glorious good?

Ultimately, hell is "God's withdrawing of his presence and his blessings from men who have refused to receive them."[27] In the end, Lewis notes, there are only two kinds of people: those who say to God, "Thy will be done," and those to whom God says, "*Thy* will be done."[28] Scottish pastor and author George MacDonald put it this way: "The one principle of hell is: I am my own."[29] MacDonald said that hell is "the best that God can do for those who will not love him."[30] If a million chances were necessary for a person to be saved from hell, Lewis says, then God would give them if they would do good.[31] No one is dragged into hell; that would be unjust.[32] (Some Christians such as John Stott, Philip E. Hughes, and John Wenham have suggested that eventual annihilation of those who resist God is a possible biblical alternative to a more traditional understanding of hell. Although the debate continues and some of the arguments are worth pondering, I remain unconvinced.)[33]

Fifth, even if people in hell are in anguish, this does not mean they would prefer to be in God's presence. Resistance to God continues in hell. In C. S. Lewis's book about heaven and hell, *The Great Divorce,*[34] heaven is a realm where some people prefer not to be. They would rather be in a gloomy, miserable place than be exposed to God's presence. Hell is having one's way, apart from God's presence. This is what Scripture affirms. According to biblical scholar D. A. Carson, "There is no hint in the Bible that there is any repentance in hell."[35] But someone might point to the parable of the rich man and Lazarus in Luke 16. The rich man (who lived selfishly during his earthly life) cried out for relief in his anguish after death. Such an act, however, does not indicate that the rich man would have preferred a God-centered existence in heaven. He, like Judas after his betrayal of Jesus, felt remorseful, not repentant.[36] He simply wanted relief from his anguish. People in hell will be quite conscious of their loss, even if they do not desire to change. It is they, not God, who are responsible for their loss. Even though they intellectually recognize how badly off they are in their condition, they still choose to remain in it. They could be compared to a drug addict who knows he has a serious problem but refuses to relinquish his habit.

Carson continues:

> Perhaps we should think of hell as a place where people continue to rebel, continue to insist on their own way, continue societal structures of prejudice and hate, continue to defy the living God. And as they continue to defy God, so he continues to punish them. And the cycle goes on and on and on.[37]

C. S. Lewis states:

> I would pay any price to be able to say truthfully "All will be saved." But my reason retorts, "Without their will, or with it?" If I say "Without their will" I at once perceive a contradiction; how can the supreme voluntary act of self-surrender be involuntary? If I say "With their will," my reason replies "How if they *will not* give in?"[38]

Sixth, those in hell have committed the infinite sin, not simply a string of finite sins. Here we must make the finite-infinite contrast, not focusing chiefly on individual sins or even a lifetime of sins. We have noted that the "finite number" of sins people commit—in contrast to the "infinite punishment" they receive—is not the issue. At issue is a mind-set or disposition that continues in the afterlife. Those who have drawn near to God in their earthly lives continue to enjoy his presence in the afterlife; those who have resisted him on earth continue in their hard-heartedness in hell. Those in hell have rejected a relationship with the gracious, self-giving God, which is the ultimate sin.

Seventh, the freedom we experience on earth is a requirement for choosing one's final destiny; we freely respond affirmatively to God's loving influence or we resist it. Not uncommonly, I've heard Christians and skeptics alike ask, "Why didn't God make all human beings as we'll be in heaven—without sin and with the ability always to choose to do good? If God can guarantee a sin-free existence for believers in the afterlife, why not make it so from the start?" The question is misconceived, and I offer the following alternatives in response to it.

Alternative 1: If heaven is a place where human beings no longer have the capacity to choose to sin but only to do good and where sin cannot take place (compatibilist freedom), then a more robust freedom (incompatibilist) is an earthly prerequisite before our choices are "sealed." Our final state is the fruit of our choice to move toward or away from God on earth. To think about sin as a possibility in heaven seems troublesome. It appears that heaven (or, more accurately, the new heavens and the new earth) must be sin-free. But if this is the case, then there cannot be robust (libertarian) freedom in heaven. But isn't such freedom essential to who we are as humans? If this is so, we have a dilemma, and neither alternative looks appealing: (1) preserve human freedom and open the real possibility for sin in heaven or (2) preserve the pristine environment of heaven but remove significant human freedom.[39] How do we go about resolving this matter?

If sinning is essentially impossible in heaven (and our freedom in heaven would merely be compatibilist freedom),[40] then the kind of freedom we have on earth (incompatibilist) is not essential to our humanness. In heaven we are not free to sin, although we will carry out what we desire—namely, the good.

If libertarian freedom is not essential to us as humans, that is, it is a kind of freedom we can live without in a heavenly state, how do we bring together both heavenly sinlessness and a reasonable understanding of human freedom in a coherent way? One possible scenario is this: It is on the basis of the robust (libertarian) freedom to sin while on earth that the redeemed finally become "sealed" as a result of their directedness toward God. That is, we live in light of the choices we have made and in which we have become entrenched. Our final state is ultimately the outcome of the choices of (robustly) free agents who have chosen (while on earth) to embrace God's loving influence or to resist it freely.

While on earth we freely make choices that affect and shape our character and spiritual condition. We make free choices that move us toward or away from God, that determine our heavenly (or damned) status. Our final bliss (or condemned status) is the result of freely made choices that have shaped the direction of our lives and our destiny. "The choices made for good or evil are directly relevant to the eternal destinies they determine for us. As we form our characters, we set our spiritual compass for that location in which the lives we desire for ourselves are most fully and naturally realized."[41] By transforming the character of the redeemed into Christlikeness in the afterlife, God simply gives us the desire of our hearts.[42]

According to this view, there *must* be the possibility for evil in order for the heavenly, sinless state to be realized. Libertarian freedom on earth cannot be avoided, even though it can be bypassed in heaven.[43]

Alternative 2: It could be that God simply foreknows that no one in heaven will freely choose to sin; God, therefore, can guarantee heaven's pristine sinlessness. Some may feel that the freedom we experience on earth must continue in heaven, as such freedom is essential to who we are as human agents. We must always have the ability to choose to act either selfishly or Godwardly. Such freedom is part of our human essence or nature; without it, we would not exist, some libertarians might argue.

A satisfying solution for those taking this view might be that God foreknows that no one in heaven will actually choose to sin or act selfishly, just as he foreknows that rebellion against him in hell will freely continue forever. What will preserve heaven as an unspoiled and untarnished realm is not some divine force or permanent sealing of God that prevents the redeemed from sinning.

The redeemed just simply will not sin, and God, being who he is (a Being who innately knows all truths, including ones pertaining to our heavenly future), knows this. He knows that sinning will not even come to mind as something the redeemed would act on.[44]

Alternative 3: To strengthen alternative 2, we could add that any consideration of the possibility of sin will be gloriously overshadowed by the joys of our union with God and the Lamb. Our magnificent experience of the unmediated presence of God and Christ will so flood our hearts that not sinning will be a "no-brainer"[45]—even though it remains a possibility. My ten-year-old son, Peter, knows more about reptiles and amphibians than most adults I know. When he is near a body of water or a wooded area, I know he will be so preoccupied with observing the natural world and with catching snakes, frogs, and salamanders that he just won't get bored. While boredom is theoretically possible, his mind is so filled with his exciting surroundings that boredom just isn't realistic!

How much more mind filling and glorious to be with the Being who is more interesting than anything else that exists! God is omni-interesting. To be in a sin-free condition, finally transformed into the image of Christ, and experiencing God's direct presence through union with him will far surpass what our Edenic ancestors experienced before the fall. In such a glorious condition, sin—even if it is a possibility—will not enter our thoughts as something viable. We must note that this wonderful environment and relationship with God will not *cause* us to refrain from sinning. We will just be so preoccupied by the pure bliss and enjoyment of the gaze of God that we will not think of sinning.

Some of the thoughts in this final point are exploratory and suggestive. Admittedly, these kinds of topics remind us to be more tentative and suggestive rather than dogmatically definitive. This is only fitting as "what we will be has not yet been made known. But we know that when he appears, we shall be like him, for we shall see him as he is" (1 John 3:2).

Again, why would a good God send people to hell? It is the best that God can do for those who refuse to love him. Hell is getting what one wants (and deserves)—no God. Hell—the absence of God—is the fruit of a life directed away from God. And heaven is for those who want to be with the loving and holy God forever.

◆ Summary

- Hell is not a place with high thermal output. Flame and darkness, if taken literally, would cancel each other out. Hell is figuratively described as the final realm of life apart from God (2 Thess. 1:9—away from God's presence). Hell is the pain of loss, not of physical sensation.
- The figurative nature of the images of hell is further reinforced by the fact that hell has been prepared for spirit beings—the devil and his angels.

- Hell is both a punishment and the outcome of a mind-set against God.
- Even if one is not fully aware of the immense anguish of hell, this does not mean that this choice is too great a weight for a person to bear—or that God's grace to choose responsibly is unavailable to all.
- God does not send people to hell; rather, people freely choose to ignore and resist God's initiating grace in their lives and as a result end up condemning themselves.
- Even if people in hell are in anguish, this does not mean they would prefer to be in God's presence. Resistance to God continues in hell. Those in hell have committed the infinite sin, not simply a string of finite sins. They have rejected a relationship with a gracious God.
- God did not immediately create a heaven-like state in which the redeemed choose not to sin for this reason: The kind of freedom we experience on earth is a requirement for choosing one's final destiny; we freely respond affirmatively to God's loving influence or we resist it.
- God could not have first created a heaven-like state in which the redeemed cannot sin. Our final state is the fruit of our choice to move toward or away from God on earth (alternative 1).
- Another scenario (alternative 2) is that God simply foreknows that no one in heaven will freely choose to sin; God, therefore, can guarantee heaven's pristine sinlessness.
- We could add that any consideration of the possibility of sin will be gloriously overshadowed by the joys of our union with God and the Lamb. Our glorious experience of the unmediated presence of God and Christ will so flood our hearts that sinning will not even enter our minds, even though it remains a possibility (alternative 3).

◆ Further Reading

Craig, William Lane, and Ray Bradley. "Can a Loving God Send People to Hell?" Debate found at http://www.leaderu.com/offices/billcraig/docs/craigbradley0.html.

Crockett, William V., ed. *Four Views on Hell*. Grand Rapids: Zondervan, 1996.

Lewis, C. S. *The Problem of Pain*. New York: Macmillan, 1962.

Murray, Michael J. "Heaven and Hell." In *Reason for the Hope Within*, edited by Michael J. Murray. Grand Rapids: Eerdmans, 1999.

Walls, Jerry L. *Hell: The Logic of Damnation*. Notre Dame: University of Notre Dame Press, 1992.

RELIGION IS NOTHING MORE THAN THE HUMAN WISH FOR A FATHER FIGURE

Television mogul Ted Turner has been known to call Christians rather insulting names such as "bozos." Minnesota governor Jesse Ventura has denounced Christians as weak-minded people. It is quite common to hear Christians and other religious adherents demeaned as thoughtless and intellectually challenged. The reason religion exists at all, the skeptic often says, is because people desire some security or hope in an unstable and frightening world. In other words, God does not really exist; we invent him because of our own wishes and needs. We long for a kind of cosmic Linus blanket and eventually come to believe that one exists to help us through life. As the *Humanist Manifesto II* puts it, "Traditional religions often offer solace to humans."[1]

These sorts of claims have been with us for quite some time. The philosopher

Ludwig Feuerbach wrote about these claims in his *Essence of Christianity,* which deeply impressed Karl Marx's thinking about religion. Marx himself called religion "the sigh of the oppressed creature" and "the opium of the people."[2] Rather than humans being made in God's image, as Genesis 1:26–27 states, humans have made God in their image, according to these atheists.

More recently, the most prominent defender of the alleged connection between religion and subconscious human desires was the psychoanalyst Sigmund Freud. He wrote in his *Future of an Illusion,* "Religious ideas have arisen from the same need as have all other achievements of civilization: from the necessity of defending oneself against the crushing superior force of nature." Religious beliefs are thus "illusions, fulfillments of the oldest, strongest and most urgent wishes of mankind. . . . The benevolent rule of a divine Providence allays our fears of the dangers of life."[3]

According to Marx and Freud, religious belief is an illusion. It is a pathetic, weak-minded, and irresponsible approach to reality. Belief in God reflects "infantile" thinking rather than mature thinking. According to Freud, religion belongs to the realm of "fairy tales."[4] Even more recently, atheist zoologist Richard Dawkins has called religious belief a virus of the "mind," a kind of defect arising in the evolutionary process.[5]

There are a number of problems—and ironies—involved in this kind of an analysis of religion. *First, this "Freudian analysis" of religion has no clinical evidence to support it.* In a 1927 letter to Oskar Pfister (an early psychoanalyst and Protestant pastor), Freud wrote, "Let us be quite clear on the point that the views expressed in my book *[The Future of an Illusion]* form no part of analytic theory. They are my personal views."[6] In addition, New York University psychiatrist Paul Vitz notes that Freud had very little psychoanalytic experience with patients who believed in God or were genuinely religious. Freud nowhere published an analysis of religious belief based on clinical evidence provided by a believing patient.[7]

Second, this viewpoint commits a logical error known as the genetic fallacy. Take the following claim as an example: "Because a mean, crotchety teacher in elementary school taught me basic math, my understanding of mathematics is therefore completely mistaken." Why is this statement flawed? Simply because of the *way* I come to believe something (the genesis of my belief) does not thereby show that the belief is false.

Or take a slightly different example. A novice at mathematics may luckily arrive at the correct answer to an intricate problem, even though the *way* he got there was full of mistakes and missteps. But we don't say, "The answer can't be correct." Rather, we say, "Although the answer is correct, *how* it was reached was methodologically incorrect." The same can be said in regard to God: Even if religious people believe in God for the "wrong" or inferior reasons, this does nothing to show that God does not exist. Such a situation may reveal an inadequate basis for belief, but evidence for God's existence is a separate question.

Let's review the claim by Richard Dawkins: Religious belief is the result of a kind of virus plaguing certain human beings. Dawkins's claim actually raises serious problems for his own "scientific" atheistic worldview: (1) He appears to believe that human genetics is a matter of design (not merely the way things happen to have evolved) and that religious belief is a departure from the way things ought to be. This presupposes, however, a kind of blueprint for how we ought to function. But it is not the place of science to tell us how something *ought* to function, merely the way it *does* function. (2) If religious believers and atheists alike are nothing more than the products of genetics, how do we come to know this rationally, and why should we think that religious believers (and for that matter, nonreligious persons) can be held responsible for their beliefs? As I argue below, God may have designed us in such a way that natural processes enable us to come to know God personally, and we are at our cognitive best when our faculties direct us toward true belief in God.[8] So it might be possible both that (1) natural processes partly contribute to the formation of religious belief and that (2) religious belief is perfectly respectable and indicates that our minds are properly functioning—according to the way we have been designed.[9]

Third, we must distinguish between the rationality of belief and the psychology of belief. Perhaps you've been told, "I know why you believe in God. You need some kind of crutch to get you through life." But such a statement addresses only the psychology of belief (why or how people come to believe in God) and not the rationality of belief (whether there are good reasons to believe in God). Even if we do find ourselves needing a "crutch" to get us through life (and reasonable self-reflection tells us we need a great deal to help us live life as we should), we can still offer reasons to believe in God that are independent of our psychological desires. Even if everyone believed in God for fallacious reasons—however problematic a scenario this would be—such a situation still would not disprove God's existence. The primary question to address when discussing God's existence with atheists or skeptics is not, "*How* do people come to believe in God?" or, "What *motivates* them to believe what they do?" Rather, it is this: "What *good reasons* are there for believing rather than not believing?"

Theologian R. C. Sproul makes this point with regard to the historical basis for the Christian faith. This is a matter independent of psychological factors: "The question of the origin of religion cannot be settled ultimately by either the psychologist or the philosopher. The question of the origin of religion is a question of history."[10] First Corinthians 15 reminds us that if Jesus did not rise from the dead, then Christianity is simply false, no matter how much comfort it gives us.

Fourth, something that brings comfort and solace should not be rejected as inevitably false. Why must something that makes us feel secure be inherently suspect? Doesn't food nourish and comfort? Doesn't belonging to a healthy family bring security and solace? Surely such longings do not make food or family bad or illegitimate. This type of argument makes no sense at all.

Fifth, the fact that human beings are often "incurably religious" may indicate a divinely placed emptiness within us that can be filled by God alone. We could not legitimately say, "I have a longing for some God-like being; therefore, this being exists." On the other hand, this longing might be an indication that God exists, which makes it worth our serious consideration. If we have been made to enjoy God and find refuge and security in relationship with him, then Freud's theory that we fabricate a father figure out of need is pointless. Our feeling that we need God has been placed within us by God himself. This engrained need may suggest that God exists. Therefore, we should not be surprised that people are so religious: They really do need God! Sociologist Peter Berger says that these are the "signals of transcendence" that point beyond themselves to a higher and greater reality: "What appears as a human projection in one [frame of reference] may appear as a reflection of divine realities in another."[11] This longing—in conjunction with the evidences for God's existence mentioned in the introduction—suggests a powerful counterargument to the atheist's psychoanalysis of the theist.

Therefore, while some may boast of being self-sufficient and claim not to need God, this attitude is both foolish and inappropriate if God does exist, sustains us in being, and desires for us to relate lovingly to him. Philosopher Blaise Pascal spoke of our being created with a God-shaped vacuum. He echoed Augustine's early "confession" of belief: "Thou hast made us for thyself, O God, and our hearts are restless till they find rest in thee." While religious diversity obviously exists (and I have dealt with this question elsewhere),[12] all such religious longings remind us that we have a deep void that cries out to be filled.

Sixth, inventing a comforting father figure is unique to Christianity. New Testament scholars have noted that Jesus set himself apart in his day by introducing God as Abba—one's personal Father.[13] In Jesus' time, Abba was a title for one's father, used alike by child *and* adult.[14] Since the tendency within first-century Judaism was to view God as the Sovereign Lord (and perhaps the Father of Israel),[15] the title Abba could have been seen as somewhat familiar and disrespectful.[16]

If this unique, personal, fatherly dimension of God is evident when contrasting the Christian movement with the Judaism of Jesus' time, it is all the more apparent when looking at the beliefs of other religions. For example, even though Allah (the God of Islam) is called "most gracious *[rahman]*" and "most merciful *[rahim]*,"[17] he cannot properly be called "Father." He is to be worshiped and feared rather than personally known and loved. When former Muslim Bilquis Sheikh learned about Jesus, she cried out to God, "My Father!" At that point, she said, "Suddenly the room wasn't empty any more. *He* was there.

I could sense his Presence."[18] This woman found something that Islam could not offer—a sense of intimacy with God and the assurance of forgiveness.

In religions such as Hinduism or Buddhism, the Ultimate Reality is often abstract and impersonal, a kind of pure consciousness or even a void or nothingness. In such a scenario, the Ultimate Reality can show no concern for us and can offer no genuine security. In fact, according to these religions, our ultimate outcome is personal extinction and loss of identity. But if Freud is right, why don't other religions emphasize the fatherhood or personal warmth of the Ultimate Reality?[19] Contrary to what Freud declared, all religious belief does not inevitably end up with a comforting father, as in Christianity. Thus, Freud's claim is inaccurate and simply does not apply to religions across the board.

On the other hand, the Christian God is not only a loving Father; he is also a holy Judge who justly punishes sin. Racial hatred, murder, or torture is not passed over lightly by a God who says to the perpetrator, "That's okay. Run along now." And when saints in Bible times encountered God, they—in terror and awe—fell down as dead, having been struck by God's majesty and purity. Such a portrayal of divine holiness does not mix well with a "tame," domesticated God who is nothing more than a loving Father.

Seventh, the father figure argument could be turned on its head and used against the skeptic: "You reject God because you don't want a heavenly Father in your life." It is interesting that while atheists and skeptics often psychoanalyze the religious believer, they regularly fail to psychoanalyze their own rejection of God. Why are believers subject to such scrutiny and not atheists?

As we have seen, the psychologizing of religious belief commits the genetic fallacy (considering a view true or false based on its origin). It is fallacious because it does not really get to the point at issue. This argument does not deal with the truth or falsity of the assertion ("God exists"); rather, it brings up something negative about the "asserter."

New York University psychologist Paul Vitz essentially says, "Let's apply this (admittedly) fallacious thinking to many hard-nosed atheists and skeptics in the past. What do they have in common?" The result is quite interesting: Many of these figures did not have a significant father figure in their lives.[20] Let's look at some of them.

- Voltaire (1694–1778): This biting critic of religion, though not an atheist, strongly rejected his father and rejected his birth name of François-Marie Arouet.
- David Hume (1711–1776): The father of this Scottish skeptic died when David was only two years old. Hume's biographers mention no relatives or family friends who could have served as father figures.
- Sigmund Freud (1856–1939): His father, Jacob, was passive and weak and a great disappointment. Freud also mentioned that his father was a sexual pervert and that his children suffered for it.

- Karl Marx (1818–1883): Marx's father, a Jew, became a Lutheran under pressure, not out of religious conviction. Karl, therefore, did not respect his father.
- Ludwig Feuerbach (1804–1872): When Ludwig was thirteen, his father left his family and took up living with another woman in a different town.
- Baron d'Holbach (1723–1789): This French atheist became an orphan at age thirteen and lived with his uncle.
- Bertrand Russell (1872–1970): His father died when Bertrand was four.
- Albert Camus (1913–1960): Albert was one year old when his father died.
- Friedrich Nietzsche (1844–1900): He was four when he lost his father.
- Jean-Paul Sartre (1905–1980): The famous existentialist's father died before Jean-Paul was born.[21]

Moreover, Vitz's study notes that many prominent theists—such as Blaise Pascal, G. K. Chesterton, Karl Barth, and Dietrich Bonhoeffer—had in common a loving, caring father.[22]

Therefore, if this skeptical father figure argument were a good one (and it is not), the Christian could respond by turning the argument on its head: The rejection of God in this hard-nosed atheism emerged because these noted atheists had no earthly father whom they saw or could trust and respect; therefore, they rejected God because they had no positive father figure on which to depend. I am not saying that theists should offer bad arguments in response to bad arguments. But obviously the sword cuts both ways.

That being said, psychological factors (such as wholesome or painful childhood memories) may indeed have a bearing on how a person comes to believe or disbelieve, Vitz reminds us. Such factors are not irrelevant and need to be fully appreciated. We all bring background issues with us when encountering religion. Sometimes these factors may actually seriously diminish or undermine one's ability to trust in the Being who is the ultimate Father figure. Perhaps in some shape or form, God is being blamed for negative personal circumstances.

I am not saying that one's negative childhood circumstances *inevitably* lead to a rejection of God—any more than positive circumstances *guarantee* that one will believe in God. However, negative family circumstances (which can make us *better* or *bitter*) may be twisted into a reason to blame God and turn from him.

Perhaps this tragic scenario is best illustrated by Madalyn Murray O'Hair (1919–1999), founder of American Atheists. She hated her father so much that she even attempted to kill him with a ten-inch butcher knife. When she failed to do so, she screamed, "I'll see you dead. I'll get you yet. I'll walk on your grave."[23] Although she was murdered, her diary was recovered. She made an admission about her own failures in life: "I have failed in marriage, motherhood, as a politician." What is most relevant is that she entered in her diary at least a half dozen times: "Somebody, somewhere, love me."[24] The heart-rendering irony is that she committed her life to fighting against the God who truly loved her.

So to those who see belief in God as a crutch, we can say, "Take up your crutch and walk!" We have not been designed for self-sufficiency but God-sufficiency. As C. S. Lewis discovered, our earthly desires go unfulfilled or merely tantalize—"promises never quite fulfilled"—because we are made for God: "Your soul has a curious shape because it is a hollow made to fit a particular swelling in the infinite contours of the divine substance."[25] That "something" each of us seeks is the God who seeks us.

◆ Summary

- Sigmund Freud's "analysis" of religious belief was based on his opinion and had no clinical evidence to support it.
- This father figure argument commits the genetic fallacy—basing the truth or falsity of a belief on its origin. While one may believe in God for the wrong reasons, this does not prove God's nonexistence. That is a separate question.
- Richard Dawkins's claim that religious belief stems from a genetic virus is inconsistent with his "scientific" atheistic worldview: He presupposes a kind of blueprint for how we *ought* to function, rather than merely providing a description of how we *do* function. This is not the domain of science.
- The second problem with Dawkins's claim is this: If religious and nonreligious believers are nothing more than the products of genetics, how do we come to know this rationally, and why should we think that religious believers (and for that matter, nonreligious persons) can be held responsible for their beliefs?
- We must distinguish the psychology of belief (how we come to believe) from the rationality of belief (which deals with the proper basis for belief).
- Why should a belief that brings comfort and solace be considered inevitably false? We find comfort in relationships, but they are not therefore illegitimate.
- The fact that humans tend to be deeply religious may reflect that we have been made for a relationship with God.
- Many world religions (such as Eastern religions or Islam) do not have a comforting father figure. Freud's argument, therefore, is not universally applicable.
- This skeptical argument can be turned on its head: Perhaps atheists do not want a father figure in their lives.
- One's background may make it difficult to trust in God, especially when the people closest to that person are unworthy of trust or no longer pres-

ent. The security of the Christian community can play a role in helping restore the ability to trust in God.

◆ Further Reading

Sproul, R. C. *If There Is a God, Why Are There Atheists?* Minneapolis: Bethany Fellowship, 1978.

Vitz, Paul C. *Faith of the Fatherless: The Psychology of Atheism.* Dallas: Spence, 1999.

———. *Sigmund Freud's Christian Unconscious.* New York: Guilford Press, 1988.

PART THREE

CHALLENGES RELATED TO CHRISTIANITY

How Can God Be Three *and* One?

An anonymous Unitarian[1] tract from 1687 asserted that the doctrine of the Trinity was absurd and illogical:

> You add yet more absurdly, that there are three persons who are *severally and each of them true God,* and yet there is but one God: this is an *Error* in counting or numbring [sic]; which, when stood in, is of all others the most brutal and inexcusable; and not to discern it is not to be a man.[2]

Three hundred years later, a poorly researched pamphlet was published by the Watchtower Bible and Tract Society (of the Jehovah's Witnesses) entitled *Should You Believe in the Trinity?* The publication declares, "To worship God on his terms means to reject the Trinity doctrine."[3]

When asked to explain the doctrine of the Trinity, some Christians throw up their hands and exclaim, "It's a mystery," without ever attempting to understand this critical and glorious doctrine. I have heard Christians blur the distinction between the Father, Son, and Holy Spirit. Some say in their prayers, "Father, thank you for dying on the cross." (The Father did not die on the cross; the Son, Jesus Christ, did.) Some Christians regard the Holy Spirit as an "It," a powerful force from God, rather than as a person who has the very nature of God.

Our worship of God is short-circuited if our understanding of God is deeply flawed. In John 4:23, Jesus said that we must worship God "in spirit" and "in truth." Remaining in fundamental error regarding one of the chief distinctives of the Christian faith is to dishonor God. (On the other hand, purely intellectualizing our faith is no virtue either.)

How can we understand the basic idea of the Trinity without falling prey to error and contradiction? How should the Christian respond to the Unitarian who charges her with believing incoherent nonsense? Let me set forth some important concepts to help clear up points that are often confused and misunderstood.

First, the Bible maintains that there is a threeness to God as well as a oneness.[4] The *threeness* of God is seen in texts such as Matthew 28:19, where Jesus commands his followers to go and make disciples of the nations, "baptizing them in the name [not names] of the Father and of the Son and of the Holy Spirit." At Jesus' baptism, the Father and Spirit are also present (Matt. 3:16–17). Paul's benediction in 2 Corinthians 13:14 reveals a threeness about God: "May the grace of the Lord Jesus Christ, and the love of God, and the fellowship of the Holy Spirit be with you all."[5] There are three self-distinctions within the Godhead.

On the other hand, the *oneness* of God is seen in passages such as Deuteronomy 6:4: "The LORD our God, the LORD is one" and 1 Corinthians 8:4, 6: "There is no God but one. . . . For us there is but one God, the Father, from whom all things came and for whom we live; and there is but one Lord, Jesus Christ, through whom all things came and through whom we live."

Second, threeness pertains to persons *whereas oneness pertains to* essence *or* nature. What makes you a human being and not a kangaroo or a warthog? Although billions of humans live on earth, we all have one and the same nature in common. It is no contradiction to say that I am one of many people who possesses the same nature that makes each of us human. Although there is a deeper unity to God than merely possessing the same divine nature (which we will explore below), for now this important distinction between person and nature helps in building a case for the coherence of the doctrine of the Trinity. Basically, Christians do not hold that there are three natures or just one person in the Godhead.[6]

The charge that Christians do not know how to count is due to the (sometimes unfortunately justified) assumption that *three* and *one* refer to the same thing. For example, a Jehovah's Witness or a Muslim might ask a Christian,

"If Jesus was divine, whom was he crying out to when on the cross he said, 'My God, my God, why have you forsaken me?'" The questioner assumes that if Jesus is God, no other persons can possess the divine nature. But Christians simply reject this. In fact, a Christian could respond with this question: "If the Father is God, to whom is he speaking when he says to the Son (in Heb. 1:8), 'Your throne, O God, will last for ever'?"

Third, to help distinguish between person and nature, we must distinguish between the "is" of identity and the "is" of description/predication. When I say, "Samuel Langhorne Clemens is Mark Twain," I can just as easily reverse these names: "Mark Twain is Samuel Langhorne Clemens." To use either name is to refer to the same person; the names are interchangeable and thus the people are identical. The *is* in each of those statements indicates identity: Mark Twain=Samuel Langhorne Clemens (and vice versa).

Let's apply this to Jesus. To say "Jesus is God" is not identical to the statement "God is Jesus." Why not? Because Jesus does not exhaust what it means to speak of God (unlike the Mark Twain example just given). Jesus and God are not identical. According to the Bible, the Father and the Holy Spirit are called divine, just as Jesus is. When we say, "Jesus is God," therefore, we are using the *is* to describe or predicate, not identify or equate. Jesus is God in that he possesses a nature that only two other persons share; therefore, there is not just one person who can properly be called God. This is the mistake that Muslims and Jehovah's Witnesses often make about Christian theology.

We have seen that we must make distinctions between the persons of the Trinity and the one nature or essence they share. Again, threeness pertains to persons and oneness pertains to nature or essence. There is only one divine nature, but there are three persons who share this same nature. For God to be God, he must possess certain qualities or properties—being all-knowing, all-powerful, all-good, and so on. Three persons—and only three—are said to possess this one divine nature and can thus be called God. Moreover, these three persons—each centers of consciousness, responsibility, and activity—are distinct from one another (i.e., Jesus is not the Father, the Father is not the Holy Spirit, and the Spirit is not Jesus). There is simply no logical contradiction when Christians say, "Three persons and one divine nature."

Fourth, the members of the Trinity are deeply interrelated, or mutually indwell one another (perichôrêsis), *and thus have a necessary and unbreakable oneness.* Earlier we used the example of various human persons possessing the same nature to explain the concept of oneness. But the oneness of God needs further clarification. Even though human beings share the same human nature, they exist separately and distinctly from one another. The members of the Trinity, however, are inseparably related.

Greek theologians used the term *perichôrêsis* (the Latin equivalent is *circumincession*) to describe the necessary interrelationships of the Trinity. Jesus spoke of being "in" the Father and the Father being "in" him to describe their unique relationship (John 10:38; 17:21; cp. 10:30). There is a "mutual abiding" in the Godhead that is unlike human relationships, however close they may be. The relationship of Father, Son, and Spirit is not one of distinct, miscellaneous persons who just happen to share a generic divine essence ("God-ness") and so happen to be grouped together.[7] Rather, they mutually, inseparably share in the life of one another in a remarkable way: "For in the divine life there is no isolation, no insulation, no secretiveness, no fear of being transparent to another. Hence there may be penetrating, inside knowledge of the other as other, but [also] as co-other, loved other, fellow."[8] So while the divine persons, Father, Son, and Holy Spirit, each fully possesses the same essence (each one can be called God), they share a common, mutually indwelling life together.

Think of a triangle (which necessarily has three angles). We cannot remove one of the angles and still have a triangle. All three angles must coexist. Similarly, the perichoretic relationship between Father, Son, and Spirit exists necessarily. We cannot remove one person from this intimate relationship and have the other two remain intact.[9] All three are necessary for this mutually indwelling, interpenetrating love to exist.

To better understand the deep interrelationship between the divine persons, consider the mutual interaction of the soul and the body. According to the biblical understanding, a deep unity exists between body and soul.[10] The body continually "informs" the soul just as the soul does the body: If I am worried in my soul, then this affects my stomach, causing it to churn; if I cut off my arm, then my soul must make certain adjustments in light of this loss.[11] Thus, a mutual indwelling and interdependence exist in the body-soul relationship. Even though body and soul are separable substances,[12] they act as one.

Fifth, because the members of the Trinity share the same essence and mutually indwell one another, they also act as one rather than in isolation from one another. All that the three divine persons do, they do as one. God acts in concord with himself.

- The Father creates (Gen. 1:1; 1 Cor. 8:6) by his Son, the Word (John 1:3; Col. 1:15–20), and by his Spirit (Gen. 1:2).
- God reveals himself and redeems humankind in a trinitarian way: The Father sends his Son by the Spirit to be conceived in the Virgin Mary; Jesus does the work of his Father (John 5:17) by the power of the Spirit (Luke 3:22; 4:18) in his earthly ministry; and the Father raises Jesus from the dead (Acts 2:24) by the power of the Spirit (Rom. 1:4).
- God creates a people in a trinitarian way: Father, Son, and Spirit indwell the believer (John 14:16, 18, 23; Rom. 8:9)—and consequently the Christian community. The Spirit is called "the Spirit of God" [i.e., the Father]) and "the Spirit of Christ" (Rom. 8:9). The Spirit reveals to us the reality and presence of God/Christ (John 14:18; 1 Cor. 2:14–15) and enables us to cry out, "Abba, Father" (Rom. 8:15; Gal. 4:6).

The fact that the Father, Son, and Spirit act in necessary agreement (rather than as three independent persons) further reinforces their unity: "The acts of God are always the acts of each member of the Trinity, one or more initiating the process and the others backing it."[13]

Sixth, even though three distinct wills exist within the Trinity, only one will is ultimately expressed, which indicates the deep unity of the Godhead. Within the Trinity, there are three distinct persons who are individual centers of consciousness and will.[14] Unlike human relationships or polytheism, in which human or gods' and goddesses'[15] wills can potentially conflict, there is only necessary harmony and unity of will in the Trinity.[16] Absolutely no conflict exists between the persons of the Trinity in this, the very closest of families. The unity of deity among the three persons of the Trinity consists, at least in part, of this deep harmony of will.[17]

There are, therefore, at least four important ways in which these three divine persons share oneness:

1. They share the same essence or nature.
2. They mutually indwell one another *(perichôrêsis* or *circumincession).* The persons of the Trinity are necessarily bound together in relation, unlike a group of humans.
3. They necessarily act in perfect harmony in creation, salvation, and so on. It is impossible for them to diverge from one another in their action.
4. Only one will is expressed even though each person of the Trinity has his own will; it is necessarily the case that there is no divergence of will in the Trinity.

Christian doctrine, therefore, should not be accused of mathematical deficiency or contradiction. Christian theologians have simply attempted to move from the data of Scripture, which affirms that (1) one God exists and that (2) three persons can legitimately be called God, to a coherent and noncontradictory doctrine that affirms oneness and threeness.[18]

On a practical note, when speaking to Muslims about the doctrine of the Trinity or the incarnation, we must be careful to avoid disputations and doctrinal wranglings. I think that such heated topics are best broached when a Muslim is truly seeking and is not taking a defensive posture. In fact, I would venture to say that many Muslims are first captivated by Jesus as they personally encounter him when reading the Gospels and seeing authentic Christian community *before* they sort out questions on the Trinity and the incarnation. Christians should focus on demonstrating the love of Christ with Muslims in the context of a personal relationship and discern a seeking heart before embarking on these topics. Furthermore, once a Christian begins to explore the depths of the doctrine of the Trinity, she begins to see how rich are the resources not only for giving philosophical answers to important questions. The doctrine of the Trinity can inform and guide us in practical matters such as familial, ecclesial, social, political, and environmental concerns.[19] Rather than shrinking back from defending the Trinity, we can present this doctrine as intellectually coherent, philosophically and apologetically fruitful, practically relevant, and personally transforming.

◆ Summary

- The Bible affirms both a threeness and a oneness of God. The threeness relates to personhood, and the oneness relates to essence or nature and to the mutually indwelling interrelationship of the members of the Trinity.
- When Christians affirm, "Jesus is God," the "is" is one of description or predication (i.e., Jesus *has* the divine nature/Godness and so do Father and Spirit); the "is" is not one of identity (such as "Mark Twain is Samuel Langhorne Clemens").
- The members of the Trinity are deeply interrelated and mutually indwell one another *(perichôrêsis)* and thus have a necessary and unbreakable oneness. (Remember the necessary relationship of three angles of a triangle. If one angle is removed, the triangle no longer exists. Note also the mutually indwelling relationship of body and soul as an analogy of intertrinitarian relationships.)
- Because the members of the Trinity share the same essence and mutually indwell one another, they also act as one rather than in isolation from one another.
- Even though three distinct wills exist within the Trinity, only one will is expressed, which indicates the deep unity of the Godhead.
- The oneness of the Trinity is evident in the following ways: (1) The divine persons share one nature; (2) they mutually indwell one another; (3) they act in necessarily perfect agreement; (4) they necessarily express one will, even though each member of the Trinity possesses his own will.

◆ Further Reading

Davis, Stephen T., Daniel Kendall, and Gerald O'Collins, eds. *The Trinity: An Interdisciplinary Symposium on the Trinity.* New York: Oxford University Press, 1999.

Morris, Thomas V. *Our Idea of God.* Downers Grove, Ill.: InterVarsity Press, 1990.

Senor, Thomas. "The Incarnation and the Trinity." In *Reason for the Hope Within,* edited by Michael J. Murray. Grand Rapids: Eerdmans, 1999.

ISN'T THE IDEA OF GOD BECOMING A MAN INCOHERENT?

O ne of my favorite Christmas carols is Charles Wesley's "Hark, the Herald Angels Sing!" One line I find profoundly gripping is, "Veiled in flesh, the Godhead see! Hail th' incarnate Deity!" Traditional Christians believe that in the person of Jesus of Nazareth there were and are two natures—divine and human. As the Athanasian Creed (ca. A.D. 500) puts it, Jesus is "perfect God, perfect man subsisting of a reasoning soul and human flesh."[1]

Some critics—such as Muslims—see this doctrine as an absurd contradiction: God has attributes or properties that are so *unlike* those of human beings. For example, God is all-knowing, whereas humans are quite limited in their knowledge. God is all-powerful, but humans—however impressive they are in certain ways—are frail and weak.

The philosopher of religion John Hick, who edited a book entitled *The*

Myth of God Incarnate,[2] sees Jesus as nothing more than a traveling preacher who was "intensely conscious of God's holy and loving presence."[3] He was "wholly human."[4] Eventually, however, the "Jesus cult" developed into the "cult of the risen Christ, transfigured and deified."[5] Jesus Seminar member Marcus Borg claims that though Jesus was the initiator of a new movement in first-century Palestine, he simply could not have said, "I am the way and the truth and the life" (John 14:6) or, "I am the light of the world" (John 8:12). Such statements are the product of the early Christian community. Psychologically sane human beings, Borg asserts, simply do not make such claims: "We have categories of psychological diagnosis for people who talk like this about themselves."[6] (Of course, the question remains, Why would early Christians proclaim a psychologically challenged Jesus, a tactic that would work only to the detriment of their message?)

Is the doctrine of the incarnation—God becoming man—a logical doctrine? Or must Christians resort to throwing up their hands and saying, "It sure looks contradictory, but it's true"? How God could become a man is certainly mysterious, and we must not diminish the wonder of this truth (1 Tim. 3:16). I do believe, though, that this doctrine is logical and not self-contradictory (which would render it false). This chapter reviews some of the biblical evidence for the incarnation and then seeks to show that Jesus the God-man is not a contradictory concept.

First, the biblical evidence for the incarnation is strong.[7] For example, the "angels of God" (Luke 12:8–9) are also called *Jesus'* angels (Matt. 13:41: "his angels"). Jesus claimed to forgive sin, which was assumed by the Jews of Jesus' day to be God's prerogative alone (Mark 2:5, 7). Jesus displaced the temple as necessary for forgiveness of sins. Jesus claimed that he was the judge of the world (Matt. 25:31–46; cp. 2 Cor. 5:10), even though the Old Testament declares that God (Yahweh) is the judge of the world (Gen. 18:25; Joel 3:12). In John 10:33, the Jews want to stone Jesus, and they state their reason: "We are not stoning you for any of these [miracles] . . . but for blasphemy, because you, a mere man, claim to be God" (John 10:33).[8] John comments that by calling God his Father, Jesus was "making himself equal with God" (John 5:18).

In the New Testament, Jesus is explicitly called God—a remarkable fact given that fiercely monotheistic Jews wrote it.[9] Jesus was even prayed to (Acts 7:59–60; 2 Cor. 12:8–9), which was also a role reserved for God. The Aramaic[10] prayer, *Maranatha* (meaning, "Our Lord, come!"), in 1 Corinthians 16:22 reveals that very early in the Christian community (by the early A.D. 50s, when 1 Corinthians was penned), Jesus' followers saw him as the hearer and answerer of prayer.

Plenty of disputes took place in the early Christian communities over which foods to eat, the place of circumcision, spiritual gifts, and the place of the law of Moses. What is remarkable is that throughout the New Testament (written mostly by monotheistic Jews)—whether the Gospels or the letters (epistles)—there is absolutely no dispute regarding the elevated, divine status of Jesus.

There is no controversy regarding whether Jesus is "Lord of all." Paul, in fact, plainly declares in 1 Corinthians 8:6 that Jesus is the "one Lord" (and thus the Creator)—a title reserved for Yahweh in the Old Testament (Deut. 6:4–6).

This brings us to an important point: Liberal scholars often place a very late date on the Gospels (after A.D. 70–80), claiming that they are purely "evangelistic tracts" that are "biased" and "theologically motivated." Even if this were true,[11] however, what these scholars regularly ignore is that the epistles were written far earlier (some less than twenty years after Jesus' crucifixion), and these epistles contain clear references to the divinely exalted status of Jesus. Furthermore, these epistles (such as Thessalonians and Corinthians) are (1) the earliest sources of information about Jesus and (2) refer to Jesus' supremacy only incidentally. These writings deal with specific issues and circumstances within particular churches, and they assume a high Christology rather than try to prove it. Historian Paul Barnett makes this point: "The letters are, historically speaking, a preferred point of entry into Jesus studies."[12]

A final point is that New Testament writers see Jesus as standing in the place of Yahweh/Jehovah. Old Testament quotations using the word *Yahweh*—rendered "Lord" *(kyrios)* by the Greek Old Testament, the Septuagint—are used in the New Testament in reference to Jesus.

References to Yahweh in the Old Testament	Jesus as Yahweh in the New Testament
Ps. 23:1: Jehovah is my shepherd.	**John 10:11:** Jesus is the good shepherd.
Isa. 6:1–5: Isaiah sees Jehovah's glory in the temple.	**John 12:41:** Isaiah sees Jesus' glory (referring to Isa. 6:1).
Isa. 40:3: A forerunner prepares the way of Jehovah.	**Matt. 3:3:** A forerunner prepares the way of Jesus.
Isa. 45:23: Every knee will bow to Jehovah.	**Phil. 2:10:** Every knee will bow to Jesus.[13]
Joel 2:31–32: Calling on the name of Jehovah brings salvation.	**Acts 2:20–21/Rom. 10:13:** Calling upon the name of Jesus brings salvation.

In Isaiah, Yahweh says, "I am the first and I am the last; apart from me there is no God" (44:6); "I am he; I am the first and I am the last" (48:12). But then in the New Testament Book of Revelation, God the Father says this about himself: "I am the Alpha and the Omega" (1:8); "I am the Alpha and the Omega, the Beginning and the End" (21:6). However, Jesus Christ also applies this Isaianic title for Yahweh to himself: "I am the First and the Last" (Rev. 1:17; cp. 2:8); "I am the Alpha and the Omega, the First and the Last, the Beginning and the End" (22:13).

Used by Yahweh in the latter portion of Isaiah, these essentially equivalent phrases—"Alpha and Omega," "first and last," and "beginning and end"—are claimed by *both* God (the Father) and Jesus. Thus, Jesus shares in the very identity of Yahweh.

Second, the evidence for Jesus' limitations and his humanity is also unmistakable. Jesus was born in Bethlehem (Luke 2:1–11). He grew and his character developed (Luke 2:52). He hungered and thirsted and grew tired (Matt. 4:2; John 4:6; 19:28). He had a human body (John 1:14; 1 John 1:1), and he is called a "man" in many places.[14] Although Jesus frequently displayed supernatural knowledge[15] and was sinless,[16] he also was not aware of certain things, such as the day of his return (Mark 13:32). Because of these limitations, some theologians have suggested that Jesus must have given up or "emptied" himself of certain divine attributes (the *kenotic* view).[17] This belief is problematic and ought to be rejected because God possesses divine attributes, for example, being all-knowing or all-powerful, essentially; that is, he cannot lose them without ceasing to be God.[18]

Third, the doctrine of the incarnation is important for our salvation. Some may be wondering, "What's the big deal about the doctrine of the incarnation? Why is it important that God became human?" That was the very question asked by medieval theologian Anselm of Canterbury (1033–1109). In his book *Why God Became Man (Cur Deus homo)*,[19] he reasoned that humans owed God what they could not pay. As humans, we *had* to pay it to satisfy God's righteous demands and be rescued from our sin and its consequences, but we could not.[20] So God the Son voluntarily and freely took on the form of a human so that he as a human could pay back what we owed with a sacrifice (on the cross)—a sacrifice that only God could make. At great cost, God become like us and absorbed the punishment of our wrongdoing so that God's righteous demands could be satisfied.[21] We humans can now have a relationship with God on that basis. So while the essence of sin is our desire to become God, the essence of salvation is God becoming man.[22] This is why the God-man was necessary for forgiveness to take place; without the incarnation, salvation and forgiveness become impossible. Johann Sebastian Bach's *St. Matthew Passion* echoes this theme:

> How amazing is this punishment:
> The good Shepherd suffers for the sheep!
> The guilt the righteous *Master* pays
> For his own servants![23]

Fourth, we must distinguish between nature and person. What makes us human? What sets us apart from chimps or chickadees? We as humans all share the same nature or essence. We noted in the last chapter that a thing's nature is what makes it what it is—whether this thing is an atom or molecule,[24] human, animal, angel, or God. Certain capacities and characteristics, or properties, make you and me human and separate us from nonhuman entities (which have their own unique capacities and characteristics). If we lacked these properties, we would not exist. Because we possess certain essential characteristics that make us what we are, we belong within a particular class. Similarly, God is all-knowing, all-powerful, all-good. These characteristics make him what he is.

What are some of the characteristics and capacities that make us human? For starters, we possess a soul or spirit or mind.[25] We have the capacity to communicate in multiple languages, to act, to be conscious, to know that 8+8=16.[26] These (and plenty more) are all properties that are essential to being human. In every possible world in which humans exist (and humans do not exist in every one of them), humans would have these properties and capacities.[27]

What do we mean by person? For the sake of simplicity, a person can be understood as a center of (self-)consciousness, activity, and responsibility. Although animals such as snowy egrets or ball pythons are conscious or aware, they are not self-conscious—that is, aware that they are aware. Although animals—along with humans—are active, animals do not have the capacity for responsible moral agency. If a king cobra or black mamba bites and kills a human being, we do not hold the snake morally responsible for its actions. So it cannot be called a murderer. Persons also have an intrinsic dignity; their personhood confers dignity upon them. They are not to be treated, therefore, as mere objects or a means to our own ends. Human beings are persons, but they are not the only persons who exist. We can also properly speak of divine persons such as Father, Son, and Spirit, or angelic persons.

What is the relationship between person and nature? A person has a nature.[28] I, as a person, possess something that makes me what I am. You as a human person have a human nature, the very same nature I have. We are two human persons sharing the same human nature. Jesus of Nazareth, however, is one person who has two natures. One of these natures is identical to our human nature; Jesus shared our very humanity and identified with us. The other nature is divine. Jesus was and is fully God and fully human.

Fifth, we must further discern between what really (or necessarily) makes us human ("fully" human) and what is just common (but not essential) to humans ("merely" human); this will enable us to understand how God could become human without contradiction. What do you think of when you try to describe human beings? You may be thinking, "Humans have hair and eyes and arms and legs. They live on the earth; they inevitably go wrong morally. Then they eventually die." But are these characteristics essential to being human? Do these characteristics make us what we are such that we cannot exist without them? Certainly not. We know persons who have had their arms and/or legs amputated. I recently heard the sad story of a child who was born with no eyes. Did this birth defect make the child less human? Of course not. Fully functioning bodies are common—they could even be *universal*—to human beings, but they are not essential.[29]

What about doing wrong ("to err is human") or dying ("all men are mortal")? According to the Bible, God made sinless human beings, and one day God's people will be made sinless once again. That is, we will still possess our humanness (what is essential to us) even though we will not sin.[30] And what about death? Remember that bit of logic from Philosophy 101 days?

> All men are mortal.
> Socrates is a man.
> Therefore, Socrates is mortal.

Even though death is sweeping and appears to be universal and exceptionless, mortality is not essential to humans, even though it is widespread. After all, the biblical record reminds us that the prophets Enoch (Gen. 5:24) and Elijah (2 Kings 2:11) did not experience death. Moreover, believers who are alive at Christ's return will not see death (1 Thess. 4:17). Death is not essential to human beings.[31]

You may be wondering, "What is the point of these distinctions?" Simply this: What we usually assume about human nature is not or may not be, in fact, essential to human nature. Realizing this fact can help us see the logical consistency between the divine and the human in Christ.

This brings us to the most crucial point about Jesus' two natures. Someone who is fully divine can also be fully human without contradiction—if we distinguish between "common" human characteristics and "essential" ones. That is, even though human beings are born, get tired, hunger, thirst, and die, these charactertistics are not essential to our existence. (For example, these types of limitations will not be the lot of God's people in the new heavens and new earth.)[32] It is possible that someone could be a human being without these limitations. Therefore, when the Son of God came to earth in the person of Jesus of Nazareth, he did not become merely human—that is, contingent, created, liable to sin, non-omnipotent, non-omnipresent, and so on. Rather, he became fully or essentially human: He possessed a human nature with all its characteristics and capacities that truly make us what we are. In other words, what is essential to human nature does not exclude the possibility of being fully divine.

Sixth, the image of God in human beings is what makes the incarnation possible. In a beautiful creation psalm, the writer says that God made the human being "a little lower than God" (Ps. 8:5 NASB). Made in God's image (Gen. 1:26–27),[33] we share certain attributes or properties with God—relationality, personality, rationality, morality, creativity—even though in diminished form. We read in the New Testament that Jesus Christ himself is the very image of God (2 Cor. 4:4; Col. 1:15). When we bring these strands of biblical truth together, we see that the image of God in us makes the incarnation possible. Why? Because certain essential characteristics of human beings—that is, those properties that make us essentially human—belong to the larger category of what it means to be divine. Human nature is thus a subcategory of the divine.

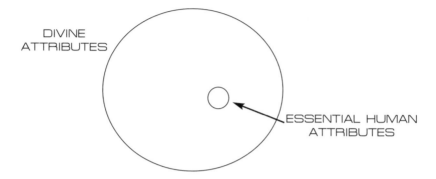

We have all heard the fairy tale about the prince who is cursed and becomes a frog; it appears that he has two natures—natures that are truly incompatible with each other. But a frog-man is far different from a God-man.[34] The mental capacities and qualities of the frog and prince are so radically different that no such union could occur.

However, the attributes of human beings to some degree resemble those of God (e.g., their relationality, their ability to reason and choose and act as morally responsible persons); therefore, a divine-human union is possible. New Testament scholar F. F. Bruce aptly writes, "It is because man in the creative order bears the image of his Creator that it was possible for the Son of God to become incarnate as man and in His humanity to display the glory of the invisible God."[35] One theologian put it this way: "If human beings are made in the image and likeness of God (Gen. 1:26–27), there must be something divine about every human being. If, and this is our case, the divine Logos could assume a humanity, there must be something human about God."[36] In other words, even though the human and the divine are poles apart in terms of greatness, they are not necessarily mutually exclusive. While human beings are in themselves limited or finite, this is not a necessary or essential property that makes us human. We do not *have* to have this characteristic to be human.[37] Apart from the person of Jesus, this characteristic is common or universal, but that does not make it necessary.

Seventh, Jesus had two consciousnesses: One was a developing, first-century Jewish human consciousness, and the other was eternal and divine. Imagine a spy who is going on a dangerous mission; in his mind he carries top-secret information that would be valuable to the enemy. So that he will not divulge secrets by succumbing to torture if he is caught, this spy is given a limited-amnesia producing pill as well as an antidote for later use.[38] The spy would still possess the vital information in his mind while under the influence of the amnesia pill, but he temporarily and voluntarily would not draw on the knowledge to which he normally has access.

Similarly, during Jesus' mission on earth, he had the full, undiminished capacities of divine knowledge and power and had access to those capacities as necessary. But Jesus in his pre-incarnate state voluntarily chose to limit the use of those powers in order to accomplish his overall mission. He did not *lose* certain divine attributes; rather, he voluntarily suppressed or gave up access to them for a time. They were latent within him. As theologian J. I. Packer expresses it, "The impression [in the Gospels] . . . is not so much one of deity reduced as of divine capacities restrained."[39] Before coming to earth, the Second Person of the Trinity had chosen that "all his intrinsic powers, all his attributes, would remain latent within him during the days of his flesh."[40] It is like a parent who doesn't play his hardest in a game against his child. He deliberately restrains himself from utilizing his full powers.

Have you ever had the experience of coming out of a dream and simultaneously still dreaming but also being conscious of the fact that it is just a dream and not reality at all? Or take self-deception. On the one hand, a person knows what is right; on the other, he consciously convinces himself to go against the conscience that echoes in the background of his mind.[41] These analogies give some indication of how two levels of awareness can work together and overlap in one person. Obviously, these analogies take us only so far, but given the uniqueness of the incarnation, this is to be expected. We can, however, build on such analogies to express the point.

Consider the twofold consciousness we have as we are coming out of a dream: At one level, we are "within" the dream, and at another we are "outside" the dream simultaneously. Could this not be an analogy of how Christ's divine and human consciousnesses worked together? We can compare the two levels of awareness in a dream (one subconscious and the other conscious) to that of Jesus' *two* consciousnesses. Our conscious awareness would compare to Jesus' human awareness, and our subconscious would compare to Jesus' divine awareness. When the Son of God took on human form, the divine consciousness did not cease but continued in its distinctively eternal, divinely aware dimension.[42] This divine awareness in no way was—indeed could not have been—interrupted at the incarnation. The Son's union and communion with Father and Holy Spirit necessarily continued. In this level of divine awareness, the Son was also—as he is unceasingly—sustaining the universe and fully aware of all things.[43]

Yet in his human consciousness, Jesus grew and developed an earthly, first-century, Jewish awareness (Luke 2:52).[44] New Testament scholar R. T. France states that the biblical portrait of Jesus is of "a real man, with real emotions and human reactions, who had to learn obedience to the will of God and did not find it easy, whose knowledge was limited, and who lived and spoke as a first-century Palestinian Jew."[45]

Certainly, significant interaction took place between Jesus' earthly/human consciousness and his divine consciousness. Perhaps we could compare it to the glow of divine light that streams through a cloth curtain. In his human awareness, Jesus was not cut off from certain heavenly illuminations.[46] We must be careful, therefore, not to compartmentalize or dichotomize the human and the divine. For example, we must not say, "Jesus suffered as a human being but not as God." God does indeed suffer. He can be deeply touched, being the relational God that he is.

On the other hand, Jesus did not regularly rely on his divine consciousness as he lived his life on earth. The primary realm in which Jesus operated was the human consciousness, with the extra depth of his divine awareness.[47] And Jesus, being fully human, freely and fully depended on the Spirit's power as he sought to carry out his Father's purpose.[48]

Eighth, prior to the incarnation, the three persons of the Trinity all agreed on what the nature of Jesus' self-limitations would be. Gerald Hawthorne correctly points out that before the incarnation, the Second Person of the Trinity with the other persons of the Godhead made a conscious decision to set aside what might diminish his ministry of humiliation and redemption. Before the Second Person of the Trinity came to earth, he had already chosen what he would renounce or surrender, and all the members of the Trinity were in complete harmony concerning this decision.[49]

Ninth, understanding the Trinity helps to resolve certain problems raised by critics about the incarnation. When I regularly visited a Muslim mosque for a couple years, I often heard questions such as these:

- "If Jesus was God, who was running the universe when he was a baby?"
- "If Jesus was God, who was in control of the universe when he was on the cross?"
- "How could God die?"
- "If God 'so loved the world,' why did he send his Son rather than come himself?"

As already mentioned, Jesus operated in two spheres of awareness—a human one (which grew and developed while on earth) and a divine one (which remained constant and operative). There was certainly interaction between these two spheres of consciousness. However, for the sake of Jesus' mission on earth, he (in his human consciousness) freely—though temporarily—gave up access to certain aspects of his divine knowledge.

Jesus, being divine and mutually indwelling the other members of the Trinity, was still governing the universe as a baby and while dying on the cross. And the death he died, he died as a mere (and not "full") human being and not literally *as God*, who alone is necessarily immortal—that is, immune to death and decay (1 Tim. 6:16).[50] Furthermore, because of the mutually indwelling relationship of Father, Son, and Spirit, each person of the Trinity experienced pain; each suffered deep pain in the crucifixion. Some might argue that God does not suffer, as he is impassible. But this is not a biblical notion.[51] New Testament scholar D. A. Carson asks, if God does not suffer, "why does the Bible spend so much time depicting him as if he does?"[52] Rather, the full sweep of the biblical evidence "pictures God as a being who can suffer."[53] That is, God can be emotionally touched by our experiences and actions but not crushed by them.[54] Alvin Plantinga is right when he says:

> As the Christian sees things, God does not stand idly by, cooly observing the suffering of his creatures. He enters into and shares our suffering. He endures the anguish of seeing his Son, the second Person of the Trinity, consigned to the bitterly cruel and shameful death of the cross. Some theologians claim that God cannot suffer. I believe they are wrong. God's capacity for suffering, I believe, is proportional to his greatness.[55]

In fact, it is in the very act of Jesus' suffering, humiliation, and death on the cross that we see most clearly the all-giving God. If you want to know what God is really like—and how great is his love toward us—look at the cross and witness the shame and anguish Jesus endured. In the depths of such suffering, God is most obvious.[56] Therefore, we can say that the Father and the Spirit felt deep pain with the Son in his crucifixion and anguish. Jesus did not bear this suffering alone. God the Father and the Spirit—not simply the Son—were deeply involved in the work of the cross. Second Corinthians 5:19 makes this clear: "God was reconciling the world to himself in Christ."

Variations on the model of the incarnation presented in this chapter certainly exist, and some people may object to the model of two consciousnesses of Christ: "Where does the Bible speak of two consciousnesses in Jesus of Nazareth? Where does the Bible differentiate between fully human and merely human?" Scripture does not always answer all our questions as we attempt to harmonize the range of biblical affirmations about this and many other topics. We may have to utilize, for example, philosophical resources to assist us in this endeavor. I assert, however, that this chapter presents a model that is both consistent with Scripture and logically coherent.

◆ Summary

- The doctrine of the incarnation affirms that the person of Jesus of Nazareth contained two natures—one divine and the other human.
- Because the image of God in us is a subcategory of the divine, it is not a contradiction that God could take on humanness.

- We must distinguish the merely human from the fully human: Although most human beings commonly have certain features (arms, hair, fingers), what is *essential* for them to be human is that they have a human soul/mind and possibly a body at some point.
- Jesus had two distinct consciousnesses, one human and the other divine (remember the analogy of how a person can be aware of both the conscious and the subconscious when coming out of a dream).
- We must be careful of pushing analogies too far, for one person with two natures and thus two consciousnesses or awarenesses is unique.
- Jesus' earthly awareness can be compared to the conscious, and the divine to the subconscious.
- In Jesus' human awareness, he had a first-century Jewish consciousness in which he grew and developed. This mind was the primary source of Christ's earthly behavior and speech, which accounts for certain limitations (such as Jesus' ignorance about his return).
- In his divine awareness, he experienced an unbroken, all-knowing, and continuous consciousness in which he remained in constant communion with his Father. In his human awareness, Jesus did not generally draw on this level of consciousness (although there were certainly breakthroughs of heavenly illuminations to his human mind from the divine). In his divine awareness, he continued to mutually indwell the other members of the Trinity and to govern and sustain the universe.
- The act of taking on human form did not diminish the Son's divine capacities. (Remember the spy who takes an amnesia-producing tablet if caught: If he takes the tablet, he does not lose the information; he gives up temporary access to it.) For the most part, the full divine capacities remained latent within Jesus during his earthly mission (as when a parent does not utilize his full powers when playing with a child).
- Prior to Jesus' incarnation, the three persons of the Trinity all agreed on what the nature of Jesus' self-limitations would be, and the persons of the Trinity were involved in Jesus' work on the cross ("God was reconciling the world to himself in Christ").

◆ Further Reading

Bauckham, Richard. *God Crucified: Monotheism and Christology in the New Testament.* Grand Rapids: Eerdmans, 1998.

Hawthorne, Gerald F. *The Presence and the Power.* Dallas: Word, 1991.

Morris, Thomas V. *The Logic of God Incarnate.* Ithaca, N.Y.: Cornell, 1986.

———. *Our Idea of God.* Downers Grove, Ill.: InterVarsity Press, 1990.

Senor, Thomas. "The Incarnation and the Trinity." In *Reason for the Hope Within,* edited by Michael J. Murray. Grand Rapids: Eerdmans, 1999.

15

IF JESUS IS GOD, HOW COULD HE *REALLY* BE TEMPTED?

an God sin? If God has the potential to sin, then it appears he is not perfectly good. But if God cannot sin, then it seems he is not really free or all-powerful—since there is at least one thing God cannot do.[1]

But such a complaint is easily dislodged. In the first place, we must be careful not to separate God's goodness from God's power. An all-powerful being who is evil rather than good would not be worthy of worship. Maximal greatness involves more than sheer power or information storage (in the case of God's omniscience). Goodness is a kind of hub that connects and holds together the various divine attributes. Second, what the skeptic considers "the power to sin" really turns out to be powerlessness. St. Anselm argued this way: If God were able to sin, this would be a deficiency since "[God's] powerlessness puts him in another's power."[2] The ability to sin, therefore, would reveal a deficiency in God's character, making him less than necessarily good.

To assume that the inability to sin is a defect in God is a misunderstanding about God's power. Consider Alexander the Great, who conquered the world. To say of Alexander, "He cannot lose in battle," does not reveal a deficiency in him but rather a deficiency in his enemies. In the words of Anselm, "Thus when I say that I can be carried off or conquered against my will, this is not my power, but my necessity and another's power. For to say, 'I can be carried off or conquered,' is the same thing as to say, 'Someone is able to carry off or conquer me.'"[3] God's inability to sin should not be viewed as a deficiency in his omnipotence any more than a general's inability to lose a battle should be seen as a lack of power or ability.

God is necessarily or essentially good. He cannot be otherwise. This means that doing wrong is impossible for God (this is known as divine *impeccability*); therefore, God cannot even be tempted to do wrong. If this were the case, then there would be a power greater than God. It is impossible for God to be morally overwhelmed by evil. James 1:13 makes this quite clear: "Let no one say when he is tempted, 'I am being tempted by God'; for God cannot be tempted by evil, and He Himself does not tempt anyone" (NASB).

The skeptic (as well as the Christian) may ask, "Wasn't Jesus himself tempted in the wilderness?" (Matt. 4:1–11). Hebrews 2:18 says that since Jesus himself "was tempted in that which He has suffered, He is able to come to the aid of those who are tempted" (NASB). Doesn't this imply that Jesus could in fact have sinned? If Jesus *could not* have sinned, then wasn't his endurance of temptation merely a matter of playacting?

The Bible, of course, portrays Jesus' temptations to sin as real. Jesus certainly *felt* a vulnerability and experienced struggle in the face of conflict—either to choose the easy way out or to choose the more difficult way of self-denial and death. And although the Bible does not really answer this question for us, we do not have to despair of some reasonable resolution. Some may say, "It's just a puzzle," which may mean nothing more than, "It's self-contradictory, and I don't know how to deal with this problem"! In light of the discussion in the previous chapter, however, we can piece together an answer.

First, the ability to sin does not make a person essentially human. After all, it certainly appears that Christians in their postmortem state will not be able to sin even though they will still be fully human.[4] Having the ability to sin, therefore, while it is common among human beings, may not be essential to being fully human. It does not make us what we are. It is not one of the characteristics or properties that we *must* have to be human. Jesus, therefore, did not need to have the ability to sin to be fully human.

Does that mean Jesus was playacting when he was tempted? Let's look at this matter more closely.

Second, when Jesus came to earth, he voluntarily set aside access to certain things; one item of knowledge he gave up being aware of was his inability to sin. The skeptic's question is a legitimate one: "If Jesus is God, why was he ignorant of certain things?" For example, we read Jesus' words in Matthew 24:36: "No one knows about that day or hour [of Jesus' return/*parousia*], not even the angels in heaven, *nor the Son,* but only the Father" (emphasis added). When Jesus requested the name of the demon he was confronting in Mark 5:1–20, it appears that Jesus' knowledge was limited.[5]

Jesus was not only ignorant of the timing of his return; he was also ignorant that he could not ultimately deviate from the Father's will. In the Garden of Gethsemane, Jesus faced the anguish of taking on the "cup" of God's wrath, taking the curse not only for Israel's sins and its "exile" but the sins (and "exile") of the world.[6] Jesus prayed for a less-devastating alternative: "My Father, if it is possible, may this cup be taken from me. Yet not as I will, but as you will" (Matt. 26:39). We have argued that the biblical evidence for Jesus' divinity is plentiful. It would be impossible, therefore, for him to turn aside from doing the will of his Father. On the other hand, the biblical evidence also reveals that Jesus was unaware that he could not deviate from doing his Father's will. Theologian Gerald O'Collins points out that the fact of Jesus' growth in self-knowledge and self-identity and his struggles in prayer (such as his agony in Gethsemane and his cry of abandonment on the cross) "supports the conclusion that the divine reality was not fully and comprehensively present to the [human] mind of Jesus."[7]

Was Jesus able to sin? No. Why not? Because Jesus was not merely human. He was also God and therefore could do no wrong. At the same time, Jesus' struggles and temptations were real. Let's now move to resolve this tension.

Even though Jesus was not able to carry out a sinful act as a result of temptation, for the temptation to be meaningful, he had to be ignorant of the fact that it was impossible for him to sin. This temporary ignorance was part of Jesus' earthly mission. Recall the example from the previous chapter of the spy who takes the amnesia-producing pill: Although he chooses to give up temporary access to vital information, the information is potentially accessible to him rather than lost.

Similarly, Jesus voluntarily surrendered access to the expression of certain divine attributes. When he became a man (being weak, hungry, and tired), he chose to limit access to his divine knowledge (e.g., ignorance of his second coming, ignorance that he was essentially good) so that he could suffer real temptation and experience human limitation—even though he at any time could have chosen to be aware of these things.

Admittedly, we are treading on the sensitive area of Jesus' incarnation, but it seems apparent that "if he simply saw the divine reality in all its entire scope and beauty, real struggles in prayer would be ruled out. So too would genuine obedience. . . . Whatever else was happening in Gethsemane and on the cross, we can be sure that Jesus was not merely pretending to struggle through prayer to maintain his obedience."[8]

The point is this: Christ did not know that he could not sin. Part of his *voluntary* ignorance in his human awareness must have included being unaware that he was necessarily good.[9] God the Father did not reveal to him that he could not sin, and Jesus chose to set aside this knowledge in his pre-incarnate state. While sinning was not an *actual* possibility for Christ, Jesus could truly experience temptation because he did not know it was impossible for him to sin. Some Christians may ask if this is indeed coherent: How could Jesus know he was divine yet not know that he could not sin?[10] However, we could ask the same thing about Jesus not knowing the time of his second coming: How could Jesus know he was divine (which would presumably entail an awareness of his omniscience) yet not know this fact? If we see that Christ voluntarily limited access to this knowledge as part of his mission to earth, then we can affirm *both* that Jesus understood he was standing in the place of God and that he temporarily gave up access to certain truths about his capacities.

Third, since Jesus did not know he could not sin (being God), this made temptation very real for Jesus; although his being God would have prevented him from actually carrying it out, acting on the temptation seemed a possibility for Jesus. Imagine that you enter a room and close the door behind you. You do not realize it, but the door immediately locks with a two-hour time lock. You consider leaving once or twice, but in the end you freely choose to stay in the room for the full two hours. After you read a newspaper and some magazine articles, you decide to leave. By this time, the lock has automatically been released by the timer and you freely walk out the door. Why did you stay in and not try to go out? Because you freely decided to stay. Would you have been able to leave? No. Perhaps the analogy is becoming apparent: Christ freely chose by his human will to resist temptation; that is, his divine will did not overwhelm or impose itself upon his human will.[11] Here we see the difference between *being* and *knowing:* In Jesus' nature or being, it was impossible for him to sin; yet the temptation was very real to him because he did not know that sinning was impossible for him:

> Jesus could be truly tempted and tested, provided that he did not know that he could not sin. If he had known that he could not sin, it would be difficult, if not impossible, to make sense of genuine temptations; they would be reduced to make-believe, a performance put on for the edification of others. It was quite a different situation to be incapable of sin and not to know that.[12]

We have seen that there is a way to deal with the reality of Jesus' temptation, even though he was God and it was impossible for him to sin. Even though Christ was not able to carry out a sinful act as a result of temptation, for the temptation to be real, he had to have at least thought that it was possible for him to sin. Christ in his human awareness voluntarily limited access to his divine knowledge so that he could suffer real temptation; Christ did not know that he could not sin. Christ freely chose by his human will to resist temptation; that is, his divine will did not overwhelm or impose itself upon his human will.

I have heard Christians say, "Of course Jesus was able to conquer sin; he was God, wasn't he?" Here we must not transform Jesus into a Docetic Jesus, one who seemed to be human but was not. Many Christian communities tend to dehumanize Jesus. For example, the Christmas song "Away in a Manger" declares of the infant Jesus, "no crying he makes." The assumption is that other babies cry, soil their diapers, and need their runny noses wiped, but not Jesus! (My wife and I have taught our children to alter the words to "*some* crying he makes.")

Jesus lived his life in dependency on the empowering of the Spirit and, therefore, is an example for how we too can live victoriously over sin. Just as Jesus was "led by the Spirit" (Luke 4:1), we too as believers are to be "led by the Spirit" (Rom. 8:14). Just as Jesus (though not internally damaged by sin) needed the Spirit's empowering to rise above the limitations of human weakness and frailty, so do we as believers. Jesus' temptation was not artificial; his victory over it was real. His overcoming did not come automatically, springing neither from the absence of an inner downward pull toward sin nor from some necessity in his being divine. Rather, his victory was the result of a moment-by-moment commitment to the will of his Father: "Jesus met and conquered [Satan's temptations] not by his own power alone but aided in his victory by the power of the Holy Spirit."[13]

There is not a built-in contradiction in the incarnation, nor was the temptation of Jesus merely playacting. We can affirm the full deity and full humanity of Jesus as well as a kind of dual awareness, one in which Jesus was fully knowing and another in which he had voluntarily limited himself in his knowledge so that he could realistically endure temptation. In his incarnation and temptation, he became like us in every way—except without sin.

◆ **Summary**

- The fact that God is unable to sin is not a defect. Rather, the ability to sin would reveal that another entity could overpower God.
- The ability to sin is not essential to humans—only common to humans. Jesus, therefore, did not need to have the ability to sin to be fully human.
- When Jesus came to earth, he voluntarily set aside access to certain things; one item of knowledge he gave up access to was his inability to sin (cp. his temptation in the wilderness, the Garden of Gethsemane).

- Since Jesus did not know he could not sin (being God), temptation was very real for Jesus. Although his being God would have prevented him from actually carrying it out, acting on the temptation seemed a genuine possibility for Jesus.
- Imagine not knowing you are in a time-locked room. Even though you cannot open the door, you freely choose to stay inside. In the same way, Jesus' divine will did not overwhelm his human will.

◆ Further Reading

Hawthorne, Gerald F. *The Presence and the Power.* Dallas: Word, 1991.

Morris, Thomas V. *The Logic of God Incarnate.* Ithaca, N.Y.: Cornell, 1986.

———. *Our Idea of God.* Downers Grove, Ill.: InterVarsity Press, 1990.

O'Collins, Gerald. *Christology: A Biblical, Historical, and Systematic Study of Jesus.* New York: Oxford University Press, 1995.

◇ 16 ◇

THE GENESIS CREATION ACCOUNT CONTRADICTS CONTEMPORARY SCIENCE (PART 1)

Hungarian physicist and Benedictine priest Stanley Jaki suggests that the Judeo-Christian worldview provided fertile ground for the birth of modern science.[1] Newton, Copernicus, Galileo, and their ilk were theists who believed firmly in the rationality and orderliness of God's creation, the distinction between creature and Creator, and the difference between rational humans and animals. Their conviction that miracles are possible if God exists did not detract them from studying the universe he had made. Chinese, Greek, Babylonian, and Egyptian civilizations had no such resources within their worldview to give birth to modern science.

Toward the end of his book, Jaki refers to young-earth, or recent, creationism, which maintains that the universe is roughly ten to fifteen thousand years old and that God created everything in six twenty-four-hour days (144 hours): "Being busy with creation science, or the science about the manner or timetable of creation, is possibly the most self-defeating strategy a Christian can adopt in an age of science."[2] He urges recent creationists not to "make a strategic error" by becoming overly preoccupied with the *how* of creation or by limiting the age of the earth to a few thousand years, especially when the universe shows many signs of being quite old. Thus, these young-earth creationists should defend the simple doctrine that "in the beginning God created the heavens and the earth."

This much seems clear: The greatness of God's creative genius is not diminished if he created gradually rather than instantaneously. God's majestic power is not lessened if he acts indirectly rather than directly. (If the stars, galaxies, and planets as well as earth's mountains and landscapes were created over billions and millions of years rather than instantly, would they fail in their ability to inspire awe? To ask the question is to answer it.) Also, there is nothing about the word *create (bara')* that requires instantaneity.[3] Nor are the truthfulness and historicity of the creation account diminished if the early part of Genesis is not exactly a straightforward historical narrative.

What are the indications of the universe's antiquity? We could list the following: the rate of its expansion, the rate of its cooling from initially high temperatures, the arrival of light from distant galaxies,[4] the fossil record (geologists witness the fossilization process taking place in our own day with regularity), continental shifting (plate tectonics), mountain building, and so on. Arguments for a young universe based on a shrinking sun, the amount of cosmic dust, the diminishing of the earth's magnetic field, and the like appear to lack solid scientific support.[5]

Recognizing that most scientists—whether Christians or not—find young-earth creationism incredible and the weight of scientific evidence against it, Christian astrophysicist Hugh Ross asks, "Is it any wonder that individuals trained in the sciences, especially those with little or no Christian background, find it difficult to make their way back into the churches?"[6]

In April of 1999, I spoke with a man who claimed that he had rejected Christianity because he could not intellectually hold to a young-earth creationism. Around the same time, I received a phone call from a young Christian woman whose fiancé (also a Christian) believed that the universe was billions of years old. However, she grew up in a church in Romania that considered such a view heretical. She wanted to know if she should go ahead and marry this man. Such stories can be multiplied.

While I can understand how young-earth creationists come to hold their views based on Genesis 1, it may be worth asking, Is the young-earth interpretation of Genesis 1 the only legitimate interpretation for orthodox Christians to embrace? Old Testament scholar Victor Hamilton remarks, "The literal understanding of 'day' is not necessarily a more spiritual and biblical interpretation, and therefore is not inherently preferable."[7] What to do?

I believe, first, that the text of Genesis allows for a less rigid interpretation of the word *day* (*yôm* in Hebrew) than the twenty-four-hour one. I respectfully disagree, therefore, with my "yomist" friends on this matter.[8] Second, the ultimate issue here is not young- versus old-earth creationism or even creation versus evolution (although I myself do not find biological evolution compelling).[9] Rather, the crux is naturalism (all reality can be explained by and operates according to natural laws and processes) versus supernaturalism (a reality exists *beyond* and is not reducible to nature—God, miracles, and so on). What is most critical is *that* God created; *how* he created is a secondary matter. If it is true that God created, then supernatural revelation and miracles are possible and naturalism is false.

How we interpret Genesis 1 may create another barrier—or open a door—for the unbeliever in his or her spiritual journey. I believe, therefore, that we should undertake this discussion with the broader picture in mind. In this chapter, I make a few preliminary points before dealing with the specifics of the Genesis text in the next chapter. In these chapters, I hope to show that Scripture and science are not at odds.

First, Genesis recounts history (such as Adam and Eve as the first humans) and thus is not mythological; its historicity is reinforced by the New Testament's understanding of the Old. Besides authoring fresh material, Moses probably used and adapted archival records (on clay tablets, etc.) and oral traditions passed on through the patriarchs.[10] The genealogies of chapters 5, 10, and 11 are indicative of the historicity of people such as Adam, Cain, Enoch, Noah, and Abram. Also, the clause "this is the account" (NASB) or literally, "these are the generations" or "this is the history of" (Gen. 2:4; 5:1; 6:9; 10:1; 11:27; 25:12; 37:2) is significant. It is a device used throughout Genesis to recount cycles of historical events and the genealogies of particular people. Further, the New Testament assumes the historicity of Adam and Eve (Luke 3:38; Acts 17:26; Rom. 5:12–19; 1 Cor. 11:8–9; 15:21–22; 2 Cor. 11:3; 1 Tim. 2:13–14). Thus, we cannot dismiss these people as mythic characters.

Second, even though Genesis 1:1–2:4a is most likely a historico-poetic genre rather than straightforward prose, it should not be deemed inferior to a straightforward historical narrative. The early part of Genesis appears to be a combination of poetry and historical narrative. Charles Hummel calls it a semi-poetic narrative cast in a historico-poetic framework.[11] Evangelical Old Testament scholars such as Bruce Waltke, Derek Kidner, Gordon Wenham, and Meredith Kline claim that this portion of Genesis is poetic in nature,[12] although it is not "full-fledged Semitic poetry."[13] Gordon Wenham states that Genesis 1–3 recounts "an absorbing yet highly symbolic story."[14] Bruce Waltke asserts that the prologue of Genesis is history but not pure historical narrative.[15] Moses, whose audience is a group of agrarian Hebrews, does not speak with scientific or photographic precision. He speaks in simple, observational language. Still, his historico-poetic history of creation should not be considered inferior communication or somehow unworthy of God; after all, the psalms and prophetic books are highly symbolic and poetic but communicate historical events such as the exodus and the Babylonian exile.

If the early portion of Genesis is semi-poetic, we have to make adjustments in our approach to this text. As Meredith Kline argues, "The semi-poetic style, however, should lead the exegete to anticipate the figurative strand in this genuinely historical record of the origins of the universe."[16] Biblical scholar Vern Poythress notes that the "natural reading" of the Genesis text "attends closely to the Bible's actual meaning within the Ancient Near East." A person using this method does not read "the text only against the background of one's own modern world and life."[17] Rather, the "natural reading" takes into account the cultural and literary context in which it was written.

The prologue of Genesis (1:1–2:4a) is tightly packed and highly structured, using the symbolic numbers three, seven, and ten. Genesis 1:1 contains seven Hebrew words, and the first section of Genesis is divided into seven sections.[18] Genesis 1:2 contains fourteen (twice seven) words. The two key words in Genesis 1:1 occur in Genesis 1:1–2:4a in multiples of seven: *God (elohim)* occurs thirty-five times, and earth/land *(eretz)* is found twenty-one times. The paragraph on the Sabbath has thirty-five words. The prologue of Genesis, anticipating the ten "words" or commandments in Exodus 20, is carefully arranged around ten divine commands. In addition, other occurrences fit into this numerical symbolism:

- "And God said": 10 times
- "Let there be": 7 times
- "make": 7 times
- "firmament": 21 times (7 times 3)
- "according to their kind": 10 times
- "and it was so": 7 times
- "and God saw that it was good *[tob]*": 7 times; the word *tob* [good] is a contrasting wordplay or pun on *tohu* [desolate] in 1:2)
- God "blessed": 3 times
- God "creates": 3 times

Given this tightly knit structure of the early portion of Genesis, it seems sensible to consider this passage something other than straightforward historical narrative, though it is historical. Moses used an economy of words, and he did not necessarily describe everything that happened within a particular "day." Perhaps more was done on each day than what Scripture records, and perhaps what God did overlapped days.

> It is a great mistake to insist that not a single animal could possibly have been created before all the plants were created simply because the third day reports on plants and the fifth and sixth days report on animals. To insist on this kind of conclusion is to overlook the fact that Moses is speaking very generally.[19]

Third, since the biblical writers regularly utilized observational ("phenome- nalistic") language, we must not erroneously believe that the early chapters of Genesis are a scientific textbook. The Judeo-Christian tradition has affirmed that God has revealed himself to us through his work in nature and through his Word (Scripture and Jesus Christ). Since these aspects of revelation stem from a truth- ful God, we are correct in seeing them as harmonious and noncontradictory. It may be the case, therefore, that scientific discovery can inform our under- standing and thus requires us to rethink our interpretation of Scripture.

For example, Psalms 93:1 and 96:10 declare that the world cannot be moved. Psalm 19:5–6 says that the sun runs its course daily. Obviously, the biblical writers speak of natural phenomena from an observational point of view. Sim- ilarly, today we say, "What a beautiful sunrise," instead of the more accurate "earth turn." Belief in the Bible's authority does not mean that the Bible must speak with technical precision about nature, no more than we do when we talk about "sunrise" and "sunset."[20] In other words, we are left to discover sci- entifically the sense of what is being said in Scripture. Just as theologians in the past had to adjust their interpretations of Scripture, having learned through scientific discovery that the earth is neither stationary nor the center of the universe, perhaps we should make certain adjustments in our interpretation of Genesis in light of the many indicators of the antiquity of the universe.[21] (This is all the more true in light of an analysis of the Genesis text itself.)

Even in the sixteenth century, John Calvin was aware that students of the Bible can make this book appear silly by insisting on the literal truth of sim- ple observational language recorded in the text. For example, despite the evi- dence from astronomy, some well-meaning Christians might assert, based on Genesis 1:16 (which speaks of the sun and the moon as "the two great lights") that the moon must be bigger than Saturn (which it is not). Commenting on this passage, Calvin astutely writes:

> Moses does not here descant [i.e., discourse at great length], as a philosopher, on the secrets of nature, as may be seen in these words. First, he assigns a place in the expanse of heaven to the planets and stars; but astronomers make a distinc- tion of spheres, and, at the same time, teach that the fixed stars have their proper place in the firmament. Moses makes two great luminaries; but astronomers prove, by conclusive reasons, that the star of Saturn, which, on account of its great distance, appears the least of all, is greater than the moon. Here lies the differ-

ence; Moses wrote in a popular style things which, without instruction, all ordinary persons, endued with common sense, are able to understand; but astronomers investigate with great labour whatever the sagacity of the human mind can comprehend. Nevertheless, this study is not to be reprobated, nor this science to be condemned, because some frantic persons are wont boldly to reject whatever is unknown to them. . . . Had he spoken of things generally unknown, the uneducated might have pleaded in excuse that such subjects were beyond their capacity. . . . Moses, therefore rather adapts his discourse to common usage. . . . There is therefore no reason why janglers should deride the unskilfullness of Moses in making the moon the second luminary; for he does not call us up into heaven, he only proposes things which lie open before our eyes. Let the astronomers possess their more exalted knowledge; but, in the meantime, they who perceive by the moon the splendour of night, are convicted by its use of perverse ingratitude unless they acknowledge the beneficence of God.[22]

Francis Schaeffer has counseled along these lines:

We must not claim, on the one hand, that science is unnecessary or meaningless, nor on the other hand, that the extensions [i.e., interpretations] we make from Scripture are absolutely accurate or that these extensions have the same validity as the statements of Scripture itself.[23]

Fourth, the primary thrust of Genesis is not scientific but theological; it serves as a critique of and a corrective for the mythologies of the ancient Near East. The Babylonian epic of creation begins:

When the heaven(-gods) above *[Enuma elish]* were as yet uncreated,
The earth(-gods) below not yet brought into being,
Alone there existed primordial Apsu [the great male ocean] who engendered them.

According to Public Broadcasting System specials or popular interpretations of how ancient religions accounted for the creation/origin of the world ("cosmogony"), the common assumption is that Genesis is just like other ancient accounts. The implication is that the Genesis account is just another myth. While some similarities exist between Genesis and ancient creation epics (e.g., the creation of dry land, heavenly lights, and humankind; the gods resting), the differences are far more striking and noteworthy:

- Whereas the divine spirit and cosmic matter are coexistent and coeternal in creation epics, in Genesis, God creates matter and exists independently of it; whereas light emanates from the gods in the Babylonian epic, God creates light in Genesis.[24]
- The Babylonian creation story is an elaborate story that "features a succession of rival deities" rather than a simple monotheistic account.[25] Gen-

esis defines the God of Israel as the one Creator, as opposed to the many gods in the ancient orient who were limited in power, knowledge, and morality.[26] God created the sun, moon, and stars, which were often thought to be gods in their own right.

• The Genesis account portrays God as the sole sovereign, whereas the Babylonian epic exalts Marduk as the chief god of the Babylonian pantheon, depicting how he became supreme.

• Near Eastern epics depict the creation of the universe as the result of a conflict of wills, in which one party is victorious. These ancient cosmogonies do not distinguish between "nature" and human beings.[27]

As U. Cassuto points out, the Near East creation epics tell about the origin of the gods who came before the birth of the world and human beings. They speak of "the antagonism between this god and that god, of frictions that arose from these clashes of will, and of mighty wars that were waged by the gods."[28] Also, these epics "connected the genesis of the world with the genesis of the gods and with the hostilities and wars between them; and they identified different parts of the universe with given deities or with certain parts of their bodies."[29]

Ancient Near East scholar Kenneth Kitchen has noted the contrast between the simple creation account in Genesis and the more elaborate ancient creation epics. As a general rule of thumb with such things, the simpler the earlier: "Simple accounts or traditions may give rise (by accretion or embellishment) to elaborate legends, but not vice versa."[30]

A further difference between Genesis and the ancient Near Eastern epics is that the creation account in Genesis 1–2 presents a threefold theological emphasis:

1. the identity of the Creator, who is also the God of Israel, not part of a pantheon of gods
2. the origin of the world (Gen. 1:1)
3. the tying of the work of God in the past to the work of God in the future (e.g., the creation account parallels the building of the tabernacle in the Pentateuch)[31]

As we look at Genesis 1–2, therefore, our focal point should be primarily theological rather than scientific, noting the broader biblical principles of God's providence, the orderliness of creation, and humans' role as stewards of God's creation.[32]

Fifth, animal death occurred before human beings existed; with the fall, human death entered the world. From an examination of the fossil record, it seems clear that animal death occurred before human beings existed.[33] This is reinforced by certain biblical passages. Note the "creation psalm"—Psalm 104. It appears that before the fall, lions were predators: "The lions roar for their prey and seek their food from God" (v. 21). Verse 29 even implies death before the fall: "When you hide your face, they are terrified; when you take away their breath, they die and return to the dust." There is no clear biblical indication that carnivorous activity is the result of sin and could not have existed before the fall;[34] rather, as Psalm 104 suggests, all organisms have their place in the food chain: "[The] Scripture makes no mention of the sudden introduction of death or violence into the animal world."[35] This is further reinforced by God's discourse with Job about the beauty, order, and glory of his creation. We read of the hawk spying out prey from rocky crags (39:28–29); nestlings suck the blood of it, "and where the slain are, there is he." God also created the "fierce" leviathan, with "fearsome teeth" (41:1, 10, 14). No herbivore here! Job 38:39 speaks of the prey of the lion and of lions crouching in wait in a thicket (38:40). Animal death and the food chain are presupposed as part of God's creation—without apology or qualification. However, the fall of Adam did usher in human death, which Romans 5:12 affirms. And while the paleographical/geological evidence bears out that carnivorous animals—not to mention thorns and thistles or earthquakes and hurricanes—existed before the fall, it was only after the fall that human beings became vulnerable to and endangered by them.

Sixth, human beings and various animals were meat eaters before the flood of Noah. It is commonly argued that humans and all animals prior to the Noahic flood were vegetarians. In Genesis 1:29, God gives human beings every kind of tree and plant for consumption. After the flood, Genesis 9:3 affirms that "every moving thing that is alive shall be food for you" (NASB). Does this mean that God inaugurated meat eating, that all animals were herbivores before the flood of Noah, as some allege? Not so, according to Old Testament scholar Gordon Wenham. It merely ratifies or confirms the legitimacy of meat eating.[36] "Genesis . . . is not primarily interested in whether people were originally vegetarian but in the fact that God provided them with food."[37] Henri Blocher suggests that Genesis does not move from prohibition of meat eating (in Genesis 1) to permission (Genesis 9). This shift in emphasis is more likely stylistic: Genesis 1 omits this feature—though the food chain is not an evil—to suggest the perfection of harmony in the creation. Genesis 9 adds this aspect of permissibility to convey the feeling that the peace has been broken.[38]

There is further biblical evidence to suggest that meat eating took place before the flood. God tells human beings to "rule over the fish of the sea" (Gen. 1:28). What could this mean apart from permission to eat them? Abel kept sheep, presumably to eat (4:2–4). Noah himself distinguished between clean and unclean animals (7:2), which clearly assumes the edibility of meat prior to the flood.

I began this chapter talking about being wise in how we approach the relationship of science and the biblical text. While, as Christians, we affirm that the Bible is authoritative, it does not follow that all our *interpretations* of it are. Even Augustine warned Christians about the damage they could do to their testimony by being ignorant of the sciences and making unjustified pronouncements based on an interpretation of the Bible that needed to be seriously adjusted:

> It is a disgraceful and dangerous thing for an infidel to hear a Christian, presumably giving the meaning of Holy Scripture, talking nonsense on these topics; and we should take all means to prevent such an embarrassing situation, in which people show up vast ignorance in a Christian and laugh it to scorn. . . . If they find a Christian mistaken in a field which they themselves know well and hear him maintaining his foolish opinions about our books, how are they going to believe those books in matters concerning the resurrection of the dead, the hope of eternal life, and the kingdom of heaven, when they think their pages are full of falsehoods on facts which they themselves have learnt from the experience and the light of reason?[39]

◆ Summary

- *That* God created is more important than *how* he created. The crucial issue we must address is naturalism versus supernaturalism, not creation versus evolution or old- versus young-earth creationism.
- God's majesty is not diminished if he creates over a lengthy period of time or if he creates indirectly rather than directly.
- The truth, power, and historicity of God's creation are not undermined if a genre other than historical narrative was used in Genesis.
- Genesis recounts history and thus is not mythological; its historicity is reinforced by the New Testament's understanding of the Old.
- Even though Genesis 1:1–2:4a is most likely a historico-poetic genre rather than straightforward prose, it should not be deemed inferior to a straightforward historical narrative.
- Since the biblical writers regularly utilized observational ("phenomenalistic") language, we must not erroneously believe that the early chapters of Genesis are a scientific textbook.
- The primary thrust of Genesis is not scientific but theological; it serves as a critique of and a corrective for the mythologies of the ancient Near East.
- Animal death occurred before human beings existed; with the fall, human death entered the world.
- Human beings and various animals were meat eaters before the flood of Noah.

◆ Further Reading

Blocher, Henri. *In the Beginning: The Opening Chapters of Genesis.* Trans. David G. Preston. Downers Grove, Ill.: InterVarsity Press, 1984.

Moreland, J. P., and John Mark Reynolds, eds. *Three Views on Creation and Evolution*. Grand Rapids: Zondervan, 1999.

Ross, Hugh. *Creation and Time: A Biblical and Scientific Perspective on the Creation-Date Controversy*. Colorado Springs: Navpress, 1994.

Sailhamer, John. *Genesis Unbound: A Provocative New Look at the Creation Account*. Sisters, Ore.: Multnomah, 1996.

Young, Davis. *Christianity and the Age of the Earth*. Grand Rapids: Zondervan, 1982.

THE GENESIS CREATION ACCOUNT CONTRADICTS CONTEMPORARY SCIENCE (PART 2)

Historian Mark Noll has pointed out an interesting phenomenon within American evangelicalism: Many—though not all—who insist on a "biblical literalism" when reading creation texts of Genesis tend to approach the Book of Revelation in the same straightforward way. To make his point, Noll characterizes young-earth creationism as having an all-or-nothing attitude about interpreting certain texts.[1] If there is any ambiguity about interpreting certain words or phrases ("day," "evening," "morning" in Genesis; "two witnesses," "1,000 years," "144,000," or "1,260 days" in Revelation), then we cannot properly interpret any text or understand the author's intention, so the claim goes. When interpreting Scripture, however, we cannot treat all types of literature within Scripture identically. We cannot interpret poetry or prophecy in the same manner as historical narrative.[2]

For instance, Craig Blomberg of Denver Seminary comments on Revelation, which is partly prophetic (and partly apocalyptic) in nature: "There is an approach to interpreting Scripture that requires that all texts be taken literally unless there is clear evidence of the use of figures of speech, but however helpful this approach may be for other literary genres, it is almost certainly more misleading than helpful when one approaches prophecy."[3]

When it comes to Genesis, we may be misreading Genesis's creation texts if we treat them as a straightforward historical narrative. If, as many biblical scholars believe, this portion of Scripture is a unique type of literature, then we must not use interpretive principles for historical narrative to interpret it.

While we may certainly find reasons for thinking that the word *day (yôm)* in Genesis 1:1–2:4a could be interpreted as a twenty-four-hour period of time,[4] this is not the only legitimate interpretation of the text.[5] In the preceding chapter, we established the theological and literary context for discussing the specifics of Genesis 1:1–2:4a. Biblical history (such as the historicity of Adam) and sound theology are not at all undermined by treating *day* in an indefinite or more flexible sense. Augustine himself considered the days of creation to be epochs, and he cautioned against dogmatism about the nature of these days: "What kind of days these were it is extremely difficult or perhaps impossible for us to conceive, and how much more to say!"[6] As biblical scholars such as Gleason Archer, Derek Kidner, and Bruce Waltke have argued, there are sound biblical reasons, apart from the scientific evidence, for taking the word *day* to be an extended or indefinite period of time rather than a literal twenty-four-hour day. Christian thinker Francis Schaeffer counseled that *day* in Genesis 1 should be held with some openness.[7]

Before I plead for more interpretive room regarding the days of Genesis, let me briefly put forth another intriguing alternative that assumes (1) the universe is billions of years old (in affirmation of what scientific study appears to have established) and (2) day in Genesis 1:1–2:4a is a twenty-four-hour period (still taking the young-earth creationist's position on day).[8] My point in doing so is this: Even holding that the Genesis "days" are twenty-four hours does not require a recent-earth interpretation.

John Sailhamer presents his "Textual Creationist" model in his book *Genesis Unbound*. He believes that this approach to Genesis 1–2 fits remarkably well with "current scientific models of the universe"—namely, the big bang, the antiquity of the universe, geological/ice ages, the extinction of dinosaurs before humans were created, and so on.[9] The primary purpose of the early chapters of Genesis is not to describe how God made the world/universe. Rather, it is to describe two acts: (1) the creation of the universe in Genesis 1:1 (which could have spanned billions of years and thus was not instantaneous) and (2) the preparation of the land for God's people in Genesis 1:2–2:4a (which took a much shorter period of time). While "heavens and earth [or sky and land]" in 1:1 is a particular figure of speech (called a *merism*) expressing totality ("God created *the works!*"), by itself the word *earth (eretz)* in 1:2, which is better translated "land," refers to the land God will later promise to Abraham in Genesis 15:7—the land extending from the region of Egypt/Cush (Ethiopia)[10] to the borders of the Tigris and Euphrates Rivers (cp. Gen. 2:11–14). This is the Garden of Eden.

Sailhamer challenges another common but unexamined assumption that most people bring to Genesis 1:1–2:4a (implicit in our English translations). Genesis 1:2 does not refer to some formless mass that God shaped into the world as we know it today (a misperception that can be traced to the influence of Greek thought on the Septuagint's translation, which affected the Latin Vulgate—all the way to the King James and modern versions).[11] Sailhamer follows the medieval Jewish exegetes, such as Ibn Ezra and Rashi, who dissented from the Hellenistic "global reading" of Genesis 1:2ff. Sailhamer makes a strong—but commonsense—case that Genesis 1–2 be read in the broader context of Genesis itself and also the entire Pentateuch, with its emphasis on God's preparing a land and a people to inhabit it; the God of Israel is none other than the Being who created everything.

I myself tend to think that the Genesis days are indefinite periods of time (for reasons given below), but I find Sailhamer's approach refreshing, text sensitive, and worthy of serious consideration. Either of these approaches, though, avoids what appears to be in strong conflict with the findings of contemporary science. Again, Scripture is authoritative, and it can help guide and inform scientific research rather than always be guided by it. But it is also true that the findings of science can help correct our interpretations of Scripture. Throughout church history, certain interpretations of Scripture have needed to be modified in light of the findings of science (e.g., the earth does move, and it revolves around the sun). We are dealing with God's two books—God's *Word* and God's *works,* neither of which is ultimately in conflict. This means that theology and science can learn from and inform one another.

First, if the genre of the early portion of Genesis is indeed historico-poetic or not purely historical, then it is unfair to make unwarranted literary demands on it. Arthur Custance makes the commonly heard claim that an ordinal ("first, second, third," etc.) before the word *day* always refers to a literal twenty-four-hour day in Hebrew.[12] Therefore, any reading but the 144-hour creation week is illegitimate. But two responses are in order. For one thing, this is not true. For instance, Hosea 6:2 uses the word *day* preceded by an ordinal in reference to an extended period of time: "After two days [God] will revive us; on the third day he will restore us." Here "third day" is not a literal twenty-four-hour day. Rather, day is obviously used figuratively, and here it makes a theological point:[13] The Old Testament usage of "the third day"—while frequently literal—

connotes salvation, rescue, or divine help.[14] This is why 1 Corinthians 15:4 speaks of Jesus being "raised on the third day according to the Scriptures," giving a fuller theological sense to "third day" than just a literal reading.

For another thing, if it is true that the early part of Genesis is a unique literary genre, then to appeal to other uses of the ordinal-plus-day configuration to prove that day in this part of Genesis must be a twenty-four-hour period is an imposition on the Genesis text. For the sake of argument, suppose that the Greek (and not the Hebrew) text uses the ordinal-plus-day arrangement to refer to a twenty-four-hour day in many cases. But then suppose that this same arrangement is used throughout the Book of Revelation—a highly symbolic work of prophetic-apocalyptic literature (particularly 4:1–22:8).[15] Typically, numbers (such as 3, 7, 10, 12, and their multiples) and vivid, bizarre images in the apocalyptic literature of John's day were used symbolically. Thus, we would begin with the assumption that something is figurative unless there were good reasons to take it literally. My point is this: It would be wholly unwarranted to say that day must mean twenty-four hours when this particular literature calls for treating such numbers symbolically.

Second, the word day *is flexible within the text of Genesis itself.* The word *yôm* can be used of a literal twenty-four-hour period (Gen. 7:4) but also of the hours of daylight (Gen. 29:7) or of an indefinite period of time (Gen. 35:3). But even early in Genesis, within the creation account itself, day is used for a lengthy period of time—namely, the entire creative process from day one through the sixth day:[16] "These are the generations of the heavens and the earth in the *day* the LORD God made earth and heaven" (Gen. 2:4, author's translation). Although the NIV does not adequately capture this meaning, *day* is used for a longer period of time than twenty-four hours.

Third, the seventh day has not yet ended. We are told that God rested on the seventh day, but there is no "evening" and "morning" as with the other days. The implication is that the Sabbath continues even today, which is a remarkable length of time. If the seventh day is not twenty-four hours but quite lengthy, could not the same case be made for the others?[17] Gordon Wenham rightly cautions that

> in speaking of his creating the world in six days, we do not identify [God's] mode of creation with human creativity nor need we assume his week's work was necessarily accomplished in 144 hours. By speaking of six days of work followed by one day's rest, Gen 1 draws attention to the correspondence between God's work and man's and God's rest as a model for the Sabbath, but that does not necessarily imply that the six days of creation are the same as human [i.e., twenty-four-hour] days.[18]

Fourth, the fact that "evening" is mentioned before "morning" is unusual and might have symbolic—sacramental—significance. "There was evening and there was morning" is repeated throughout the creation text. This arrangement is an unusual usage of grammar, since the Hebrew day began in the morning and ended in the evening.[19] It seems that evening is mentioned first—then morning—in order to make a connection with the worship of God by his people. For example, Genesis 1:14 indicates that the lights were for days and seasons and years. This is the very language used later in the Pentateuch for Israel's celebrations and holy days (such as Passover or the Day of Atonement) when evening is mentioned first (as the beginning point of the day itself) and then the morning or the day after.[20] Meredith Kline suggests that the order of evening followed by morning thus implies that these days have a sense of holiness or sacramentalism. This would be another likely indicator that *yôm* should not be taken literally. The connotation of ceremonial sanctity strongly suggests a figurative meaning.[21]

Fifth, the sixth day itself is crowded with activity, far more than could be achieved in a twenty-four-hour period. If we take the creation days as twenty-four-hour periods, we run into problems with the text. For example, Genesis 2:9 speaks of God causing trees to grow,[22] but this growth did not take place in a short moment. Such growth was not like that portrayed in time-lapse photography in which a flower or shrub appears to grow from a sprout into a mature plant in seconds! Several factors regarding the sixth day indicate a lengthy period of time, at least more than twenty-four hours.

Factor 1: Genesis 1:26–28 indicates that both man and woman were created on the sixth day, that they had some time to get acquainted, that God blessed them and commanded them to have dominion over other living creatures. He also told them they could eat from the herbs and trees for food (1:29). Here we have the outline of a crowded day. But there's more.

Factor 2: Genesis 2 goes into greater detail about the sixth day, which makes things even more crowded. God told Adam that he could freely eat of any of the trees (2:16) but not of the tree of the knowledge of good and evil (2:17). Then Adam gave names to all the animals and birds (2:20), which presumably required time to examine each of the animals (which would most naturally include observing its physical features, its behavior, and its habits) and think up a name for it. Given the thousands of species of animals that exist today (not to mention multitudinous ones that are now extinct) prompts us to question seriously how Adam could name all of them in so brief a period. Today there are, modestly speaking, approximately 8,600 species of birds, 5,300 species of reptiles, and 2,500 species of amphibians—not to mention the huge number of insect species.[23]

Factor 3: Adam presumably had to notice the social and mating habits of the animals in order to recognize that he himself had no equal (2:20). Then God put Adam into a deep sleep and created Eve from his side. The new couple would have more than likely wanted to get acquainted before dropping off to sleep after an exhausting day. Old Testament scholar Gleason Archer asks, "Who can imagine that all of these transactions could possibly have taken place in such a short space of time?"[24] It seems best to maintain that the days of Genesis are *indefinite* rather than specifiable. This is reinforced by yet another factor.

Factor 4: When Eve finally arrived on the scene, Adam cried out, "At last!" or "Now!" (*happaʿam* [2:23]), a word that indicates a significant passing of time. Furthermore, "at last" is found in other Old Testament passages in which a considerable period of time elapsed. Take, for instance, the arrival of Leah's "vindication," when she *at last* gives birth to children to offset Jacob's favoritism of her younger sister, Rachel (Gen. 29:34–35). When Jacob arrives in Egypt to see his long-lost son Joseph still alive, he says that *at last* he can depart this life (Gen. 46:30).[25]

It seems that evidence for the antiquity of the universe does not contradict Genesis, for the term *day* could be understood as an indefinite period of time. Science does not undermine Scripture but is in harmony with it.

◆ Summary

- Recent-earth creationism may be one permissible reading of the Genesis text, but it is unfair to say that is is the *only* one. The text of Genesis itself allows the word *day* to mean indefinite periods of time.

- One view worth considering is John Sailhamer's "textual creationism," which assumes (1) the universe is billions of years old and (2) day in Genesis 1:1–2:4a is a twenty-four-hour period. The recent-earth creationist reading of the creation texts (in which day is twenty-four hours) is not the only one.

- In Hebrew, an ordinal ("first, second, third") before *yôm* (day) does not always refer to a twenty-four-hour period (e.g., Hosea 6:2).

- If the genre of the early portion of Genesis is indeed historico-poetic or not purely historical, then it is unfair to make unwarranted literary demands on it (such as the ordinal-*yôm* configuration).

- The seventh day has not yet ended (there is no "evening" and "morning" as with the other days). If the seventh day is not twenty-four hours but quite lengthy, could not the same case be made for the other six days?

- The fact that evening is mentioned before morning is unusual and might have symbolic—sacramental—significance. Therefore, the text may not be a straightforward historical narrative.

- The sixth day seems quite lengthy (Adam names thousands and thousands of animals, gets acquainted with their mating habits, realizes that he is alone, and so on; when Eve is finally created, he cries out, "At last!" or "Now!"—which indicates the passage of a long period of time).

159

◆ Further Reading

Blocher, Henri. *In the Beginning: The Opening Chapters of Genesis.* Trans. David G. Preston. Downers Grove, Ill.: InterVarsity Press, 1984.

Moreland, J. P., and John Mark Reynolds, eds. *Three Views on Creation and Evolution.* Grand Rapids: Zondervan, 1999.

Ross, Hugh. *Creation and Time: A Biblical and Scientific Perspective on the Creation-Date Controversy.* Colorado Springs: Navpress, 1994.

18

HOW COULD
A LOVING GOD
COMMAND GENOCIDE?

erd Lüdemann, a German theologian who recently became an atheist, wrote that "the command to exterminate is extremely offensive, even if at that time it was given by God in a highly personal way." Lüdemann wonders how such acts could have anything to do with a merciful God.[1] Such a command has also had repercussions throughout Western history. During the time of the Crusades, this "holy war" mentality was implemented to put to death Jews and Muslims.[2]

Let's look at the biblical text itself. Note what Deuteronomy 20:16–18 says regarding the destruction of various clans and nations[3] within the land of Canaan:

Only in the cities of these peoples that the LORD your God is giving you as an inheritance, you shall not leave alive anything that breathes. But you shall utterly destroy them, the Hittite and the Amorite, the Canaanite and the Perizzite, the Hivite and the Jebusite, as the LORD your God has commanded you, in order that they may not teach you to do according to all their detestable things which they have done for their gods, so that you would sin against the LORD your God[4] (NASB).

How do we respond to critics who wonder how God could allow the Canaanites (a people consisting of seven smaller nations)[5] to be exterminated? And even if the adult population was wicked, why unleash such destructive fury on innocent children? Was such an act just, or was it immoral?

First, war was a part of life in the ancient Near East. When I moved to the city of Chicago to begin graduate school, my roommate Kent (who had become a well-seasoned city driver by then) told me, "There are only two kinds of drivers in Chicago—the quick and the dead!" I found out that to drive in the Windy City I needed to be cautious and quick—and, at times, aggressive—in order to survive.

In the ancient Near East, it was often the case that, all things being equal, a nation had to be quick—alert to the maneuverings and plottings of surrounding nations and tribes—or it would be dead! "War was a normal state in the ancient world of the Near East."[6] For Israel, it was "a natural—if unpleasant— part of the world in which they lived."[7] For example, the biblical city of Bethel, one famous archaeologist noted, was destroyed four times in a period of two hundred years (1200–1000 B.C.).[8] One scholar summarized the general situation for Israel this way: "Israel did not fight for her faith but for her existence."[9]

Second, we cannot come to terms with such divine commands unless we understand the historical context of God's saving plan for the entire world through the establishment of the people of Israel. The reason most people caricature the Israelites as bloodthirsty, shekel-grubbing, land-hungry nationalists is that they have isolated Israel's conquest from the Pentateuch's teaching on Israel's foreign policy.[10] God's command to destroy the Canaanites was linked to his promise to Abraham and his offspring that they would possess this land (Gen. 15:7). God's ultimate plan was not an isolated, nationalistic agenda. Rather, from the beginning God intended that through Abraham and his descendants, all the nations of the earth would receive God's blessing: "And all peoples on earth will be blessed through you" (Gen. 12:3). In the New Testament, the fulfillment of this promise came through Jesus Christ, whose sacrificial substitutionary death brought Jews and Gentiles alike into a new community of God's people (Eph. 2:11–22). This fulfillment took place when the historical stage was perfectly set—in the "fullness of time" (Gal. 4:4–5).

But for the cultural and religious context to be properly set—in order to make theological sense of the death of Jesus, the very climax of the human story—God mandated that a particular ethnic group inhabit the land, namely, the nation of Israel. God also had to create a history and an identity for this people, through which the Savior of the world would come. And God's promises to Abraham, Isaac, and Jacob—which involved the blessing and salvation of all the peoples of the earth—would be greatly hindered apart from the removal of the perverse culture surrounding this people.[11]

Therefore, in light of Israel's situation in the ancient Near East, the demand (in many cases) to take up arms in self-defense or protection of ethnic identity, and the importance of establishing a vehicle for universal salvation (i.e., Israel), Israel's purpose in warfare becomes clearer. What we see here is the outworking of progressive revelation: In the unfolding of salvation history, God begins with the historical givenness of Israel's situation and moves the nation through the gruesomeness of war to clear the way for the salvation in Christ.

Third, it was only after much patient waiting that God used the Israelites to punish an evil Canaanite civilization and granted escape to those who sought it (such as Rahab and her family). Some critics assume that the Israelites wiped out an innocent, decent civilization. Nothing could be farther from the truth!

Even when God made his promise to Abraham to give him the land, God told him its fulfillment had to wait until the sin of the Amorites (who lived in Canaan) had "reached its full measure" (Gen. 15:16). This time of waiting would last roughly 430 years, which meant that Israel would have to endure slavery in Egypt. Why was this the case? God was allowing time for the Canaanites to turn to him in repentance and faith. This divine compassion was shown to the ancient city of Nineveh when the city's inhabitants took seriously Jonah's warnings of divine judgment for their wickedness. God gave the same opportunity to those in Jericho, although only Rahab and her family finally responded. Inhabitants of this city recognized that it was the true God who had miraculously delivered Israel from slavery in Egypt by allowing them to pass through the Red Sea (Josh. 2:9–13).[12] Furthermore, the promise of compassion rather than judgment pertains to *any nation* willing to turn to God and abandon its evil lifestyle (Jer. 18:7–10).

At any rate, 430 years was plenty of time for the guilt of the Canaanites to accumulate and for this culture to turn from its vile practices to serve the true and living God. Hope was being held out to them, but it could not go on indefinitely. Beyond this point, justice could no longer be delayed.

Fourth, because of the wicked lifestyle and false idol worship of the Canaanites, it may well have been the case that the truth of monotheism and ethical purity in Israel could have been preserved only through the destruction of these corrupting rival cultures. God told the Israelites not to make a covenant with the Canaanites or to follow after their gods or their evil practices (Exod. 23:24, 32). According to Leviticus 18:30, the land of Canaan was full of "detestable customs." What *kinds* of evil practices characterized the Canaanites? Archaeologist William Foxwell Albright has listed some of them. Besides infant/human sacrifice, we see "their orgiastic nature-worship, their cult of fertility in the form of serpent symbols and sensuous nudity, and their gross mythology."[13] These practices had a polluting or defiling effect on this culture such that "the land vomited out its inhabitants" (Lev. 18:25). The destruction of the Canaanites was an execution of justice once God's patience could wait no longer; the wickedness of the Canaanites was much greater than that of surrounding pagan nations.

Also, the divine "dedication to destruction" *(hêrem)* was due not to the irrevocable and fixed edict of God but to the evil resolve of the Canaanites themselves to reject the rule of God. In the words of J. P. U. Lilley:

> The Canaanites in general would never accept the Israelite doctrine of God and submit themselves to its discipline; the exceptional case of Rahab only points the contrast. A whole way of life is at stake. Debased religion has corrupted Canaanite thought and practice . . . and no way will they be persuaded to abandon it. Their society is ripe for judgment.[14]

Such a punishment from God was just and coincided with God's plan to establish a land, history, and religion for Israel, through which a rescuer of the nations would come. For example, if Israel struck an alliance with Moab or Ammon, the Israelites would actually take sides against God (Deut. 23:6). To make peace with one would mean making an enemy with the other.[15] There was an obligation, therefore, to drive out the Canaanites so that Israel's worship would not be corrupted. Apart from the Canaanites' wickedness, an even greater consideration was that the Israelites avoid the moral pollution of the Canaanites' practices.[16]

Mimicking the false worship and immoral practices of ancient Near Eastern cultures was a real temptation for the Israelites before their exile to Babylon in 587/586 B.C.[17] The Canaanites, whose culture was particularly vile in comparison to their neighbors, needed to be destroyed *(hêrem,* as the Hebrews called it) as an entire culture and people. The Canaanites were the most serious threat to the true religion of Israel, which would impinge on successful preparation for the coming of the Messiah.

In the foreknowledge of God, it was precisely because of the wickedness of the Canaanites that Israel could inhabit this land. The Old Testament scholar Peter Craigie has written that there were two primary reasons for the divinely commanded total destruction of these cultures: (1) The Israelites were instruments of God's judgment; the conquest was not only the means by which God granted his people the Promised Land but also the means by which he executed his judgment on the Canaanites for their sinfulness (cp. Deut. 9:4). (2) If the Canaanites survived, their unholy religion could turn Israel aside from serving the Lord.[18] That is why Yahweh says, "You are to be holy to me. . . . I have set you apart from the nations to be my own" (Lev. 20:26); and "Do not follow any of the detestable customs that were practiced before you came and do not defile yourselves with them" (Lev. 18:30; cp. 18:3).

For the Israelites, coexisting with the Canaanites would present an ethical dilemma. Although the biblical commands are themselves considered harsh,[19] not carrying them out would have undermined the very theocracy and plan of salvation that God had established.

Fifth, God's command to destroy the Canaanites reflected God's right to give and to take life, on the one hand, and God's compassion, on the other. The obvious question is, Why didn't God command the Israelites to wipe out the adults only and to spare the infants and children? Perspective is important here. Among other divine blessings, life itself is a gift from God the Creator, and he is perfectly justified in giving and taking life as he sees fit. God does not owe anyone a minimum of seventy years of life. The philosopher Charles Taliaferro wisely writes:

> If there is a robust sense in which the cosmos belongs to God, then God's moral standing from the outset is radically unequal to ours. . . . Arguably our rights are at least hedged if the ownership of God is taken seriously. Being thus beholden to God would not seem to entitle God to create beings solely to torment them, but if life is indeed a gift from God which no creature deserves . . . , then certain complaints about the created order may be checked.[20]

God was under no obligation to create. And, having created, God is not under obligation to sustain the universe. We live, move, and have our being in him as a gift. As the author and giver of life, God has certain prerogatives. Moreover, the eradication of certain incorrigible, immoral cultures may actually be viewed as a mercy on the history of humanity (think of the defeat of Nazism or the fall of Soviet communism). It may be in the best interests of the human race for one culture to give place to another. And what of the infants and children killed in the process? Theologically speaking, these infants and children, upon death, entered into a heavenly existence with God and were spared the corrupting influences of a Canaanite culture. From the divine perspective, perhaps this was all that could be done with so perverse a culture.[21]

Sixth, unlike its neighbors, Israel did not fight wars for war's sake, and Israel's soldiers were to fight only when certain personal moral duties were attended to. God made certain moral demands of Israel's soldiers. The Crusades began at the end of the eleventh century and continued into the thirteenth century. Jerusalem had been captured by Muslim (Seljuk) Turks in 1071. Announcing *Deus vult* ("God wills it") and guaranteeing the salvation of anyone who died in the fighting, Pope Urban II[22] in 1095 promoted a campaign in the name of God to fight against the Turks. Through this effort, the Holy Land was recaptured in 1099. One crusader, after entering Jerusalem, wrote in his journal about the horrific killing of Muslims and Jews:

> The amount of blood that they shed on that day is incredible. . . . Piles of heads, hands, and feet were to be seen in the streets of the city. . . . It was a just and splen-

did judgment of God that this place should be filled with the blood of unbelievers, since it had so long suffered from their blasphemies.[23]

Not infrequently, people suppose that the ancient Israelite armies were bloodthirsty savages, like the Crusaders, who indiscriminately plundered, pillaged, and raped. Although raping women and ravaging the land were common practices in ancient Near Eastern warfare, this was not so for Israel. Israel did not fight for the sake of bloodletting or destroy for the sake of destroying.[24] Any rape would have been intolerable and punished by death.[25] There were even laws about leaving fruit trees standing rather than cutting them down (Deut. 20:19–20). Israel's warriors were also to uphold certain holy requirements, to keep themselves from "everything impure" (Deut. 23:9).

Israel as a nation was to be holy, not morally reckless—even in its warfare. For example, instead of consulting Yahweh, Joshua presumptuously attacked Ai (Josh. 7:1ff.). Because Achan had taken some of Jericho's plunder (all of which was to be destroyed under God's ban), the Israelite army was not morally prepared to fight. On the other hand, Israel remained committed to its obligation not to destroy the soon-to-be-attacked Gibeonites, who had earlier made a deceitful pact with God's people. Joshua had agreed to this without consulting God (Josh. 9:14), and even though breaking the treaty would have caused fewer logistical headaches, Israel did the right thing. Still earlier, Israelites went to fight their enemies after God expressly told them that they would have to wander in the wilderness for forty years. As a result, they were repulsed (Num. 14:39–45; Deut. 1:41–45). Later, when Israel fought the Philistines, instead of trusting in God, they treated the ark of the covenant as a talisman and hoped for a magical military defeat of their enemies; the Israelites themselves were trounced (1 Sam. 4:1–10).

In all these wars, the Israelites were to depend on God (e.g., remember the battle against Ai) rather than human power to win the victory (e.g., 2 Chron. 35:22, when Josiah foolishly proceeded to fight against Egypt for no good reason). The point? The Israelites were to fight only in the way God wanted them to: in dependence on him and in moral purity.

We can also note that the land of Canaan itself was not Israel's by right, as though they deserved possession of it. The Promised Land was a gift, and the means of possessing it came by God's direction and empowerment. And lest we think that Israel was chosen because of its righteousness to be the means of divine punishment against the Canaanites, Deuteronomy 9:4–5 makes clear that it was the wickedness of these nations—not Israel's own moral standing—that enabled Israel to possess the land.

Seventh, if Israel turned from the God with whom it had made a covenant, then Israel would become subject to the same threats of punishment and judgment that its Canaanite predecessors had been under. Living under God's rule (a "theocracy") entailed two things for Israel: (1) Other nations were prohibited from undermining God's covenant relationship with Israel. Because Israel made an exclusive covenant with Yahweh at Mount Sinai,[26] they were prohibited from making unilateral political alliances with other nations (which, by implication, would mean that they recognized and approved of their gods). To do so would be an act of disloyalty to Yahweh.[27] Any provocation or threat to Israel's well-being—such as kings Sihon and Og in Numbers 21—brought down God's judgment.

Also, (2) Israel would fall under God's judgment if it compromised its covenant with Yahweh. After the southern kingdom of Judah turned from Yahweh to idol worship and its associated ritual immoralities, God said he would send the Babylonians (Chaldeans) to carry out divine punishment against the Israelites. The prophet Habakkuk retorted that the Babylonians were even more wicked than Judah's inhabitants! Again, the punishment was not based on Babylon's righteousness but on Judah's wickedness.

God had repeatedly warned that if Israel deserted the covenant they had made at Sinai, he would treat them like the other nations (Deut. 28:15ff.; Josh. 23:14–16). God did not show favoritism toward Israel ("Israel can do no wrong"), for even during the wilderness wanderings under Moses' leadership, God on various occasions struck down many—sometimes thousands and thousands—of the disobedient and complaining Israelites by sickness, pain, and death. When Israel abandoned its covenant with Yahweh and worshiped the gods of the surrounding nations, God carried out judgment and wrath (Jer. 21:3–7). The invading enemies would show "no mercy or pity or compassion" (21:7) on Israel and Judah and would carry them off into exile.

Eighth, Israel was to offer terms of peace before fighting (Deut. 20:10). In most of the wars, the Israelites were defending themselves and were not the aggressors; frequently, they were mistreated by their enemies who often sought to eradicate them. In conducting its affairs with nations in the Promised Land, Israel's first obligation to the surrounding nations was to offer them terms of peace (Deut. 20:10: "When you march up to attack a city, make its people an offer of peace"). If the city complied, the people would go into forced labor; if the city refused, then Israel would make war against it.

Each genuine "Yahweh war" was always initiated by Yahweh himself and never Israel.[28] When Israel initiated war without divine approval, the consequences provoked God's dismay. Contrary to what many assume, Israel did not initiate—through God's direction—most of their battles; rather, they fought defensively.[29] For example:

• The Amalekites attacked Israel in the wilderness (Exod. 17:8), and Israel had to defend itself.

- The Canaanite king of Arad initiated an assault on Israel and took some Israelites captive (Num. 21:1).
- Moses sent messengers to Sihon, the king of the Amorites, and asked permission to pass peacefully through his land, promising not to touch anything of theirs. Sihon rejected these "words of peace" (Deut. 2:26) and mustered his troops to fight against Israel; so Israel took control of Sihon's territory (Num. 21:21–32).
- When Moses and the Israelites entered Bashan, Og the king came out to meet them in battle (Deut. 3:1); so the Israelites defended themselves and took possession of this territory as well.
- Five kings attacked Gibeon precisely *because* of its peace pact with Israel (Josh. 10:4: "Come . . . help me attack Gibeon, . . . because it has made peace with Joshua and the Israelites"). So Joshua defended Gibeon and subdued these kings.
- Vengeance is taken on Midian for its deliberate attempts to lead Israel astray through idolatry and immorality (Num. 31:2–3; cp. 25; 31:16).

As mentioned earlier, even the city of Jericho had an opportunity to repent—*forty years,* in fact. The inhabitants knew about God's marvelous deliverance of Israel from Egypt (Josh. 2:8–14), yet only Rahab and her family turned to the true God (6:25). As we read Deuteronomy, we find that to some degree, "blessing may fall upon those nations who cross Israel's path, if they respond wisely to Yahweh's people."[30]

Furthermore, God prohibited Israel from conquering other neighboring nations that Israelites could have conquered if they were fighting for the sake of fighting: Moab and Ammon, because Abraham's nephew Lot was their forefather (Deut. 2:9, 19); and Edom, because their father Esau was Jacob's brother (Deut. 2:4; 23:7), despite the fact that Edom had earlier refused to assist the Israelites (Num. 20:14–21; cp. Deut. 2:6–8).

Ninth, the enemy nations of Israel are seen by God as potential objects of his mercy, if they would humbly respond. They could receive God's mercy during Old Testament times or later through the work of Jesus Christ, through whom these believing Gentiles would be incorporated into God's people.[31] We saw earlier that God's plan was to keep Israel morally pure and religiously uncontaminated so that she could be the means of blessing and salvation to the surrounding nations. Isaiah 19 tells of God's ultimate plan to embrace Israel's enemies—Egypt and Assyria—as "my people" and "my handiwork" (v. 25). This is something that takes place in the new covenant era through the work of Jesus and the gift of his Spirit to all nations (cp. Eph. 3:6, which states that the Gentiles are "co-heirs" with Israel in receiving God's salvation; cp. Acts 15:13–18).

Even in the Old Testament, God cries out in compassion for Gentile nations such as Moab (Isa. 15:5; 16:9), something that would have shocked the initial Hebrew audience. God's ultimate concern is to see "all nations"—the "ends of the earth"—experience "the salvation of our God" (Isa. 52:10). This reflects the kind of message evident in the Book of Jonah: God's concern for the spiritual well-being and salvation of Israel's hated enemy, Assyria (Nineveh). Therefore, even if divine judgment on pagan enemies who threatened Israel's well-being—and Israel itself—was necessary to preserve Israel from moral and religious corruption, this judgment was for the ultimate good and blessing of humankind (Gen. 12:3).

Tenth, the divinely given command to wage war was unique and unrepeatable. Although so-called Christians have misused Old Testament commands to justify crusades or pogroms against the Jews, these commands by God were obviously limited to the establishment and preservation of Israel as the only true theocracy. We cannot justify genocide today on the basis of Old Testament commands, nor can Israel use these commands to justify its modern-day wars: "The idea of the people of God engaging in warfare against other allegedly 'pagan' nations is no longer an option because the original basis of national distinctiveness (as expressed in Deut. 7:6) does not apply to the multinational community of the followers of Jesus."[32]

◆ Summary

- War was a part of life in the ancient Near East. Israel had to fight to survive.
- God's commands to destroy cannot rightly be grasped unless we understand the historical context of God's saving plan for the entire world through the establishment of the people of Israel as a theocracy.
- Only after much patient waiting did God use the Israelites to punish an evil Canaanite civilization and grant escape to those who sought it (such as Rahab and her family).
- God's command to destroy the Canaanites reflects God's right to give and take life, on the one hand, and his compassion, on the other. Infants and children who were killed went to heaven and were ultimately spared the corrupting influence of Canaanite religion and culture.
- Unlike its neighbors, Israel did not fight wars for war's sake, and Israel's soldiers were to fight only when certain personal moral duties were attended to. God made certain moral demands of Israel's soldiers.
- If Israel turned from the God with whom it had made a covenant, then Israel would become subject to the same threats of punishment and judgment that its Canaanite predecessors had been under.
- Israel was to offer terms of peace before fighting (Deut. 20:10). In most of the wars, the Israelites were defending themselves and were not the aggressors; frequently, they were mistreated by their enemies who often sought to eradicate them.

- The enemy nations of Israel are seen by God as potential objects of his mercy, if they would humbly respond. They could receive God's mercy during Old Testament times or later through the work of Jesus Christ and their incorporation into God's people.
- The divinely given command to wage war was unique and unrepeatable and is unjustified in our day.

◆ **Further Reading**

Longman III, Tremper, and Daniel G. Reid. *God Is a Warrior.* Grand Rapids: Zondervan, 1995.

Millar, J. Gary. *Now Choose Life.* Grand Rapids: Eerdmans, 1998; Downers Grove, Ill.: InterVarsity Press, 2001.

Wood, John A. *Perspectives on War in the Bible.* Macon, Ga.: Mercer University Press, 1998.

DOESN'T THE BIBLE CONDONE SLAVERY?

n 1846, the American educator Samuel Gridley Howe witnessed an event that, he said, "chilled me to the marrow of my bones." A black girl had been brought to a New Orleans prison by her master to be whipped by the common executioner. There was no trial, judge, or jury—only the master's demand that she be beaten. Naked and lying flat on her face, she was on display for all the prisoners to see. She was tied by her thumbs and her feet while she was severely whipped: "Every stroke brought away a strip of skin . . . while the blood followed it."[1] She writhed and shrieked, screaming to her master to stop the whipping. What further shocked Howe was the indifference and even laughter of those in the prison.

When we hear of such horrific treatment of human beings, which was quite common in the antebellum South,[2] we are shocked at such inhumanity and cruelty. We thus admire the courageous leadership of Abraham Lincoln, who declared in his Emancipation Proclamation that on 1 January 1863, "all persons held as slaves" within the rebel states "shall be then, thenceforth and forever free."

Unfortunately, it is not unusual to hear people associate such miserable treatment of slaves with the slavery common during biblical times. Not infrequently I am asked the questions, "Why don't we read about the condemnation of slavery in the Bible? Why isn't the abolition of slavery introduced as a kind of social program in the Bible? Why are biblical writers silent on the matter, even appearing to endorse it?"

First, slavery during biblical times was different from slavery in the old South. To assume that slavery during biblical times was the same as it was in antebellum America is a gross misunderstanding. Slavery in the Old Testament was not, as one Old Testament scholar put it, "the horrible institution known by the same name in modern western countries."[3] Instead, it often (though not always) approximated employer and employee relationships, although the slave was generally considered the property of his master.[4]

During the first century A.D., approximately 85 to 90 percent of Rome's population consisted of slaves.[5] Although slaves were considered the property of their masters and did not have legal rights, they had quite a range of other rights and privileges, including (1) the potential of starting a business, (2) the possibility of earning the monetary means to purchase freedom *(manumission)* from their masters, or (3) the right to own property (known as the *peculium*).[6]

Slaves performed a variety of tasks. Some were civil or imperial servants who had prestigious roles and commanded power and respect. There were indeed slaves at the other end of the spectrum who, for example, worked in mines under horrible conditions. Between these extremes were temple slaves, pedagogues/"tutors," artisans, and business agents.[7]

Although many slaves were able to purchase their freedom, a good number of them chose not to do so because of the security their masters offered them (clothing, food, shelter, good employment). To leave one's master was a move toward significant vulnerability. During Paul's time, the master-slave relationship provided sufficient benefits and opportunities such that it dampened any thoughts of revolutionary behavior. One freed slave had inscribed on his tombstone: "Slavery was never unkind to me."

New Testament scholar Ben Witherington has documented ancient attitudes toward slavery.

- No former slaves who became writers ever attacked slavery as such.
- Slave revolts never sought to abolish the institution but only protest abuses.
- More often than not, it was *free* workers rather than slaves who were abused by foremen and bosses. (After all, an owner stood to have an ongoing loss if he abused his slave.)[8]

Though slave owning was certainly not ideal and social reform would need to be implemented, we must not wrongly associate this practice in the biblical world with antebellum slavery in the South or in the West in general.[9]

Second, since slavery was so thoroughly entrenched in the ancient Near East, this practice was mitigated, limited, and controlled in the law of Moses instead of abolished.[10] Certain regulations and restrictions regarding slavery were implemented in the law of Moses at Mount Sinai. Even though freedom from slavery was an ideal status in Israelite society (e.g., as seen in the regular release of slaves every seventh year and in the year of Jubilee every fifty years), slavery was not easily eliminated. For one thing, foreign slaves were typically obtained through one nation's victory in warfare over another. And these foreigners somehow had to be assimilated into a society without enabling them to rise up in rebellion against their new masters or simply leaving them alone in their own land, where they could muster forces and launch a counterattack. Given the economic realities that produced slavery,[11] God instituted laws for Israel that applied to their current situation. While many laws in Israel were a remarkable departure from and improvement on the practices and laws of its neighbors, the law of Moses reflected some of the cultural principles and practices common in the ancient Near East.[12] Jesus himself referred to the law of Moses when he spoke of divorce as being less than ideal: It was permitted—not commanded—because of human sin and hard-heartedness (Matt. 19:8). Therefore, given that such practices would not be eradicated because of human sin and certain undesirable but entrenched dimensions of ancient Near Eastern cultures, they at least needed to be regulated and limited.[13] In fact, in making such concessions, the Old Testament itself recognized the ultimate inconsistency and abnormality of slave owning[14] (as it did divorce).[15] God told the Israelites that they should not keep their fellow countrymen in slavery beyond six years because "you were slaves in Egypt" (Deut. 15:15).

Third, the law of Moses addressed abuses since, according to the Bible, masters did not have absolute rights over their slaves. Harriet Beecher Stowe wrote that in the antebellum South, masters had absolute control over every facet of the life of their slaves: "The legal power of the master amounts to an absolute despotism over body and soul."[16] Moreover, "there is no protection for the slave's life," she noted.[17]

On the other hand, the biblical demands concerning those who had slaves and servants assumed that the power of the master was not absolute, even though this was the general assumption in the ancient Near East. In fact, a master could lose his life if he killed his slave (Exod. 21:20, 23). If a master inflicted bodily injury on his slave (such as knocking out his tooth or eye), the slave was automatically released (Exod. 21:23–26). The slave—whether foreign or Hebrew—had a day of rest each week (Exod. 20:10; Deut. 5:14).[18] All slaves in Israel were to be involved in the religious life and celebrations of the nation (Deut. 12:12, 18). Any demeaning or oppressive treatment of slaves was condemned as wrong by biblical writers; slaves who had run away from harsh masters were not to be returned but were to be harbored and protected (Deut. 23:15–16).

Furthermore, during Old Testament times, some destitute Israelites—out of desperation—sold themselves into slavery to pay back their debts. But they could be held in slavery for only six years, after which time they were set free (Exod. 21:2; Deut. 15:12; Jer. 34:14).[19] In addition, Israelite slaves could not themselves be sold by their masters (Lev. 25:42).

Fourth, the Bible affirms that slaves had full personhood, dignity, and rights alongside their masters, a significant advance compared to the surrounding ancient cultures. Unlike the antebellum South, in which slaves who escaped from masters who had severely mistreated them were to be returned to their masters, Deuteronomy 23:15–16 exhorts, "If a slave has taken refuge with you, do not hand him over to his master. Let him live among you wherever he likes and in whatever town he chooses. Do not oppress him." The continued oppression of a runaway slave was prohibited.

In the Book of Job, the master Job speaks of the full humanity of those who worked under him as slaves:

> If I have denied justice to my menservants and maidservants
> when they had a grievance against me,
> what will I do when God confronts me?
> What will I answer when called to account?
> Did not he who made me in the womb make them?
> Did not the same one form us both within our mothers?
>
> 31:13–15

Biblical scholars have noted that the recognition in the Old Testament of slaves having legal rights and intrinsic worth as human beings was nothing short of revolutionary in its day. Christopher Wright declares of the slave in the Old Testament, "The slave was given human and legal rights unheard of in contemporary societies."[20] This was a radical advance in the ancient Near East. "We have in the Bible," another scholar notes, "the first appeals in world literature to treat slaves as human beings for their own sake and not just in the interests of their masters."[21]

Similarly, in the New Testament, the apostle Paul (as well as the other New Testament writers) had a revolutionary perspective on slavery within a first-century setting, especially seen in his rejection of the assumption that slaves are property. In Ephesians 6 and Colossians 4, he gives "household rules" not only for slaves but for masters as well. On the one hand, Paul reminds slaves in Ephesians 6 to remember that they are ultimately serving God, their heavenly Master. On the other hand, he tells masters to "treat your slaves in the same way," namely, as persons governed by a heavenly Master (Eph. 6:9). New Testament commentator P. T. O'Brien points out that "Paul's cryptic exhortation is outrageous" for his day.[22] For Paul, threatening, terrifying, manipulating, or demeaning slaves was unacceptable. In addition, in one of Paul's vice lists (1 Tim. 1:9–10, which expounds on the fifth through the ninth commandments in Exodus 20 and Deuteronomy 5), he condemns "slave traders" (NIV), or slave dealers, as violators of the eighth commandment ("You shall not steal").[23] Paul makes clear his own position on slave trading, which tends to go unnoticed by critics.

Paul also reminds Christian masters that they themselves are *fellow slaves* of the same Lord, who is impartial. Masters should not mistreat their slaves just because slaves are lower on the social ladder: "In an unprecedented fashion, slaves are treated as ethically responsible persons (cp. Col. 3:22–25) who like their masters are members of the body of Christ."[24] As Christians, slave and master alike belonged to Christ, in whom there is "neither slave nor free" (Gal. 3:28; Col. 3:11). Spiritual status was and is more fundamental than social status. Lower social standing does not diminish our value in God's eyes either as human beings or as Christian believers.

Fifth, biblical writers did not speak directly against slavery for the same reason that Jesus did not speak directly against the rule of Rome: Social reform was secondary to certain internal, attitudinal transformations. Beginning in the Old Testament and continuing into the New, we see an undermining of the basis of slavery in the surrounding culture. Regarding the Old Testament, "while not actually abolishing an institution which was universal in the ancient world, the Old Testament law did considerably humanize and even . . . undermine it, as a result of Israel's experience of liberation from Egypt."[25]

The New Testament takes this emphasis even farther. While Jesus was certainly the founder of a revolutionary movement, he went about it in a way that turned people's expectations on their heads. Jesus did not introduce a social or economic blueprint for reform to replace the existing order. Consider what Jesus said about the use of money: Rather than mandating fixed financial percentages or an amount to give, save, and spend, Jesus instead advocated specific attitudes such as contentment and generosity over those of envy, greed, and consumption. As New Testament scholar R. T. France writes, "The recorded teaching of Jesus contains no explicit attack on, or even reference to, the current socio-political system as such, still less a concrete proposal for its reform. . . . His concern is with the basic orientation of a man's life."[26] When in place, these attitudes offer—in seed form—economic hope for individuals and communities and a limiting of corruption and oppression within various social structures.

Similarly, Paul does not directly address the abolition of slavery, which would have created massive social upheaval by leaving vast numbers of persons unemployed in the Roman Empire. Historian and biblical scholar N. T. Wright suggests that one might as well protest against the mortgage system in the West.[27] Paul's approach, rather, is subtle: He commends certain perspectives and attitudes (e.g., that slaves and masters are equally human and, within the Christian community, are brothers and sisters in Christ) that also offer a glimmer of hope for future social changes where inequalities and injustices exist. For instance, Paul reminds Philemon that his newly converted slave Onesimus is a brother in Christ—on the same spiritual footing—and Paul pleads with him to be treated as such. Another passage offers seeds for reforming the slavery system: 1 Corinthians 7:20–22. Although an interpretive issue certainly comes into play here,[28] a plausible case can be made that Paul is encouraging slaves to acquire their freedom whenever it is possible.

Furthermore, a number of slaves in Christian congregations known to Paul are specifically mentioned in his letters. For example, in Romans 16, Andronicus and Urbanus are noted, and these names were used almost exclusively of slaves.[29] But because Christian masters and slaves were brothers and sisters in Christ, there could be harmonious living. And there was no spiritual basis for prohibiting slaves from taking leadership positions in the church, even over their masters. But the real rub came with Christian slaves of pagan masters. If one could gain freedom in such a situation, Paul recommended this (as in 1 Corinthians 7).

The New Testament reminds us that all human beings are made in God's image (James 3:9), and all believers are brothers and sisters in Christ—an even stronger reason for not treating other persons as property. When Paul sends the runaway slave Onesimus home to his master Philemon, he does not say, "Take him back as a fellow human being who has rights"—true as that was. Rather, Paul asks Philemon to receive back Onesimus as a brother in Christ: "Instead of forbidding slavery, [Paul] imposed fellowship."[30] Thus, any institution or social structure that undermines human dignity, freedom, and the right to worship one's ultimate Master is incompatible with Christianity and must be resisted.

The Christian statesman John Stott offers a response to the apparent condoning of slavery by God:

> To permit [slavery's] continuance like divorce "because of the hardness of your hearts" is not the same as to condone it. No. The nineteenth-century campaigners opposed slavery not on the ground that the Bible's tolerant attitude was a temporary cultural lapse, but on the ground that slavery conflicted with the biblical teaching on the dignity of human beings made in the image of God. For the same reason [as with divorce] the Old Testament law carefully regulated it, making it more humane and providing for manumission [i.e., obtaining legal freedom from a master], while the New Testament went further, demanding "justice" for slaves (Colossians 4:1) and declaring that Christian slave and slave-owner are "brothers" (Philemon 16; 1 Timothy 6:2). Thus, principles were laid down in Scripture with which slavery was perceived with steadily increasing clarity to be incompatible.[31]

In other words, the New Testament undermines slavery *indirectly,* acting like yeast in a batch of dough. Slaves were given a place of honor within the Christian community, and over time this new point of view could have an impact on the larger society.[32] The Bible actually opens the door for a reversal of social structures in which oppressive social structures are condoned. When Paul commands Christian masters to call their slaves "brother" or "sister" and to show compassion, fairness, and patience, the worm is already in the wood for altering the social structure.[33] No longer did "ownership" mean privilege and status for the master but responsibility and service.

Sixth, one could easily imagine that making the abolition of slavery a plank of early Christian dogma—within the context of Roman rule—might have offered a misguided or false reason for joining the church. Perhaps the early Christian leaders exercised wisdom by not turning Christianity into a socio-political movement.[34] Maybe you've heard of "rice Christians," those in developing nations who, in order to get material/monetary assistance, "convert" to Christianity. Of course, this is no conversion at all. It is simply a crass means to get assistance. Similarly, if a slave joined the church merely because of some promised agenda to abolish slavery, he or she would join for the wrong reason and could obscure the message of the gospel. And, of course, such a movement would easily be quashed by a powerful Roman Empire, which was typically quick to suppress such rebellions.

God's revelation about the matter of slavery is progressive. It takes into consideration the givenness of this institution in the ancient Near East. God makes important demands on the Israelites, stressing that slaves are not property but human beings who have the same rights before their Creator (Job 31:13–15). In the New Testament, masters are responsible to God for how they treat their slaves, and freedom from slavery is encouraged if the opportunity arises (1 Cor. 7:21). Furthermore, masters and slaves within the church are brothers and sisters in Christ, a concept that has revolutionary social implications.

◆ Summary

- Even though slaves were considered property during biblical times, slavery was different from what it was in the antebellum South.
- Because of the universality of slavery in the ancient Near East and the great difficulty in overhauling the system, the Bible offered humanizing and legal measures to control and limit the practice of slavery.
- The law of Moses addressed abuses of slavery since masters did not have absolute rights over their slaves.
- The Bible affirms that slaves had full personhood, dignity, and rights alongside their masters, a revolutionary departure from and moral advance beyond the surrounding ancient cultures (cp. Job 31:13–15).

- New Testament writers did not speak directly against slavery for the same reason that Jesus did not speak directly against the rule of Rome: Social reform was secondary to certain internal, attitudinal transformations.
- Biblical writers offer, in seed form, the basis for societal transformation—especially by affirming that slaves are equal to their masters before God and, if believers, are in the same spiritual family.
- Making the abolition of slavery a plank of early Christian dogma—within the context of Roman rule—might have offered a misguided or false reason for joining the church.

◆ Further Reading

Bauckham, Richard. *The Bible in Politics: How to Read the Bible Politically.* Louisville: Westminster John Knox, 1989.

Kaiser, Walter C. *Toward Old Testament Ethics.* Grand Rapids: Zondervan, 1983.

Wright, Christopher J. H. *God's People in God's Land: Family, Land, and Property in the Old Testament.* Grand Rapids: Eerdmans, 1990.

THE GOSPELS
CONTRADICT EACH OTHER

John E. Remsburg was a well-known traveling lecturer on "free thought" during the late nineteenth century. He authored books on Thomas Paine and criticism of the Bible and was what we could call a "left-wing fundamentalist."[1] We are certainly familiar with the derogatory term "right-wing fundamentalists." They are called "Bible thumpers"—rigid conservatives or traditionalists who tend to see everything as simply black-and-white, from interpreting the Bible to determining how every detail of life should be lived. They seem to have the dreaded fear that someone, somewhere, somehow is enjoying himself![2]

Unfortunately, many skeptics reject the intellectual integrity of Christian belief because of the black-and-white demands right-wing fundamentalists make. On the other hand, left-wing fundamentalists are alive and well today.

They make the same kind of mistake as their conservative counterparts—except they are dogmatic skeptics. Many of the alleged "contradictions" and "distortions" within the Gospels, according to left-wing fundamentalists, turn out to be the result of serious misunderstandings of what counts for an actual discrepancy or an undermining of the Gospels' historicity. No reliable historian would reject the general reliability of a document simply because such secondary discrepancies exist.

A left-wing fundamentalist such as Remsburg notes, for instance, the Gospels' variations concerning the inscription on Jesus' cross: The one in Mark 15:26 ("The king of the Jews") differs from the one in John 19:19 ("Jesus of Nazareth, the King of the Jews");[3] therefore, it appears there is a serious problem with the Gospels' reliability.[4] Remsburg also discounts the holy family's departure from Egypt (Matt. 2:15) as a "fulfillment" of Hosea 11:1 ("Out of Egypt I called my son"): This Old Testament text "clearly refers to the exodus of the Israelites from Egypt."[5]

In addressing a sampling of left-wing fundamentalist charges in this and the next chapter, I will offer some suggestions to deal with these issues. But first, we should note that the study of biblical history should be approached with a critical realism, not a naïve literalism. If anyone has watched even one game of baseball, he or she should know that what is a strike to the home plate umpire is not always obvious to the batter, and what the umpire calls a ball is sometimes disputed by the pitcher and the catcher. Of course, the umpire's judgment ultimately prevails—despite the protestations of the players or their dust-kicking managers. Sometimes strikes are clear; other times they are not. Making a judgment is required.

The study of the Gospels also requires making a judgment. When we study them—as we do other purported historical texts—we need to make certain interpretive judgments. Sometimes these judgments are straightforward and clear; other times they require some critical discernment. Some people—whether believers or skeptics—may approach their study in a naïve manner; they assume the interpretive "balls and strikes" are obvious. On the one hand, a believer might argue that the way an event is described is exactly the way it happened. For instance, when the believer reads about the voice at Jesus' baptism in Matthew 3:17 ("This is my Son, whom I love; with him I am well pleased"), he assumes that this is precisely what was said (although he will allow that it was said in Aramaic rather than English!). On the other hand, a skeptic will point to the parallel passage in Mark 1:11 (where it says, "*You* are my Son, whom I love; with *you* I am well pleased") and charge that these accounts are clearly contradictory. The same sort of charge could be made about the various accounts of Peter's confession[6] or the inscription on Jesus' cross.[7]

In this case, the believer (the "right-wing fundamentalist") and the skeptic (the "left-wing fundamentalist") are beginning with a faulty assumption of naïve realism or literalism ("what you see is exactly what you get"). But there is another way to approach history: critical realism.[8] Critical realism maintains that there is a past reality outside the historian and the documents he studies (realism), but there is often an interactive process between the available data and the historian (critical). The fact that variations in parallel Gospel accounts exist means we must abandon the naïve approach to doing history. But even if the believer is inaccurate in saying that "This is my Son" is exactly what was said (after all, we have slight variations in other Gospels), the critical realist can affirm that this is the gist of what the heavenly voice reportedly said—without concluding that the Gospel accounts are wrong. On the other hand, the skeptic expects too much when requiring that all the parallel accounts be identical. (In fact, if they were identical, this would strike us as suspicious. Perhaps the Gospel writers engaged in a collaborative plot in order to suppress any variation.)

Before looking at possible disagreements within the biblical text, let me underscore what I said earlier: Even if the New Testament writers actually contradict one another regarding secondary historical details, this does not undermine their general historical reliability as a source about the person and work of Jesus. Unlike the Muslim, who cannot be in error about the Qur'an's reliability (which has come under serious fire recently),[9] the general historical reliability of the Bible—which would include data concerning the person and work of Jesus of Nazareth and his saving significance—is not diminished even if errors in secondary details exist. For the Muslim, the Qur'an is eternal and purely divine. The Christian believes that the Bible, though divinely inspired, was also written by humans, and he thus allows for the use of documents, variation in writing style, and so on. The Muslim has far less wiggle room. Therefore, we can gain solid historical information from the Gospels and other New Testament writings (especially Acts).[10]

Amazingly, some people reject the reliability of the entire Gospel of Luke,[11] for example, by appealing to historical difficulties such as the census of Augustus in Luke 2:1 (despite the Gospel's remarkably accurate eye to detail); or they might appeal to the apparent discrepancy between John and the Synoptic Gospels regarding the timing of the Last Supper.[12] Even if these were insurmountable problems, it would hardly be justification for overthrowing the general reliability of the Gospels. For example, the meticulous documentation and historical/archaeological verification of Luke's Gospel and Acts (which are a unity rather than two distinct works), provide a solid basis for seeing Luke as an eminently reliable ancient historian.[13] John's Gospel also takes care to note important geographical, cultural, and topographical information—much of which has been archaeologically verified (Solomon's Portico, the Sheep's Gate, the Pool of Siloam, and so on). This is significant: Since most scholars think John wrote *after* the destruction of Jerusalem, the author of this Gospel must have been thoroughly familiar with the customs and the layout of Palestine/Jerusalem before Jerusalem was decimated; he was not simply fabricating his story from a distance. In both Luke-Acts and John, therefore, both writers emphasize the significant theme of *witness* and "its ability to induce faith."[14] They want the readers to take seriously their attempt at accuracy and their desire to persuade people of the life-changing truth of the gospel of Jesus. To repeat the thrust of these introductory matters: The Gospels present a reliable historical account of the ministry of Jesus.

How then do we go about harmonizing alleged conflicts and discrepancies in the Gospels without straining historical believability? By considering a Gospel writer's particular emphases, by paying attention to his audience, by noticing his literary strategies, and by examining the social and cultural context of his work—not to mention a host of other scenarios (which we cannot cover here).

First, harmonization is often possible when we note the strategic emphasis (or "theology") of a particular evangelist. You are probably familiar with the book *Men Are from Mars, Women Are from Venus*.[15] Although disputed by some in the past, general differences (although varying in degree) between males and females are obvious. Even if marriage partners share many similar interests and a common outlook on life, they will often see and assess situations, relationships, and personal conversations differently.

But this is not true only in a male-female scenario. This is true of historians, who write from a particular perspective and with a particular purpose in mind. When a historian sets about her task, she limits her research; that is, she hones in on a particular topic or thesis and then makes judgments about what is relevant to her work and what is not. She simply cannot include everything. Similarly, New Testament writers should not be faulted for, say, not mentioning the virgin birth or the empty tomb here or there; in many cases, it is likely that they simply assumed their audience knew about it and thus did not feel they needed to cover old terrain.

Furthermore, the argument "Paul does not explicitly mention the virgin birth;[16] therefore, it did not happen"[17] is not acceptable. An absence of evidence is not evidence of absence, and it is clear that Paul was interested in the birth of Jesus (Rom. 1:3; Gal. 4:4–5). Also, a Christian could reply to a skeptic, "What if the apostle *did* mention it?" The skeptic would likely not see this as evidence in favor of the virgin birth anyway.[18]

Ironically, when Gospel writers focus on particular themes, critics accuse them of distortion, embellishment, or complete fabrication. Since I have dealt with some of these erroneous charges elsewhere,[19] I will focus specifically on how editorial and literary judgments made by the evangelists need not be construed as distortion.

Let's look at a particular theological emphasis in Mark's Gospel to carry this point farther. Mark emphasizes the "messianic misunderstanding"—that Jesus' messiahship could not be understood apart from his death on the cross.[20] Consequently, in this Gospel, Jesus frequently silences those who announce that he is the Son of God or who want to tell about his miracles (1:24–25, 34, 43–44; 3:11–12; 5:43; 7:36; 9:9; and so on) lest his mission be misconstrued as having a political, anti-Roman, revolutionary agenda. Even Jesus' disciples consistently fail to see what the Messiah is really supposed to accomplish. At the climax of the Book of Mark (8:29), Peter sets forth Jesus' true identity ("You are the Christ"). At that point, Jesus, for the first time, teaches the disciples about and clarifies the necessary suffering role of the Messiah—and his resurrection (9:12; 9:31; 10:33–34). In a series of three lessons, Jesus uses the disciples' mistakes and prideful behavior (8:32–33; 9:33–34; 10:35–41) to teach them lessons in discipleship, self-sacrifice, and humility. In doing so, as the humble and suffering Messiah,[21] he sets himself up as the example they should follow (8:34–9:1; 9:35–10:31; 10:42–45).

Because Mark uses such lines as, "[Peter] did not know what to say" (9:6) or, "Don't you understand this parable?" (4:13)—lines that were omitted in other Gospels[22]—we should not surmise that Matthew and Luke (who used Mark's Gospel as one of their sources in writing)[23] ignored these occurrences. Mark has a particular emphasis (or, some might say, a "theology") on bungling disciples.

When Jesus walks on the water (Matt. 14:24–33; Mark 6:47–52), Mark says, "They were completely amazed, for they had not understood about the loaves [feeding the five thousand]; their hearts were hardened" (vv. 51–52); Matthew's recounting ends, "And those in the boat worshiped him, saying, 'Truly you are the Son of God.'" Many critics see this as an irreconcilable contradiction. But this need not be so. Mark uses this incident to highlight how the disciples had not learned to trust Jesus in light of his recently performed miracle of feeding the five thousand. Matthew stresses their awe and worship of the One who controls nature. But as we see elsewhere, it is possible that one can be filled with fear and with joy simultaneously (Matt. 28:8)—or be amazed at God's greatness with an admixture of fear (Luke 9:43, 45). Some may be amazed by Jesus' teaching and take offense at him as well (Matt. 13:54, 57; cp. Luke 4:22–28). A key passage is Luke 5:26 (after the paralytic was healed): The crowds were "glorifying God" while "seized with astonishment" and "filled with fear" (NASB). Mark and the other evangelists indicate that a mixture of belief and unbelief can coexist within a person (e.g., Mark 9:24: "I do believe; help me overcome my unbelief"). In fact, the evangelists all point out how people (1) recognize Jesus' identity to some degree and yet (2) fail to see the significance or implications of his identity.[24]

Some people see serious and problematic conflicts in the virgin birth accounts and in the genealogies of Jesus. But these do not seem insurmountable. Again, Matthew and Luke are employing different strategies. While there are differences between the virgin birth stories (e.g., in Matthew, Joseph is notified by an angel while Mary is the one informed in Luke), they can be harmonized. When we compare the stories, we see that Matthew is looking at the situation from Joseph's point of view.[25] Joseph was engaged to a woman who was, it appeared, to give birth to an illegitimate child. Much of Matthew's birth narrative is preoccupied with clearing up the matter to Joseph's moral satisfaction. Hence, the necessary angelic visitation. Luke writes from Mary's perspective and captures her joy at the privilege of giving birth to the fulfiller of the hopes of Israel. Luke focuses on the joyous news, not Joseph's dilemma.

And what about discrepancies between the genealogies of Jesus in Matthew 1:1–17 and Luke 3:23–37? Most likely is this suggestion: Matthew, who presents Jesus as the Messiah and Son of David—the fulfillment and climax of Old Testament history and prophecy—tracks the royal line of David's descendants.[26] Luke simply gives us the particular biological line to which Joseph belonged.[27] Moreover, "son of" in these genealogies—as with genealogies in the Old Testament, in which "x begat y"—need not imply a direct father-son connection; rather, it allows for the skipping of generations (cp. Jesus' being called the "son of David").

Second, harmonization is possible when we note the cultural context. Left-wing fundamentalists often assume that the Gospels must present us with the exact words of Jesus; when they do not read identical words in parallel passages, they think they have found a discrepancy. For one thing, since Jesus spoke primarily Aramaic rather than the language of the New Testament (Greek), the Gospels do not give us the exact words of Jesus anyway—except for Abba ("Father"), Rabbi ("Teacher" [literally, "my great one"]), or *Eloi, Eloi, lama sabachtani?* ("My God, my God, why have you forsaken me?"). Let's move on to some examples that will reveal the importance of cultural context.

Jesus, in the Sermon on the Mount, says: "Therefore everyone who hears these words of mine and puts them into practice is like a wise man who built his house on the rock" (Matt. 7:24). The parallel passage in Luke 6:47–48 speaks of a man "who dug down deep and laid the foundation on rock." Matthew was writing to Jews familiar with building homes in Palestine: They did not dig foundations. Luke's Gentile audience, however, would have been familiar with digging a foundation before building. Luke has adapted the message to his audience. Rather than keeping the exact words of Jesus *(ipsissima verba),* Luke captures Jesus' intention or exact voice *(ipsissima vox)* to communicate architectural stability to his particular audience. The same is true in Mark 2:4, where Mark recounts that the friends of a paralytic dug through the mud roof of a house in first-century Palestine; Luke talks of removing tiles from the roof (Luke 5:19), which would have been understandable to Greeks, whose roofs were tiled.

Another event recorded in the Gospels raises the question, Who came to Jesus? In Matthew 20:20–21, we read that the mother of the sons of Zebedee came to Jesus to request a high promotion in Jesus' kingdom; however, Mark 10:35–36 records that "James and John, the sons of Zebedee" came to Jesus to make this extravagant request. Who really approached Jesus?

The mother was acting as her sons' representative, or ambassador (the Hebrew word is *shaliach*). While the mother actually asked, it was as though her sons were speaking since they had put her up to it. We see this idea of a representative when comparing Matthew 8:5–13 (in which a Roman centurion approaches Jesus) and Luke 7:1–10 (in which a delegation of Jewish elders comes on his behalf). To the first-century Jew, this is no contradiction. Even in our own day, when a press secretary speaks for the White House and the news media then proclaim that "the president said," they are utilizing this representative motif. This motif is even stronger in Scripture. Exposure to the cultural background of this motif, therefore, clears up this discrepancy.

Another example in which a reader should keep in mind the cultural background of an event involves Jesus' birth. Was he born in a stable or a home? Jesus Seminar member Marcus Borg claims that Jesus was born "in a stable" according to Luke but in a home according to Matthew.[28] As it turns out, this simply is not true. Contrary to the traditional Christmas story, Jesus was born in a home. Borg's claim is based on the notable mistranslation of Luke 2:7: "There was no room for them in the inn." This rendering goes against Luke's intention. First, there would have been no inns in a backwater town like Bethlehem. Second, the word for inn *(katalyma)* is the same one for "guest room [of a private home]"[29] mentioned in Mark 14:14 and Luke 22:11—the room where the Last Supper was eaten. Also, this word is different from the one in Luke 10:34 (*pandocheion*=inn), where the beaten man was taken by the compassionate Samaritan. This inn was on a main thoroughfare between Jerusalem and Jericho, I might add. Third, Joseph, no doubt a considerate husband, would have taken ample time to find Mary a place to give birth, and Luke 2:6 indicates just this: "And it came about that while they were there, the days were completed for her to give birth" (NASB). Everything seems natural, and there is no mad dash to find a decent birthing room. Fourth, in a culture that valued hospitality, Joseph would have insulted his relatives by going to an inn. Rather, he would have stayed with relatives, who would readily have made room for his expectant wife—even if the guest room was crowded and the birth had to take place in the main living area, to which animal sheds were typically attached.[30] Finally, when the wise men arrive, they come to a house (Matt. 2:11). (Most people assume that the magi came much later, hence the "house." Why not the simpler solution of the house being one and the same as in Luke's account?)

Part of understanding the cultural context is realizing that New Testament writers did not use quotation marks to indicate precise verbatim quotations. Rather, they often summarized certain statements or speeches. For example, when we compare Matthew's statement about the voice at Jesus' baptism—"This is my Son" (3:17)—with Mark's—"You are my Son" (1:11)—why think this is a contradiction when the meaning is the same? One or the other could simply be summarizing, which is acceptable.

In the Book of Acts, Luke condenses the sermons of Peter, Stephen, and Paul, which were in fact much longer; but this abbreviated version is perfectly legitimate and historically responsible. The same defense is true concerning the variations in Peter's confession or those in the inscription on Jesus' cross.[31]

Further, certain Gospel information may be recounted *thematically* rather than chronologically. Gospel writers are not compelled to follow a chronology of events—especially when they have a theological or literary purpose in mind. Yet left-wing fundamentalists often give the impression that the Gospel material must be purely chronological, or else it is not historical. But biblical scholars know that, for example, Matthew thematically clusters his information into two general categories: (1) Jesus' teaching/discourse material[32] and (2) Jesus' ministry (e.g., Matthew 8–9 presents a string of healings and exorcisms).[33] We must allow the biblical writers freedom to include, exclude, and edit particular material according to a particular theme they want to emphasize.

Additional resolutions could be offered to the problems raised by left-wing fundamentalists. Some problems are resolved easily; others take more work; still others require further evidence. However, ample resources such as reference books and commentaries deal with most of these kinds of questions.

While left- and right-wing fundamentalists tend to miss the more "fundamental" issues in biblical criticism (they tend to be naïve—rather than critical—realists), what they do correctly emphasize is the significance of history for the Christian faith. Without the historical workings of God through the exodus, the Davidic dynasty, the prophets, the incarnation, and the death and resurrection of Jesus, the Christian faith cannot survive.

◆ Summary

- The study of biblical history should be approached with a critical realism, not a naïve literalism (as is the case with left-wing fundamentalists): There is a past reality outside the historian and the documents he studies (realism), but there is often an interactive process between the available data and the historian (critical).

- Harmonization is often possible when we note the strategic emphasis (or "theology") of a particular evangelist.

- Any writer of history must hone in on a particular topic or thesis and then make judgments about what material is relevant to his work and what is not.

- Harmonization is possible when we note the cultural context of a biblical event.

- Certain Gospel information may be recounted thematically rather than chronologically (e.g., Matthew distinctly groups teaching material and narrative).

◆ Further Reading

Blomberg, Craig. *The Historical Reliability of the Gospels.* Downers Grove, Ill.: InterVarsity Press, 1987.

Bock, Darrell. *Can I Trust the Bible?* RZIM Critical Questions Booklet Series. Norcross, Ga.: Ravi Zacharias International Ministries, 2001.

Green, Joel B., Scot McKnight, and I. Howard Marshall, eds. *Dictionary of Jesus and the Gospels.* Downers Grove, Ill.: InterVarsity Press, 1992.

Stein, Robert. *Studying the Synoptic Gospels: Origins and Interpretation.* Grand Rapids: Baker, 2001.

———. *The Synoptic Problem.* Grand Rapids: Baker, 1987.

Twelftree, Graham H. *Jesus the Miracle Worker.* Downers Grove, Ill.: InterVarsity Press, 2000.

OLD TESTAMENT "PROPHECIES" ARE TAKEN OUT OF CONTEXT IN THE NEW TESTAMENT

ave you ever read a passage in the New Testament that seemed to have been taken horribly out of context from the Old? It is not unusual, therefore, to hear critics claim that New Testament writers were sloppy in their use of the Old Testament, that they mined it for anything they could find to reinforce their belief that Jesus was the long-awaited Messiah, that they were historically and culturally insensitive, ripping out of context whatever Old Testament passages suited their agenda, calling it "fulfillment" of prophecy.

Matthew, for instance, cites the verse, "Out of Egypt I called my son" from the prophet Hosea (11:1); because many usually think of "prophecy" in terms of prediction-fulfillment, they wrongly assume that Hosea was predicting Jesus' departure from Egypt once Herod was no longer a threat (Matt. 2:15). However, in the original context, Hosea was referring to the exodus of Israel from Egypt—not to Jesus.[1]

Or take the passage Isaiah 7:14, in which Isaiah is addressing Ahaz, the king in Jerusalem, who is fearful of an invasion from the Northern Kingdom of Israel and its partner, Syria. Isaiah presents Yahweh's message: "The virgin [or maiden] will be with child [i.e., conceive] and will give birth to a son, and will call him Immanuel." Matthew quotes this passage, and many believe that Matthew means for this text to refer exclusively to Jesus the Messiah. But the context of Isaiah 7:14 indicates that this child would be born in Ahaz's day and that this child would be a sign visible to Ahaz and his court: "Before the boy knows enough to reject the wrong and choose the right, the land of the two kings you dread will be laid waste" (7:16); "Before the boy knows how to say 'My father' or 'My mother,' the wealth of Damascus [Syria] and the plunder of Samaria [Israel] will be carried off by the king of Assyria" (8:4). The threat of these two kings will be taken care of by God—by means of the Assyrian army. Although Matthew and Luke clearly depict the birth of Jesus by the Virgin Mary, evangelical scholar Craig Blomberg notes, "The fact that the son was to be born in Ahaz's day (Isa. 7:15–16) implies at least a provisional fulfillment in Isaiah's lifetime."[2]

In Matthew 2, we read how Herod had the boys of Bethlehem under age two put to death. (Given that the population of Bethlehem was roughly one thousand, the number of infants killed, it is commonly agreed, would have been around ten or twelve.) Matthew cites this as a fulfilled prophecy of Jeremiah. Yet if we look at the context of Jeremiah's original quotation (Jer. 31:15), we see that Rachel's weeping refers to the Babylonian invasion of Judah and its exile in 587/586 B.C.[3] Jeremiah does not seem to predict that Herod would kill Bethlehem baby boys at all. How, then, should we interpret the New Testament understanding of "prophecy" and "fulfillment"?

First, Jewish interpretation of the Old Testament during Jesus' time was nuanced: There were four basic approaches to interpreting Scripture. Many critics of the Bible claim that the "fulfilled prophecies" regarding Jesus were simply lifted out of their original context in order to "prove" a point about Jesus. But these critics fail to understand the way that first-century Judaism handled and interpreted Scripture. This treatment of the Old Testament was not simply a phenomenon among early Christians who were trying to make sense out of their experience with Christ based on the Old Testament Scriptures. They were familiar with certain approaches to interpreting Scripture used by the rabbis of the day: the literal, midrash, pesher, and allegorical.[4] If we understand this, we will not be confused by the apparent "quoting out of context" methodology that New Testament writers seemed to use.[5]

1. literal: The scriptural text is taken in its most straightforward sense. When used in this way, the Scriptures were taken quite literally, almost

woodenly at times. An example of this straightforward method of interpretation is Jesus' quotation of Deuteronomy 6:4 (in Mark 12:29): "Hear,
O Israel, the Lord our God, the Lord is one. Love the Lord your God...."
The New Testament interprets this passage just as it was used in its original context.

2. midrash: discovering a thought or idea not seen on the surface of the
text. The word *midrash* literally means "to search out, investigate."
When a writer used this procedure, he attempted to go beyond the literal sense of the text to the spirit of the text—a sense that is not always
immediately obvious. Someone using this approach begins with a text
or phrase, extends its meaning, and draws out its implications. For
example, Hebrews 3 and 4 elaborate on the word *rest* found in Joshua
11:23; 14:15; 23:1; and Psalm 95 to stress our rest in Christ and the ultimate rest that is to come.

3. pesher: "This situation refers to that situation." The word *pesher* means
"solution, interpretation." *Pesher* is the this-is-that approach: When a
situation arose that was comparable to a situation in Scripture, the rabbi
would say, "This is that." In other words, the situation that the prophet
talked about is this one in the present day. For example, Jesus said to
the unbelieving Jews of his day, "You hypocrites! Isaiah was right when
he prophesied about you: 'These people honor me with their lips, but
their hearts are far from me'" (Matt. 15:7–8; citing Isa. 29:13). According
to the pesher method, "This [your hypocrisy] is that [of which Isaiah
spoke]." Isaiah did not literally predict that Jesus would deal with hyp-
ocritical Pharisees, fulfilling this passage. Rather, Jesus used the situation of Isaiah's time to illustrate the same situation in his own day.

4. allegorical: "That person/situation represents this person/situation."
This method of interpretation was often fanciful and was rarely used
by the New Testament writers. In Galatians 4:21–31, Paul makes the
story of the conflict between the Egyptian servant Hagar and her mis-
tress Sarah (from Genesis 21) into an allegory, which the author of Genesis certainly did not intend. In this allegory, Hagar represents the law
of Moses and Sarah represents the promise of God to Abraham.[6]

The first Christian preachers did not distinguish between the first three of
these methods; they naturally utilized many of the traditional rabbinic methods of interpretation. But we must also take stock of the fact that they were
not given to fanciful interpretations, as many rabbis of the day were.[7]

*Second, the accusation that early Christians "plundered" the Old Testament
for texts that resembled Jesus' situation and ministry is a distortion of the evidence.* Left-wing fundamentalists will point to Matthew's use of Isaiah 7:14 as
an indication of "ripping a text out of its context" to "prove" that Jesus fulfilled Scripture. They will go so far as to say that Matthew himself fabricated

the virgin birth. But why is it that Luke, who also asserts a virgin birth, does not quote this Old Testament text? As N. T. Wright notes, this "plundering" argument "looks thin."[8] And when Matthew cites Hosea 11:1, "Out of Egypt I called my son," the evangelist was well aware of what skeptics fail to give him credit for—that Hosea was speaking of Israel's exodus from Egypt.

Such an accusation itself rests on a faulty assumption of what fulfillment means—a theme we will explore next.

Third, in the majority of cases, the term fulfillment *in the New Testament does not mean a fulfillment of a prediction; it has a much broader usage.* When Christians see a book entitled *All the Messianic Prophecies of the Bible,*[9] they most likely conclude that all the Old Testament verses cited in it predict the coming and ministry of the Messiah. But this is too hasty and needs qualification. Not all prophecy is predictive, and not all fulfillment implies completion of prediction. When Jesus explained to the disciples that "Everything must be fulfilled that is written about me in the Law of Moses, the Prophets and the Psalms" (Luke 24:44), or when he said, "Do not think that I have come to abolish the Law or the Prophets . . . but to fulfill them" (Matt. 5:17), what did Jesus have in mind?

The Greek word for "fulfill" *(plêroô)* means something much broader than "the completion of a prediction."[10] In fact, most instances of the word *fulfill* do not imply prediction at all. Fulfillment is part of the very fabric of the New Testament, which sees Jesus and his work bringing to fruition the significance of the entire Old Testament.[11] We cannot limit fulfillment to the completion of a prediction.

Consider Matthew 5:17 (which says Jesus comes to fulfill the Law and the Prophets). The law of Moses contains a handful of instances that actually *predict* the coming Messiah.[12] We cannot say that the law actually predicted that the Messiah would come and do certain things. Rather, fulfillment here has the sense of embodying, bringing to completion, or perfecting. Jesus fulfilled the law of Moses not only in that he perfectly lived out the intent, or purport, of the law. Rather, he brought to final conclusion all that the law stood for— the sacrificial system, the priesthood, the feast days, the Jubilee year, the Sabbath, and so much more.[13] All of these things in the law are not predictive, but, as the Book of Hebrews makes clear, these are a shadow of the substance/fulfillment found in Christ.

When an Old Testament passage seems to have been taken out of context by a New Testament writer who refers to Jesus' person and work, we can see with greater clarity what the writer is attempting to do by substituting certain words for fulfill, such as complete, embody, typify. When we see a clause such as, "This was to fulfill what was spoken by the prophet," we can read it as, "This was to bring to completion what was spoken by the prophet." This does not exclude, obviously, the predictive element of some prophetic passages, but it does allow for the much broader and richer understanding of fulfillment in the mind of the New Testament writers.

Consider Psalm 22. The cry of Jesus on the cross (Matt. 27:46) was originally the cry of David. David was the one who felt abandoned and was himself mocked (22:6–8). He was a righteous sufferer, and Matthew used this situation as a picture of Jesus. Jesus fulfills or embodies or perfectly epitomizes such suffering. He is the ultimate fulfillment of the experiences and feelings that David underwent. Concerning references (in John 19, for example) to divided garments (v. 24), casting lots for clothing (v. 24), and crucifixion (i.e., pierced hands and feet [v. 16 in light of Ps. 22:16, 18]), John Wenham notes:

> This is not logical proof of [Christ's crucifixion] from the fulfillment of [predictive] prophecy; but to the believer, who knows that the Scriptures are from God and that the events of the Passion were ordered by God, it is a coincidence that can be scarcely accidental.[14]

Regarding these sufferings of David in Psalm 22, Doug Moo comments, "It is not always clear that David would always have been aware of the ultimate significance of his language; but God could have so ordered his experiences and his recordings of them in Scripture that they become anticipatory of the sufferings of 'David's greater son.'"[15]

In Matthew 15:7–8, Jesus lashes out against religious leaders who honor God with their lips but whose hearts are far from him. He cites Isaiah, declaring that Isaiah prophesied about these leaders. But, it should be obvious that Isaiah did not prophesy predictively regarding Jesus' opponents but of Isaiah's contemporaries. Jesus was not saying that the situation in his day was a fulfillment of a prediction. Rather, the situation in which Isaiah found himself was typified or fulfilled in Jesus' parallel situation. As John Wenham notes, "Matthew is often concerned rather with the fulfillment of what is prefigured, than with the fulfillment of predictions."[16]

Fourth, Jesus as well as the other New Testament writers interpreted the Old Testament in a Christocentric manner: Jesus is the perfect picture or the completer of foreshadowed historical situations, images, and personages of the Old Testament. The New Testament writers saw the content of the Old Testament become clear in light of Jesus' claims and work. As we have seen, Hosea was thinking of Israel—not Jesus—when he wrote, "Out of Egypt I called my son" (Hosea 11:1). But Matthew viewed Jesus as the embodiment—the fulfillment—of what God intended for Israel. Therefore, he could apply this passage to Jesus as God's ultimate Son: "And so was fulfilled what the Lord had said through the prophet, 'Out of Egypt I called my Son'" (Matt. 2:15).[17]

We must more often than not think of fulfillment in terms of types or foreshadowings of things to come.[18] Old Testament prophecies regarding historical events, acts, or persons—usually related to Israel—are patterns repeated in New Testament events, acts, or persons (that are centered around Jesus) to make a theological point.[19] In the words of R. T. France, Jesus

> uses *persons* in the Old Testament as types of himself (David, Solomon, Elijah, Elisha, Isaiah, Jonah) or of John the Baptist (Elijah); he refers to Old Testament *institutions* as types of himself and his work (the priesthood and the covenant); he sees in the *experiences* of Israel foreshadowings of his own; he finds the *hopes* of Israel fulfilled in himself and his disciples and sees his disciples as assuming the *status* of Israel; in Israel's *deliverance* by God he sees a type of the gathering of men into his church, while the *disasters* of Israel are foreshadowings of the imminent punishment of those who reject him, whose *unbelief* is prefigured in that of the wicked Israel, and even, in two instances, in the arrogance of the Gentile nations.[20]

Jesus sees himself as the fulfillment of various Old Testament patterns. In his life and death, Jesus repeats the history of Israel, though on a higher plane. For example, Jesus' temptation while in the wilderness for forty days repeats Israel's time of testing in the wilderness for forty years. Jesus selects twelve disciples as symbolic of a new community/new Israel, pointing back to the twelve tribes of Israel. However, there is not merely repetition but also continuity in Jesus' fulfilling work. He conceives himself as being Israel and/or the head of a new people, which finds its identity in him. He takes over Israel's role and destiny, carrying it to fulfillment.[21]

The idea behind this typology in Scripture is the assumption that God's operations in past history have a theological bearing on the present in Christ; in Christ, earlier "foreshadowing" historical events (e.g., the exodus, the giving of the law) are given theological significance[22] (i.e., Jesus comes as the new Moses to deliver his people and goes up the mountain to give his new community their "law"). The Old Testament language is not "used up" or "fulfilled" in a single event.[23] A New Testament author, therefore, saw similarities between Old Testament events and Christ's (or even his own) situation, revealing theological significance. He said, therefore, without thinking in terms of prediction, "This situation is a fulfillment of Scripture."[24]

Fifth, the Old Testament does indeed contain certain clear predictions of the Messiah or the coming new covenant era that are specifically fulfilled and have a one-to-one correspondence with their prediction. Simply because we have spoken about fulfillment of the Old Testament in broad, nonpredictive ways does not mean that the Old Testament contains no predictions. Micah 5:2–4 indicates where the Messiah was to be born—Bethlehem. The biblical scholars summoned by Herod the Great certainly believed that Bethlehem was the Messiah's birthplace (Matt. 2:5; cp. John 7:42). We read of a prophet to come in Deuteronomy 18:18–19 and implied in 34:10–12. Isaiah 52:13–53:12 speaks of the coming suffering Servant (Acts 8:30–35; 1 Peter 2:23).[25] The triumphal entry of Jesus on a donkey (John 12:14–15) is the fulfillment of a prediction

(Zech. 9:9). Jesus' burial in a rich man's grave (Matt. 27:57–60) fulfills the prediction in Isaiah 53:9. Malachi 3:1–5 speaks of a coming messenger, but this messenger is depicted as carrying out the work that only Yahweh can do. Prediction-fulfillment connections do exist, though the truth remains that the notion of fulfillment in the New Testament is more complex than we perhaps first realized.

Sixth, we should not seek to imitate the Jewish methods of interpretation but rather utilize the grammatical-historical approach to discover how the apostolic writers handled the text. While we must be wise and careful students of how New Testament writers handled the Old Testament, we should study the words and literature of Scripture as they were intended by the author within his historical situation.[26] This would be akin to the "literal" approach first-century interpreters took. However, we must be careful not to imitate the other rabbinic methods of interpretation (midrash, pesher, and allegory) common within first-century Judaism. Otherwise, we open ourselves to an arbitrary approach that has no controls to guide it.

We should discover how the apostles interpreted the Old Testament, but we must not imitate their approach in all its features. Klyne Snodgrass nicely summarizes some of the concerns raised:

> The abuse of the Old Testament message is all too common in Christian history. Clearly the proximity of the apostles to the ministry, death, and resurrection of Jesus places them in a unique category. . . . We must be guided by the author's intention. We do also, however, read the Scriptures in light of the person and work of Christ. We must resist superimposing Christian theology on Old Testament texts and should feel no compulsion to give every Old Testament text, or even most of them, a Christological conclusion. But we will have failed if we do not ask how Old Testament texts function in the whole context of Scripture.[27]

◆ Summary

- Jewish interpretation of the Old Testament during Jesus' time was nuanced: There were four basic approaches to interpreting Scripture: the literal, midrash, pesher, and allegorical.
- The accusation that early Christians "plundered" the Old Testament for texts that resembled Jesus' situation and ministry is a distortion of what actually took place. The New Testament authors were not unaware that, for example, "Out of Egypt I called my son" referred to Israel's exodus from Egypt.
- In the majority of cases, the term *fulfillment* in the New Testament does not mean a fulfillment of a prediction; it has a much broader usage: embody, typify, epitomize, reach its climax, and so on.

- Jesus as well as the other New Testament writers interpreted the Old Testament in a Christocentric manner: Jesus is the perfect picture or the completer of foreshadowed historical situations, images, and personages of the Old Testament.
- Even though fulfillment means more than "completing a prediction," the Old Testament does contain certain clear predictions of the Messiah or the coming new covenant era that are specifically fulfilled and have a one-to-one correspondence with their prediction.
- We should not seek to imitate the Jewish methods of interpretation but rather utilize the grammatical-historical approach to discover how the apostolic writers handled the text.

◆ Further Reading

France, R. T. *Jesus and the Old Testament.* Reprint ed. Vancouver: Regent College, 1992.

———. *Matthew: Evangelist and Teacher.* Downers Grove, Ill.: InterVarsity Press, 1999.

Longenecker, Richard. *Biblical Exegesis in the Apostolic Period.* 2d ed. Grand Rapids: Eerdmans, 1999.

Silva, Moisés. "The New Testament Use of the Old Testament: Text Form and Authority." In *Hermeneutics, Authority, and Canon,* edited by D. A. Carson and John Woodbridge. Grand Rapids: Zondervan, 1986.

Snodgrass, Klyne. "The Use of the Old Testament in the New." In *New Testament Criticism and Interpretation,* edited by David Alan Black and David S. Dockery. Grand Rapids: Zondervan, 1991.

CONCLUSION

n writing this book, I condensed and summarized answers to the various challenges skeptics level against believers. This has obvious benefits: The answers are accessible both in format and style. But there are drawbacks: Plenty more could be said—volumes written—about each of these topics. I am conscious of the fact that where brevity abounds, nuance and qualification should abound all the more. But as Shakespeare said, "'Tis better to be brief than tedious."[1] So I'll have to take my chances.

We began by discussing assaults on the objectivity of truth and reality, and we found that truth and reality are inescapable and undeniable—even in attempts to avoid them. The next topic involved worldviews: Which worldview—theism, naturalism, or Eastern monism—does the best job of coherently answering a wide array of questions and putting the pieces of life together for us? It certainly seems that naturalism and Eastern pantheism are insufficient and ill equipped to do so. Rationality; objective moral values; moral responsibility and freedom; human significance, dignity, and identity; meaning in life; and even the horror of evil are far less difficult to understand in a theistic context. Can these matters be reduced strictly to natural entities and processes? Or should the monist reject as illusory morality, evil, or logical laws that make discourse possible? It seems that neither alternative is the proper path. Rather, theism is the way.

The theism I advocated is not a generic, one-size-fits-all theism but a robust trinitarian theism, in which we reflect the image of a relational, loving, and good God. This God entered into human history and drew near to us in the person of Jesus Christ, "the image of the invisible God" (Col. 1:15) and "the exact representation of [God's] being" (Heb. 1:3). The fundamental doctrines of the Trinity and the incarnation—so disappointingly and grievously ignored by many who name the name of Christ—should shape our thinking and living as God's relational, embodied image bearers. These tenets of the Christian faith—in addition to God's gracious revelation in Scripture—are not only defensible but truly glorious in what they display. Through God's empowering Spirit, these doctrines can motivate and transform the ways in which the Christian community worships, lives, and engages culture.

Despite inescapable and lingering questions and mysteries that confront us in our particular intellectual and spiritual pilgrimages, we can defend the Christian faith with integrity and honesty. Reasons for belief are available for those who seek. Yet plenty of skeptical arguments can be constructed and loopholes discovered for those who refuse to do so. The fact that we are called to love God with everything we have—heart, soul, mind, and strength—means that people may also turn away from God with their whole being. In subtle or not so subtle ways, they may ignore or repudiate God's loving influences in pursuit of their own agendas and then try to justify their stance by formulating skeptical arguments. We must not let these personal and volitional expressions of resistance to God prevent us from treasuring and defending Christianity's core truths and the historical gospel in the marketplace of ideas.

At the same time we defend the gospel of Christ, however, we should also make it attractive by our lives. The love of a caring and praying community, the personal integrity of Christians in the workplace, the hospitality of a believing family can illustrate and embody the message that God illustrated and embodied: "This is how we know what love is: Jesus Christ laid down his life for us. And we ought to lay down our lives for [one another]" (1 John 3:16).

NOTES

INTRODUCTION

1. Paul Copan, *"True for You, but Not for Me": Deflating the Slogans That Leave Christians Speechless* (Minneapolis: Bethany House, 1998). See a partial summary of this book in Paul Copan, *Is Everything Really Relative?* RZIM Critical Questions Series (Norcross, Ga.: Ravi Zacharias International Ministries, 1999), available at www.rzim.org or 1-800-448-6766.

2. I am thinking of Francis Beckwith and Greg Koukl, *Relativism: Feet Firmly Planted in Midair* (Grand Rapids: Baker, 1999); Jay Budziszewski, *How to Stay Christian in College* (Colorado Springs: Navpress, 1999); and to some extent (although more analytical and technical) Douglas Groothuis, *Truth Decay* (Downers Grove, Ill.: InterVarsity Press, 2000). (See my forthcoming review of *Truth Decay* in *Philosophia Christi*, series 2.)

3. C. S. Lewis speaks of these primary worldviews in books such as *Mere Christianity* and *Miracles*.

4. Peter Lipton, *Inference to the Best Explanation* (London: Routledge, 1991).

5. Alvin Plantinga, "Natural Theology," in *Companion to Metaphysics*, ed. Jaegwon Kim and Ernest Sosa (Cambridge: Blackwell, 1995), 347.

6. In John Hick, ed., *The Existence of God* (New York: Collier, 1964), 175.

7. For example, see William Lane Craig, *Reasonable Faith* (Wheaton: Crossway, 1994); idem, *God, Are You There? Five Arguments for God's Existence and Three Reasons It Makes a Difference*, RZIM Critical Questions Booklet Series (Norcross, Ga.: Ravi Zacharias International Ministries, 1999); Norman Geisler, *Christian Apologetics* (Grand Rapids: Baker, 1998); and J. P. Moreland, *Scaling the Secular City* (Grand Rapids: Baker, 1987).

8. By "simpler," I mean less convoluted or ad hoc. By "more powerful," I mean being able to explain a larger number of things and different kinds of things. For example, the theistic hypothesis offers a sufficient explanatory context for all the wide-ranging features listed above. By "more familiar," I mean that certain parallels or analogies are available to us to help explain other phenomena. For instance, I infer that a personal cause must have brought about the universe and physical time from a state of nothingness and changelessness, and I have the familiar experience of seeing personal human agents initiating or bringing about events.

9. P. James E. Peebles, "Making Sense of Modern Cosmology," *Scientific American* 284, no. 1 (January 2001): 54.

10. Ibid. Peebles claims that "the big bang theory describes how our universe is evolving, not how it began" (54).

11. See William Lane Craig, "Design and the Cosmological Argument," in *Mere Creation*, ed. William Dembski (Downers Grove, Ill.: InterVarsity Press, 1998), 332–59.

12. Freeman Dyson, "Energy in the Universe," *Scientific American* 225 (September 1971): 25.

13. For these and other features of the universe's fine-tuned characteristics, see John Leslie, *Universes* (London: Routledge, 1989).

14. Bernard Carr and Martin Rees, "The Anthropic Principle," *Nature* 278 (1979): 612.

15. Cp. Acts 26:8, where Paul asks this question about Jesus' bodily resurrection.

16. Consciousness applies to both animals and humans, although the latter possess *self-consciousness*—an awareness of one's awareness.

17. Ned Block, "Consciousness," in *A Companion to the Philosophy of Mind*, ed. Samuel Guttenplan (Malden, Mass.: Blackwell, 1994), 211.

18. John Searle, "The Mystery of Consciousness: Part II," *New York Review of Books* (16 November 1995), 61.

19. For example, see my criticisms of the atheist Michael Martin ("Is Michael Martin a Moral Realist? *Sic et Non*" and "Atheistic Goodness Revisited: A Personal Reply to Michael Martin") and his response in *Philosophia Christi*, series 2, 1, no. 2 (1999) and 2, no. 1 (2000). My essays can be found on-line at www.rzim.org.

20. For further discussion, see Stephen T. Davis, *God, Reason, and Theistic Proofs* (Grand Rapids: Eerdmans, 1997), 4–6.

21. *Epistle to Diognetus*, 5.

22. For a good example of the need for a community to reinforce the Christian message and its defense, see some of the testimonies in Kelly Monroe, ed., *Finding God at Harvard* (Grand Rapids: Zondervan, 1996).

23. This story was recounted to me by Ravi Zacharias (who knows this couple) in June 1998.

24. For further discussion on this, see my essay, "St. Augustine and the Scandal of the North African Catholic Mind," *Journal of the Evangelical Theological Society* 41, no. 2 (June 1998): 287–95.

25. Augustine, *Confessions*, 11.12.14.

26. Although his account is controversial in places, Tom Beaudoin offers a useful analysis of Generation X in *Virtual Faith: The Irreverent Spiritual Quest of Generation X* (San Francisco: Jossey Bass, 1998).

27. C. S. Lewis, *The Weight of Glory and Other Addresses* (New York: Macmillan, 1965), 6–7.

28. Ibid., 7.

29. Eric Korn, *Times Literary Supplement*, 29 August 1997; cited in *Context* 30, no. 2 (15 January 1998): 6–7.

30. For a discussion at a popular level of the hiddenness of God, see Paul K. Moser, *Why Isn't God More Obvious?* RZIM Critical Questions Booklet Series (Norcross, Ga.: Ravi Zacharias International Ministries, 2000); for a more scholarly approach, see Daniel Howard-Snyder and Paul K. Moser, eds., *The Hiddenness of God* (Cambridge: Cambridge University Press, 2001).

31. Friedrich Nietzsche, *Daybreak*, trans. R. J. Hollingsdale (Cambridge: Cambridge University Press, 1982), 89–90.

32. Norwood Russell Hanson, *What I Do Not Believe and Other Essays* (New York: Humanities Press, 1971), 313–14.

33. Aldous Huxley, *Ends and Means* (London: Chatto and Windus, 1969), 270, 273 (my emphasis).

34. Thomas Nagel, *The Last Word* (New York: Oxford University Press, 1997), 130 (my emphasis).

CHAPTER 1: IT'S ALL RELATIVE

1. See Barna Research Online at http://www.barna.org/cgi-bin/PageCategory.asp?CategoryID=16.

2. Some of these comments are taken from my booklet *Is Everything Really Relative? Examining the Assumptions of Relativism and the Culture of* Truth *Decay* (Norcross, Ga.: Ravi Zacharias International Ministries, 1999), 7–10. To obtain this and other booklets in this series, contact Ravi Zacharias International Ministries at 1-800-448-6766 or visit the web site at www.rzim.org.

3. Thanks to David Klement for this helpful insight.

CHAPTER 2: THAT'S JUST *YOUR* INTERPRETATION

1. 12 September 2000. Thanks to Danielle DuRant for calling this interview to my attention.

2. John R. Searle, *Mind, Language, and Society: Philosophy in the Real World* (New York: Basic, 1998), 17.

3. Taken from Nicholas Rescher, *Objectivity: The Obligations of Impersonal Reason* (Notre Dame: University of Notre Dame Press, 1997), 202.

4. Recounted in J. P. Moreland, *Love Your God with All Your Mind* (Colorado Springs: Navpress, 1997), 153–54.

CHAPTER 3: THAT'S JUST *YOUR* REALITY

1. Scott Smith, "Each Individual Possesses Ability to Shape [His or Her] Own Reality, Control Fate," *The Wheel*, 8 September 1998. My response was published in *The Wheel* on 15 September 1998 (www.cc.emory.edu/WHEEL/).

2. Much of the material in this and the following chapter is taken from my booklet *Is Everything Really Relative?* 11–20.

3. Augustine, *Confessions,* 11.14.

4. Truth propositions about the past ("The Hundred Years' War took place during the years 1337 to 1453") or the future ("Jesus will come again") can be said to be real even if they are not presently occurring.

5. Cited in John P. Newport, *The New Age Movement and the Biblical Worldview* (Grand Rapids: Eerdmans, 1998), 348–49.

6. Paul K. Moser, Dwayne H. Mulder, and J. D. Trout, *The Theory of Knowledge: A Thematic Introduction* (New York: Oxford University Press, 1998), 61.

7. Gary Zukav, *Soul Stories* (New York: Simon and Schuster, 2000), 15.

8. Ibid.

9. Ibid., 16.

10. Searle, *Mind, Language, and Society,* 17.

CHAPTER 4: REALITY IS SHAPED BY FORCES BEYOND OUR CONTROL

1. Francis Crick, *The Astonishing Hypothesis: The Scientific Search for the Soul* (New York: Charles Scribner's Sons, 1994), 3.

2. B. F. Skinner, "Origins of a Behaviorist," *Psychology Today* 17, no. 9 (September 1983). "If I am right about human behavior, I have written the autobiography of a nonperson" (32). Why does he think this? He says, "So far as I know, my behavior at any given moment has been nothing more than the product of my genetic endowment, my personal history, and the current setting" (25).

3. Richard Rorty, *Objectivity, Relativism, and Truth: Philosophical Papers,* vol. 1 (Cambridge: Cambridge University Press, 1991), 23.

4. Paul K. Moser, *Philosophy after Objectivity: Making Sense in Perspective* (New York: Oxford University Press, 1993), 167.

5. Keith Windschuttle, *The Killing of History* (New York: Free Press, 1996), 1.

6. Ibid., 2.

7. On such issues related to the politicization of the university, see Dinesh D'Souza, *Illiberal Education: The Politics of Race and Sex on Campus* (New York: Free Press, 1991).

CHAPTER 5: EVERYTHING IS ONE WITH THE DIVINE; ALL ELSE IS AN ILLUSION

1. Shirley MacLaine, *Out on a Limb* (New York: Bantam, 1983), 347.

2. Chandogya Upanishad, 7.52.2.

3. Brihadaranyaka Upanishad, 4.5.6.

4. Ibid., 2.5.19.

5. Ibid., 1.4.10.

6. Robin Collins, "Eastern Religions," in *Reason for the Hope Within,* ed. Michael Murray (Grand Rapids: Eerdmans, 1999), 187. Collins's chapter offers a concise perspective on and critique of Eastern religion.

7. For further discussion, see John M. Koller, *Oriental Philosophies,* 2d ed. (New York: Charles Scribner's Sons, 1985), 83–99.

8. Neale Donald Walsch, *Conversations with God: An Uncommon Dialogue,* vol. 1 (London: Hodder & Stoughton, 1995). For a critique of this book, see John Winston Moore, "Conversations with the God of This Age: Neale Donald Walsch's Connections with the Dark Side," *Spiritual Counterfeits Project Journal* 22, nos. 2–3 (summer/fall 1998). Available on-line at www.scp-inc.org/.

9. Walsch, *Conversations with God,* 8.

10. Norman Geisler and William Watkins, *Worlds Apart: A Handbook on World Views* (Grand Rapids: Baker, 1989), 103.

11. Ibid.

12. Peter van Inwagen, *Metaphysics* (Boulder, Colo.: Westview Press, 1993), 31.

13. Aristotle, *Physics,* 8.3, 253a33.

14. Cited in Vishal Mangalwadi, *The World of Gurus,* 2d ed. (New Delhi: Vikas, 1987), 253.

15. Geisler and Watkins, *Worlds Apart,* 102.

16. Collins, "Eastern Religions," 189.

17. Furthermore, even if *all* the distinctions we experience are dreams or illusions, there are clearly distinctions within our dreams themselves—for example, between a butterfly and a flower.

18. D. T. Suzuki, *Introduction to Zen Buddhism* (New York: Grove Press, 1991), 58.

19. Arthur Koestler, *The Lotus and the Robot* (New York: Macmillan, 1961), 273–74. For the sake of clarity, I have laid out the conversation in a more readable format than Koestler's account.

20. Ibid., 274.

21. Herman Hesse, *Siddhartha,* trans. Hilda Rosner (New York: Bantam, 1971), 116.

22. Geisler and Watkins, *Worlds Apart,* 103.

23. Stuart Hackett, *Oriental Philosophy* (Madison: University of Wisconsin Press, 1979), 177.

24. Walsch, *Conversations with God,* 135.

25. Ibid., 39.

26. G. K. Chesterton, *Orthodoxy,* 18th ed. (Garden City, N.Y.: Image, 1959), 76.

27. Ibid., 35.

28. Taken from Os Guinness, *The Dust of Death* (Downers Grove, Ill.: InterVarsity Press, 1973), 223.

29. Some of the following thoughts are taken from the lecture "Understanding Hindus and Hinduism," delivered in Chennai, India, by Acharya Daya Prakash Titus, 17 January 2001.

30. Found in E. Stanley Jones, *Christ of the India Road* (Lucknow: Lucknow Publishing House, 1925).

31. See Jaroslav Pelikan, *Jesus through the Centuries* (New York: Harper & Row, 1986), chap. 2.

32. For example, see Acharya Daya Prakash's self-published, *The Bhagavadgita: A Forerunner to the Gospel of Jesus*, 3d ed. (Nainital, U.P., India, 1999), and his *The Concept of Divine Sacrifice in the Bible and the Vedic Scriptures* (Nainital, U.P., India, n.d.). These booklets are available from Khristadvaita Ashrama, Dugai Marg, P.O. Bhowali, Nainital, U.P., India 263 132.

For example, note the Bhagavad Gita's themes of the divine's self-sacrifice: "the basis of all sacrifices, here in the body is Myself" (8.4), and "I am the sacrifice" (9.16); of salvation by grace (11.47); of release from sin/evil: "I shall release thee from all evils" (18.66); and complete preoccupation with the divine (8.5).

CHAPTER 6: WHY NOT BELIEVE IN REINCARNATION?

1. Mary Rubio and Elizabeth Waterston, eds., *The Selected Journals of L. M. Montgomery*, vol. 2 (Toronto: Oxford University Press, 1987), 372.

2. Wade Clark Roof, *Spiritual Marketplace* (Princeton: Princeton University Press, 1999), 209–10.

3. Bhagavad Gita, 2.22.

4. J. P. Moreland and Gary Habermas, *Immortality: The Other Side of Death* (Nashville: Nelson, 1992), 121.

5. Ibid., 121–22.

6. Ibid., 123.

7. See Graham H. Twelftree, *Jesus the Exorcist: A Contribution to the Study of the Historical Jesus* (Peabody, Mass.: Hendrickson, 1993). For a general treatment of this subject, see Clinton E. Arnold, *Three Crucial Questions about Spiritual Warfare* (Grand Rapids: Baker, 1997).

8. Rabi Maharaji, *Death of a Guru* (Eugene, Ore: Harvest House, 1986), 124.

9. Moreland and Habermas, *Immortality*, 127. The point here is not that psychic knowledge is morally neutral. We must beware of its association with demonic influence (cp. the fortune-teller in Philippi in Acts 16:16–18). Rather, I am emphasizing only that one need not experience certain events in order to have detailed knowledge about them.

10. Ibid., 128.

11. See, for instance, Stephen T. Davis, *Risen Indeed* (Grand Rapids: Eerdmans, 1993); William Lane Craig's chapter on the resurrection in *Reasonable Faith*, 255–98; Paul Copan, ed., *Will the Real Jesus Please Stand Up?: A Debate between William Lane Craig and John Dominic Crossan* (Grand Rapids: Baker, 1998); and Paul Copan and Ronald K. Tacelli, eds., *Jesus' Resurrection: Fact or Figment?* (Downers Grove, Ill.: InterVarsity Press, 2000).

12. See Joseph Gudel, Robert Bowman, and Dan Schlesinger, "Reincarnation: Did the Church Suppress It?" *Christian Research Journal* 10 (summer 1987): 8–10, 12. Some of my comments below are taken from this article.

New Age proponents frequently claim that the early church fathers believed in reincarnation and that this doctrine was taught in the Bible until it was expunged by powerful church authorities. Regarding the claim that reincarnation is found in the Bible, some point to John 9:2. Jesus is asked about the man born blind: "Who sinned? This man or his parents?" Did the disciples believe in reincarnation? After all, the blind man may have done something bad in his past life so that he was reborn blind. But this does not follow. For instance, rabbinic Judaism maintained that an unborn fetus could sin (Genesis Rabbah, 63:6, which comments on Esau and Jacob in the womb [Gen. 25:22]). Another passage used to support reincarnation is Jeremiah 1:5, where God tells the faint-hearted prophet, "Before I formed you in the womb I knew you." (Mormons use this verse to support the doctrine of the preexistence of the soul.) This is an illegitimate use of the verse, however. For the point of preexistence to be made, Jeremiah would have to say *to God*, "And before you formed me in the womb, *I* knew *you*." All this passage demonstrates is God's foreknowledge and sovereignty over human history.

Regarding the revisionist charge, some (e.g., Leslie Weatherhead) erroneously claim that early Christians believed in reincarnation and that under Emperor Justinian, anti-reincarnationists changed (or even excised) biblical texts. These alleged revisionists, though relatively successful in their project, overlooked a few passages that "show signs" of reincarnation (e.g., Matt. 17:10–13; John 3:3, 7; 9:1–3; Eph. 1:4; Rev. 3:12). This charge is a pure fabrication, however, and there is simply no textual evidence to bear this out. See F. F. Bruce, *New Testament Documents: Are They Reliable?* 5th ed. (Grand Rapids: Eerdmans, 1960). For further reading on these reincarnationist allegations regarding the church fathers, see Gudel, Bowman, and Schlesinger, "Reincarnation."

13. Francis Beckwith and Stephen Parrish, *See the Gods Fall: Four Rivals to Christianity* (Joplin, Mo.: College Press, 1997), 221.

14. Hackett, *Oriental Philosophy*, 202.

15. Robert Morey, *Reincarnation and Christianity* (Minneapolis: Bethany House, n.d.), 18.

16. MacLaine, *Out on a Limb*, 347.

17. Walter Martin, *The Riddle of Reincarnation* (San Juan Capistrano, Calif.: Christian Research Institute, 1980), 26.

18. Mark Albrecht, *Reincarnation: A Christian Appraisal* (Downers Grove, Ill.: Inter-Varsity Press, 1982), 64.

19. Of course, it is possible that people continue to resist movement toward enlightenment and remain in an increasingly depraved state over the series of reincarnations.

20. Hackett, *Oriental Philosophy*, 202.

21. Ibid.

22. For further discussion, see William Lane Craig, "Graham Oppy on the *Kalam* Cosmological Argument," *Sophia* 32 (1993): 1–11. The noted mathematician Georg Cantor himself claimed that the argument against the infinity of the past is sound. In a letter of 1887 he wrote:

When it is said that a mathematical proof for the beginning of the world cannot be given, the emphasis is on the word "mathematical," and to this extent my view agrees with that of St. Thomas. On the other hand, a mixed mathematical-philosophical proof of the proposition might well be produced just on the basis of the true theory of the transfinite, and to this extent I depart from St. Thomas, who defends the view: *Mundum non semper fuisse, sola fide tenetur, et demonstrative probari non potest* [(That) the world did not always exist is held by faith alone, and it cannot be proven demonstratively].

See Georg Cantor in *Probleme des Unendlichen: Werk und Leben Georg Cantors*, ed. H. Meschkowski (Braunschweig: Freidrich Vieweg, 1967), 125–26.

23. Krister Sairsingh, "Christ and Karma: A Hindu's Quest for the Holy," in *Finding God at Harvard*, ed. Kelly Monroe (Grand Rapids: Zondervan, 1996), 180.

24. Ibid., 183.

25. Ibid., 184–85.

26. Ibid., 187.

CHAPTER 7: IF GOD MADE THE UNIVERSE, WHO MADE GOD?

1. Quoted by Bertrand Russell, "Why I Am Not a Christian," in his *Why I Am Not a Christian and Other Essays on Religion and Related Topics* (New York: Simon and Schuster, 1957), 6.

2. Ibid.

3. Stephen W. Hawking, *A Brief History of Time* (New York: Bantam, 1988), 174.

4. John D. Barrow and Joseph Silk, *The Left Hand of Creation*, 2d ed. (New York: Oxford University Press, 1993), 38.

5. Cited in John D. Barrow, *The World within the World* (Oxford: Clarendon Press, 1988), 226.

6. By "prior" I don't mean necessarily that there were moments of time before the big bang. (By "time" I mean that which is constituted by the succession of events or happenings. If there were no events, there would be no time.) Rather, I refer to the priority of being ("metaphysical priority"): One state of being (God's timeless existence) serves as the ground for another (temporal, contingent existence). Or we could just speak of God *with* or *without* the universe.

7. Barrow and Silk, *Left Hand of Creation*, 209: "What preceded the event called the 'big bang'?. . . . The answer to our question is simple: nothing."

8. Michael Martin, *Atheism: A Philosophical Justification* (Philadelphia: Temple University Press, 1990), 106. Martin footnotes one philosopher of science, Quentin Smith, who has maintained that the universe was truly uncaused. See, for instance, his coauthored book with William Lane Craig, *Theism, Atheism, and Big Bang Cosmology* (Oxford: Clarendon, 1993). Smith has since modified his stance, moving away from the universe's uncausedness to its self-causedness—an equally baffling metaphysical outlook. See his (to my mind rather unpersuasive) defense of such a proposal in "The Reason the Universe Exists Is That It Caused Itself to Exist," *Philosophy* 74 (1999): 579–86.

9. Martin states, "Metaphysical intuitions have been notoriously unreliable. Everything from the principle of no action at a distance to microdeterminism has been intuited to be true only later to be discarded" ("Comments on the Craig-Flew Debate," 4. This is an unpublished essay from a book under review with Oxford University Press. I am grateful to Stan Wallace for furnishing me with this essay.).

10. In a letter to John Stewart in February 1754, Hume said that the idea that "anything might arise without a cause" was "so absurd a Proposition" (*The Letters of David Hume*, vol. 1, ed. J. Y. T. Greig [Oxford: Clarendon Press, 1932], 187).

11. Kai Nielsen, *Reason and Practice* (New York: Harper & Row, 1971), 48.

12. It seems, however, that an impersonal cause of the universe (such as a state of physical conditions) would be eliminated, since the cause would have to exist simultaneous with its effect:

> If the cause [of the universe's beginning] were a mechanically operating set of necessary and sufficient conditions, then the cause could never exist without the effect. For example, the cause of water's freezing is 0° Centigrade. If the tem-

perature were below 0° from eternity past, then any water that was around would be frozen from eternity. It would be impossible for the water to *begin* to freeze just a finite time ago. So if the cause is timelessly present, then the effect should be timelessly present as well. The only way for the cause to be timeless and the effect to begin in time is for the cause to be a personal agent who freely chooses to create an effect in time without any prior determining conditions. For example, a man sitting from eternity could freely will to stand up. Thus, we are brought to a transcendent cause of the universe, to its personal creator.

See Craig, *God, Are You There?* 13.

On the other hand, the skeptic may claim that a personal explanation is not "scientific." We can reply (after saying, "So what!" since science can't prove that the laws of logic or objective moral values exist) that we see evidence of personal action/agency every day. Humans have the capacity to choose and act without being physically caused to do so. The origination of their action need not be the result of prior influences and inner states (what philosophers call "efficient/producing causes")—even though these can influence decisions; rather, the buck stops with the agent who has a goal in mind in his decision making (what is called "final cause"). The agent himself is the cause of his actions. For an introductory defense of this kind of libertarian freedom, see James W. Felt, *Making Sense of Your Freedom: A Guide for the Perplexed* (Ithaca, N.Y.: Cornell University Press, 1994); see also part 1 of J. P. Moreland and Scott B. Rae, *Body and Soul: Human Nature and the Crisis of Ethics* (Downers Grove, Ill.: InterVarsity Press, 2000), which defends libertarian/incompatibilist freedom.

13. Dallas Willard, "Language, Being, and God, and the Three Stages of Theistic Evidence," in *Does God Exist?* ed. J. P. Moreland and Kai Nielsen (Nashville: Thomas Nelson, 1990), 206. This has been reprinted (Amherst, N.Y.: Prometheus Books, 1993).

CHAPTER 8: IF GOD KNOWS WHAT WE'RE GOING TO DO, THEN WE DON'T HAVE FREE WILL

1. Robert Frost, "The Road Not Taken," in *The Poetry of Robert Frost* (New York: Holt, Rinehart and Winston, 1969), 105.

2. Walt Whitman, *Complete Poetry and Collected Prose* (New York: Library of America, 1982), 297. Robert Bellah et al. have documented the dire consequences of this extreme individualism in America in *Habits of the Heart* (Berkeley: University of California Press, 1985).

3. I have in mind thinkers associated with "freewill theism" or "open theism." See Clark Pinnock, Richard Rice, John Sanders, William Hasker, and David Basinger, *The Openness of God: A Biblical Challenge to the Traditional Understanding of God* (Downers Grove, Ill.: InterVarsity Press, 1994). See also Greg Boyd, *God of the Possible* (Grand Rapids: Baker, 2000); John Sanders, *The God Who Risks* (Downers Grove, Ill.: InterVarsity Press, 1998); and David Basinger, *The Case for Freewill Theism* (Downers Grove, Ill.: InterVarsity Press, 1996).

These "openness theologians" take at face value language of God's "regretting" or "repenting/changing his mind" or his apparent surprise at certain events. Despite clear biblical affirmations that God knows the future choices of human beings, it appears that these "open theists" are utilizing a fallacious philosophical assumption (that future free choices cannot in principle be known) and imposing it on the biblical text. To be consistent, they should do what Mormons do: Take the numerous images of "God's eyes" or "God's arm"—despite the clear biblical affirmation that God is spirit—and literalize them to prove that God must have a body. Or if we take the text at face value regarding God changing his mind, then from Genesis 18:21 we should conclude that God knows neither the past nor the present—let alone the future: "I [Yahweh] will go down and see if what [the people of Sodom and Gomorrah] have done is as bad as the outcry that has reached me. If not, I will know." (I am grateful to Bruce Ware for pointing out this passage.)

For one critique of open theism, see D. A. Carson, "God, The Bible, and Spiritual Warfare: A Review Article," *Journal of the Evangelical Theological Society* 42 (June 1999): 251–69. Carson calls a book by openness thinker Greg Boyd "exegetically unconvincing, theologically troubling, historically selective, philosophically naïve, and frequently methodologically unfair" (258). For an important essay dealing with the notion that God changed his mind or repented, see H. Van Dyke Parunak, "A Semantic Survey of *NHM*," *Biblica* 56 (1975): 512–32. According to Parunak, the word *repent* has to do with "suffering emotional pain" in some contexts; in others, it has to do with "retracting blessing or judgment" based on human conduct. A change within the recipients of a promise/warning renders blessing or judgment no longer appropriate.

4. For a good discussion of the effects of sin on us, see Alvin Plantinga, *Warranted Christian Belief* (New York: Oxford University Press, 2000), chap. 7 ("Sin and Its Cognitive Consequences").

5. It is worth noting that virtually all the early church fathers (with the exception of Augustine in his later writings) held that human beings possessed the power of contrary free choice—even in a fallen state. For a catalog of citations, see Norman Geisler, *Chosen but Free* (Minneapolis: Bethany House, 1999), 145–54.

6. J. P. Moreland discusses this in *Love Your God with All Your Mind* (Colorado Springs: Navpress, 1997), 71–73.

7. Some see freedom as compatible with determinism (compatibilists). From a theological point of view, this links God too closely to evil; philosophically speaking, compatibilism does not afford a robust view of personal agency. Thus, I would opt for an incompatibilist approach in which freedom and determinism are incompatible. For some variations on these views, see David Basinger and Randall Basinger, eds., *Predestination and Free Will* (Downers Grove, Ill.: InterVarsity Press, 1986). For an explicitly compatibilist theological view, see D. A. Carson, *Divine Sovereignty and Human Responsibility* (1981; reprint, Grand Rapids: Baker, 1994).

8. The philosopher John Locke noted, "The *will* is perfectly distinguished from *desire;* which, in the very same action, may have a quite contrary tendency from that which our *will* sets us upon" (*An Essay Concerning Human Understanding* [New York: Dutton; London: Dent, 1977], 2.21.30, 118).

9. For a useful book on the subject of freedom (endorsing an incompatibilist view), see James W. Felt, *Making Sense of Your Freedom: Philosophy for the Perplexed* (Ithaca, N.Y.: Cornell University Press, 1994).

10. Viktor E. Frankl, *Man's Search for Meaning,* trans. Ilse Lasch (New York: Simon and Schuster, 1963), 105.

11. Ibid., 104.

12. Or, as Aristotle put it, *efficient* causality.

13. For the Christian who attributes the cause of actions to previous states or dispositions, an important question is, Where did Satan (before his "fall" from heaven) and Adam (before his actions in the paradise of Eden) get the *desire* for their first sin? The nature of Satan and Adam, which God originally created to be good, could not be the basis for evil. Rather, things went wrong through the exercise of free choice. See Geisler, *Chosen but Free,* 19–37.

14. Or *final* causality.

15. Some philosophers tend to present a false dilemma of choices/events either being (1) rigidly determined or else (2) utterly random. (By "determinism" is meant

that for everything that happens, there are prior conditions that necessitate certain events rather than others.) But (3) personal agency offers a third alternative. So my reasons—not necessarily my inner states, motivations, background, genetics—are the basis for my actions; therefore, my actions can be free but still have a reason. An example of such a false dilemma can be found in Ronald Nash, *Life's Ultimate Questions* (Grand Rapids: Zondervan, 1999), 326–33. Nash ignores the distinction between efficient and final causality. This false disjunction can also be found in R. K. McGregor Wright, *No Place for Sovereignty* (Downers Grove, Ill.: InterVarsity Press, 1996), 47–49.

16. We could call this model of God's foreknowledge an empirical or perceptual model (the image of "perceiving" by sight is utilized). God is viewed as the "omniperceiver." (This distinction is taken from William Lane Craig, *The Only Wise God* [Grand Rapids: Baker, 1987], 119–25.) Craig notes, "I should go so far as to say that the implicit assumption of the perceptual model underlies virtually all contemporary denials of the possibility of divine foreknowledge of free acts" (121). For example, David Basinger appears to use this perceptual model when he frequently uses the language of God "seeing" future possibilities (*The Case for Freewill Theism* [Downers Grove, Ill.: InterVarsity Press, 1996], 45–46). Basinger's use of the perceptual model is part of the reason he rejects divine foreknowledge of future free human choices.

17. Thomas Aquinas, *Summa Theologiae*, 1.14.13, *ad* 3: "Future contingent things ... are certain to God alone, Whose understanding is in eternity above time. Just as he who goes along the road does not see those who come after him; whereas he who sees the whole road from a height sees at once all those traveling on it."

18. Ibid., 1.14.13.

19. See Edward J. Khamara, "Eternity and Omniscience," *Philosophical Quarterly* 24 (1974): 212–18. I myself do not find the view of God seeing all things—past, present, and future—simultaneously in the "eternal now" as coherent for still another reason. If this "eternal present" were the case, it would be impossible for God to affirm *tensed* or *indexed* truth statements (such as, "I *am now* looking at an oak tree") as these would be undifferentiated in God's knowledge. How would God be able to differentiate between statements about past, present, and future, or how could we say that God knows something *at this time* that will no longer be true as a present-tense statement tomorrow? God would have to be *in* time (which in no way would diminish his knowledge of all truths—even of the future) in order for him to know *tensed* facts ("Ronald Reagan is not *now* president" or "Jesus *will* return at the end of the age"). It is a problem to say that all events are on par in the mind of God (past, present, and future events are equally real); certainly some events—even though God knows they *will* happen—do not yet exist.

20. See Alvin Plantinga, *Does God Have a Nature?* (Milwaukee: Marquette University Press, 1980).

21. Compare Hugh Ross's "extra-dimensional" view of God (*Beyond the Cosmos* [Colorado Springs: Navpress, 1996]). For a critique of Ross's book, see William Lane Craig, "Hugh Ross's Extra-Dimensional Deity," *Journal of the Evangelical Theological Society* 42 (June 1999): 293–304.

22. For further discussion of what it means for God to be a maximally great Being, see Thomas V. Morris, *Anselmian Explorations: Essays in Philosophical Theology* (Notre Dame: University of Notre Dame, 1987); idem, *Our Idea of God* (Downers Grove, Ill.: 1991).

23. Some may ask, "Aren't you assuming that truth statements can be made about the future? Isn't this itself the very point of contention?" I'll address this below.

24. John Calvin, *Institutes of the Christian Religion*, trans. Henry Beveridge (Grand Rapids: Eerdmans, 1979), 3.23.6, 231. Calvin, however, goes on to argue that because

God has decreed "by sovereign appointment" what will happen, the matter of fore-knowledge is irrelevant.

25. Augustine, *On Free Will*, 3.3.6.

26. Aristotle, *De interpretatione*, 9, 18a28–19b4.

27. Some may assume that because future states—such as World War III—do not presently exist, we cannot make truth statements about them. But this seems false. We can make genuine truth statements about future events and about future free human choices—even if such statements are not about the present. If I say, "There will or there will not be a Third World War," this is a truth statement that corresponds to what will (or will not) happen in the future. So we *can* assert truths about the future.

28. Linda Zagzebski, "Foreknowledge and Human Freedom," in *Companion to Philosophy of Religion*, ed. Philip Quinn and Charles Taliaferro (Malden, Mass.: Blackwell, 1997), 295.

29. See, for example, Richard Taylor, *Metaphysics* (Englewood Cliffs, N.J.: Prentice-Hall, 1963), 54–69. For a response, see Craig, *The Only Wise God*, 67–74.

30. William Lane Craig, "Tachyons, Time Travel, and Divine Omniscience," *Journal of Philosophy* 85 (1988): 135–50.

31. There is a distinction between the *necessity* in these two statements. One is *de dicto* necessity (that is, the necessity of *words*), and the other is *de re* (the necessity of *things*). In a *de dicto* scenario, we are attributing a necessary truth to a *proposition;* in a *de re* scenario, we are attributing necessity to some *object* or *thing*.

A: If God foreknows something, it will necessarily come about *(de re)*.

B: *Necessarily*, if God foreknows something, it will come about *(de dicto)*.

As we have just seen, A is false whereas B is true; that is, all that we can conclude from God's foreknowledge of human choices is that they *will* occur (B), not that they *must* (A). See Alvin Plantinga, *The Nature of Necessity* (Oxford: Clarendon, 1974), 9–13.

A further example to show the distinction is this:

De re: The number of planets is *necessarily* odd.

De dicto: Necessarily, the number of planets (i.e., nine) is odd.

In this case, the *de re* statement is false (there could have been an even number of planets), and the *de dicto* statement is true (the number of planets is nine, which is necessarily odd).

32. See Alvin Plantinga, *God, Freedom, and Evil* (Grand Rapids: Eerdmans, 1977), 65–73. Also Philip L. Quinn, "Plantinga on Foreknowledge and Freedom," in *Alvin Plantinga*, ed. James E. Tomberlin and Peter van Inwagen, Profiles 5 (Boston: Reidel, 1985), 271–87; see also Plantinga's reply (384–85).

33. Note the following argument:

1. Necessarily, if God foreknows something (x), then x will happen.

2. God foreknows x.

3. Therefore, x will happen.

It is fallacious to conclude that x will *necessarily* happen. This just doesn't logically follow from premises 1 and 2. All we can legitimately conclude is that x *will* happen. For us to conclude that x will necessarily happen, the second premise would have to read, "Necessarily, God foreknows x." Such a statement could not be true since this implies that this particular world is the *only* world God could have created, but this denies God's freedom to create freely one world and not another, that there are possible worlds God could have created.

34. For a fuller elaboration, see Craig, *The Only Wise God;* also idem, "Middle Knowledge," in *Divine Foreknowledge: Four Views*, ed. James Beilby and Paul Eddy (Downers Grove, Ill.: InterVarsity Press, 2001).

35. Of course, there are possible worlds in which no humans exist. In fact, there are possible worlds in which nothing at all exists but God, who exists in *all* possible worlds.

36. I speak about this possible-worlds view in relation to the question of the unevangelized in my *"True for You, but Not for Me,"* 127–32. For further elaboration, see Craig, *The Only Wise God.*

37. See Craig, *The Only Wise God,* 127–54.

38. I also discuss this in more detail in *"True for You, but Not for Me,"* part 5.

39. Craig, *The Only Wise God,* 74.

40. Thanks to J. Budziszewski for his comments on this chapter.

CHAPTER 9: IF GOD PREDESTINES SOME TO BE SAVED, WHAT CHOICE DO I REALLY HAVE?

1. The context of this Romans passage (which speaks of the potter being able to do what he wishes with the clay) refers back to Jeremiah 18:6–10, where the destruction or preservation of a nation or kingdom was conditioned upon the repentance of the people: "*If* that nation I warned repents of its evil, *then* I will relent [repent of] and not inflict on it the disaster I had planned" (v. 8, emphasis added).

The language in Romans 9 is not that the potter makes some vessels to destroy— potters do not do that! Rather, God makes vessels to be used, whether for noble or menial purposes (see 2 Tim. 2:19–21). All human "vessels"—even the dishonorable vessels who resist him (Pharaoh, Nebuchadnezzar, Pilate, Judas Iscariot, and so on)—can be used by God to accomplish his purposes. These vessels can thus honor God by displaying his holy judgment and wrath; God will use them to further his ends so that, in this sense, no one can resist his will.

2. Let me comment briefly on some of these verses. Ephesians 1:11 cannot be understood in some deterministic sense since people defy God (Matt. 23:37; Acts 7:51), which is contrary to what he desires and ideally wills for them. John 6:37 does not refer to a select group of people but simply those who believe in Christ—the body of believers or followers God has given Jesus; they have put their trust in him, and they have been collectively given to Jesus by the Father (see below).

In Matthew 11:25–27, the context informs us that those to whom Jesus chooses to reveal himself are those who have humbly and simply responded to God's initiating grace or drawing (John 6:44)—rather than proudly resisting it (as in Acts 7:51, where unbelieving Jews are resisting the Holy Spirit). In Acts 13:48, the context indicates it was "necessary" that the Word of God be given to Jews first, but since they repudiated the offer of "eternal life," Paul turned "to the Gentiles" (13:46). Paul mentions his commission to be "a light for the Gentiles" (v. 47). At this "the Gentiles" heard and rejoiced at the news (v. 48). Therefore, those who were "ordained" to "eternal life"—that is, Gentiles—believed inasmuch as they (collectively) had been included in God's saving plan. This "light for the Gentiles" fulfills what was foretold in the beginning of the Luke-Acts account (Luke 2:32). Therefore, we should rightly question the notion of

> some pretemporal election of certain ones so that they, and only they, come to believe. This would fit poorly in the context. The Jews' rejection of the Word of God accounted for their failure to gain eternal life. They did not consider themselves worthy of eternal life (v. 46). . . . Surely in this context Luke does not intend to restrict the application of salvation only to those appointed. Rather he shows that salvation's sphere of application must expand from only Jews to believing Gentiles.

William W. Klein, *The New Chosen People: A Corporate View of Election* (Grand Rapids: Zondervan, 1990), 110.

3. Calvin, *Institutes*, 3.22.1, 213.

4. Ibid., 3.21.5, 206. Calvin (in 3.21.6, 209) appeals to Romans 9 (which cites Malachi 1:2–3, where God says that he "loved" Jacob (father of the nation of Israel) and "hated" Esau (father of the nation of Edom). Although Calvin sees this as God's election to salvation, it actually deals with God's plan of salvation in the course of history. God chose whom he did for a particular mission—to carry out his plan for salvation to the nations through ethnic Israel (which is the thrust of Romans 9–11). God has the prerogative to choose one (Jacob) over against the other (Esau) to carry out his plans in history. This does not mean that Esau could not have repented and come to personal salvation. Furthermore, the same kind of language could have been used about Joseph (Jacob's favored son) and Judah (the fourth son of Jacob): Although Joseph was exemplary in integrity and godliness, God passed him by and chose the much less desirable character of Judah to carry on the messianic line. God's choice was not on the basis of works.

When it comes to individuals and salvation in Romans 9–11, "the issue . . . is the presence or absence of faith, not whether they were individually chosen for salvation" (William Klein, "Is Corporate Election Merely an Abstract Entity? A Response to Thomas Schreiner" [unpublished], 2). The reason most Jews are not among the elect (or "the remnant") is because of their unbelief (Rom. 11:20, 23), not because God never elected them to salvation.

Even the language of "love" and "hate" involves comparative terms (love more or less; cp. Matt. 10:37 ["loves . . . more than"] and Luke 14:26 ["hate"]). In the original context of Malachi 1:2–3, the love-hate language has to do with political alliance and enmity rather than personal emotion or affection. God is saying, "I have allied myself with Jacob, and Esau I have made my enemy" (Douglas Stuart, "Malachi," in *The Minor Prophets*, vol. 3, ed. Thomas E. McComiskey [Grand Rapids: Baker, 1998], 1284).

5. For a response to many of the truth claims of Islam, see Norman Geisler and Abdul Saleeb, *Answering Islam* (Grand Rapids: Baker, 1993).

6. Jerry L. Walls, "The Free Will Defense: Calvinism, Wesley, and the Goodness of God," *Christian Scholar's Review* 13 (1983): 25.

7. Geisler, *Chosen but Free*, 5.

8. I borrow heavily from Klein, *The New Chosen People*. Klein argues that "the first-century Mediterranean person did not share or comprehend our [Western] idea of an individual" (260). See also Klein's essay, "Paul's Use of Kalein: A Proposal," *Journal for the Evangelical Theological Society* 27 (March 1984): 53–64. Cp. H. H. Rowley, *The Biblical Doctrine of Election* (London: Lutterworth, 1952). Max Turner notes this: "God chose a people (in Christ). . . . The thought [in Eph. 1:3] is not primarily of the election of individual people to the church (though that may be implicit) . . . [but] that God eternally chose a people in Christ (us, i.e., the church)" ("Ephesians," in the *New Bible Commentary*, ed. G. J. Wenham et al. [Downers Grove, Ill.: InterVarsity Press, 1996], 1225).

9. Ibid., 259.

10. Ibid., 264–65.

11. Cp. Acts 16:14, where the Lord "opened" Lydia's heart.

12. See I. Howard Marshall, *Jesus the Savior: Studies in New Testament Theology* (Downers Grove, Ill.: InterVarsity Press, 1990), 290–92. John Wesley also noted this "personal" election as "a divine appointment of some particular men, to do some particular work in the world." Wesley did "not find this to have any necessary connexion with eternal happiness" ("Predestination Calmly Considered," in *The Works of John Wesley*, vol. 10 [Grand Rapids: Baker, 1998], 210).

13. Notice that God's choosing an individual for a mission or function does not exclude the possibility that this person may be a believer (as with the eleven believing disciples). On the other side, God's choice to harden Pharaoh's heart (Rom. 9:18: "He hardens whom he wants to harden") does not directly bear on Pharaoh's personal salvation except that his resistance of God's command would indirectly affect his salvation. The point is that God could use even the hardness of Pharaoh's heart to manifest his power and proclaim his name to other nations (Rom. 9:17). God is not hardening one whose heart would have been soft toward God through the initiating influence of the Spirit (which could be resisted). Rather, God "hardens those who reject him by hardening their hearts against him" (Klein, *The New Chosen People*, 167), but Pharaoh could not resist God's will to display his divine power. (Thus, note the line repeated in various forms to both the Israelites and the Egyptians in the Exodus narrative: "You shall know that I am the LORD" [Exod. 6:2, 7, 8, 29; 7:5, 17; 8:10, 22; 10:2; 14:4, 18; cp. 14:31 as well as 5:2, where Pharaoh says, "I do not know the LORD"!].)

In Romans 9, the "discussion revolves around those God chooses to accomplish his purposes in the world" (Klein, *The New Chosen People*, 198). It should be noted that God hardened Pharaoh's heart, but this was only *after* Pharaoh had repeatedly hardened his own heart by his own choice (Exod. 7:13–14, 22; 8:15, 19, 32). Commentator C. E. B. Cranfield notes, "The assumption that Paul is here thinking of the ultimate destiny of the individual, of his final salvation or ruin, is not justified by the text" (*Romans: A Shorter Commentary* [Grand Rapids: Eerdmans, 1985], 236).

14. P. T. O'Brien states that the "corporate dimension" to God's election must still be understood as being individual and personal as well (e.g., redemption, forgiveness, the seal of the Holy Spirit come to believers as individuals). Thus, O'Brien says that the plurals ("we," "us") in Ephesians 1 are *common*, not *corporate;* further, the corporate-election idea I am suggesting makes an either-or dichotomy between group and individual (*The Letter to the Ephesians* [Grand Rapids: Eerdmans, 1999], 99). However, in personal correspondence, William Klein responded to this argument:

> A common noun is one with which you can use modifiers such as *every* or *some,* and speak of one of a class of beings or things. The distinction [common vs. corporate] O'Brien tries to make simply will not hold up. If I say, "This class will learn Greek," the word "class" is a common noun. Of course it means that each individual must learn Greek, but I'm speaking of the entire group as a group, as opposed to my other class that studies math. If I say, "I will give my Greek class the day off, but not the math class," I'm speaking of them in corporate terms, though, of course all the individuals have the day off. Paul's point is not that individuals are specifically chosen, but that God chose this group in Christ. I don't [accept this] attempt to dismiss the emphasis on corporate entities simply with the device of common nouns. No typical speaker of English (or Greek) would understand [this] distinction.

Correspondence with William Klein from 18 July 2000.

15. Klyne Snodgrass, *Ephesians,* NIV Application Commentary (Grand Rapids: Zondervan, 1996), 49; see also Carey C. Newman, "Election and Predestination in Ephesians 1:4–6a," *Review and Expositor* 93 (1996): 237–47: "Election is corporate. . . . Some readings of divine election unfairly individualize God's work" (239).

16. Newman, "Election and Predestination," 239.

17. A. A. Solomon, "The New Testament Doctrine of Election," *Scottish Journal of Theology* 11 (1958): 408.

18. Snodgrass, *Ephesians,* 49.

19. Solomon, "The New Testament Doctrine of Election," 421; Newman, "Election and Predestination," 239.

20. The differentiation is made between "all without *distinction*" (e.g., Christ died for people of all classes and races—though not for every individual) and "all without *exception*" (i.e., Christ died for each individual). Even the Reformer John Calvin seems to have believed that Christ died for all without exception. When commenting on 1 Timothy 2:4–5, Calvin states, "By this [Paul] assuredly means nothing more than that the way of salvation was not shut against any order of men; that on the contrary, he had manifested his mercy in such a way, that he would have none debarred from it" (*Institutes,* 3.24.16).

In his commentary on Galatians, he says something similar: "For it is the will of God that we should seek the salvation of all men without exception, as Christ suffered for the sins of the whole world" (*Commentary on Galatians,* 5:12).

For further references to Calvin's apparent belief in universal (rather than limited or definite) atonement, see Geisler, *Chosen but Free,* 155–60.

21. For example, John S. Feinberg, "God Ordains All Things," in *Predestination and Free Will,* 29: "Ephesians 1:11 is perhaps the clearest expression of the notion [of divine sovereignty]." See also John S. Feinberg, "And the Atheist Shall Lie Down with the Calvinist: Atheism, Calvinism, and the Free Will Defense," *Trinity Journal* NS 1 (1980): 142–52.

22. For example, Paul asks in Romans 8:32: "Will he not . . . graciously give us *all* things?" (emphasis added).

23. This kind of biblical evidence appears to fly in the face of what the Westminster Confession states about humans "being made willing by grace" (10.1).

24. Klein, "Corporate Election," 7.

25. Klein, *The New Chosen People,* 281.

26. John Calvin admits that "by the predestination of God, Adam fell" (*Institutes,* 3.23.4, 228).

27. Marshall, *Jesus the Savior,* 299.

28. Wayne Grudem, *1 Peter* (Downers Grove, Ill./Grand Rapids: InterVarsity Press/Eerdmans, 1989), 108.

29. Does God elect a group prior to his election of individuals for salvation? Some people (such as Thomas Schreiner) maintain that for God to elect a group, he would have to elect individuals to salvation. If God chooses a group to be his people, then it is predetermined that each member of the group should come to faith. But as Klein responds, this view assumes a *determinist* view of reality. Why should we assume this? It is *faith* that is decisive for salvation, and God in his foreknowledge knows who will be saved, but this does not require that they are not free to trust in Christ. If a person is consistent on the determinist view, he will have to admit that God, by his foreknowledge, determines those who reject Christ and also their damnation, which is deeply troubling. (Taken from William Klein's unpublished paper, "Corporate Election").

One further question: Are we left with some affirmation of God's selecting some sort of *abstract* group with no individuals belonging to it (as Schreiner maintains, by appealing to the analogy of a team: "You have chosen that there be a team, the makeup of which is totally out of your control") ("Does Romans 9 Teach Individual Election unto Salvation? Some Exegetical and Theological Reflections," *Journal of the Evangelical Theological Society* 36 [1993]: 37). But this charge that corporate election implies that God selected an abstract group is not successful. Israel as a nation was chosen, and consequently, everyone born into Israel became part of God's chosen people. Similarly, God chose Christ to be the head of a new people (just as Abraham was of ethnic

Israel), and anyone who has faith in him becomes part of that group. This is why Christians are elect—because they have become part of God's chosen people "in Christ" through faith.

CHAPTER 10: THE COEXISTENCE OF GOD AND EVIL IS A LOGICAL CONTRADICTION

1. Eleonore Stump, "The Mirror of Evil," in *God and the Philosophers*, ed. Thomas Morris (New York: Oxford University Press, 1994), 239.

2. Alvin Plantinga, "A Christian Life Partly Lived," in *Philosophers Who Believe*, ed. Kelly James Clark (Downers Grove, Ill.: InterVarsity Press, 1993), 71.

3. Ibid.

4. Richard Dawkins, *River out of Eden: A Darwinian View of Life* (New York: Basic Books/Harper Collins, 1995), 132–33.

5. Edward Madden and Peter Hare, *Evil and the Concept of God* (Springfield, Ill.: Charles C. Thomas, 1968), 4.

6. R. Douglas Geivett, "A Neglected Aspect of the Problem of Evil" (paper delivered at the Evangelical Philosophical Society meeting in Orlando, Fla., November 1998), 4. My discussion of evil as a departure from the way things ought to be is taken from this essay.

7. Bill Anglin and Stewart Goetz, "Evil Is Privation," *International Journal for Philosophy of Religion* 13 (1982): 10.

8. C. S. Lewis, *Mere Christianity* (New York: Macmillan, 1952), 45–46.

9. Ibid., 9.

10. See Alister McGrath, *Suffering and God* (Grand Rapids: Zondervan, 1995), 41–45.

11. Plantinga, "A Christian Life Partly Lived," 71.

12. C. S. Lewis, *The Problem of Pain* (New York: Macmillan, 1962), 10.

13. Daniel Howard-Snyder, "God, Evil, and Suffering," in *Reason for the Hope Within*, 78–79.

14. J. L. Mackie, "Evil and Omnipotence," *Mind* 64 (1955); reprinted in Baruch Brody, ed., *Readings in the Philosophy of Religion: An Analytic Approach* (Englewood Cliffs, N.J.: Prentice-Hall, 1974), 157–68.

15. Mackie, "Evil and Omnipotence," in *Readings in the Philosophy of Religion*, 157.

16. A good introductory defense of such a freedom is Felt, *Making Sense of Your Freedom*.

17. Lewis, *The Problem of Pain*, 27–28. See also George Mavrodes, "Some Puzzles Concerning Omnipotence," in *Readings in the Philosophy of Religion*, 340–42.

18. Howard-Snyder, "God, Evil, and Suffering," 92. The point here is that human beings do not sin of *necessity*. In other words, even though they do not have to sin, they just *end up doing it* in every world God could create containing free human creatures.

19. Plantinga, *God, Freedom, and Evil*, 17–18.

20. Stephen Evans, *Quest for Faith* (Downers Grove, Ill.: InterVarsity Press, 1986), 97. This is now reprinted under the title *Why Believe?* published by Eerdmans.

21. Howard-Snyder, "God, Evil, and Suffering," 84. William Lane Craig suggests, "Given human freedom, that in any other world God could have created, the balance between good and evil would have been even worse than in this one. That is to say, any world containing less evil might also have contained less *good*. Maybe the world we presently have has in it the most good God could get for the least amount of evil (*No Easy Answers* [Chicago: Moody, 1990], 83).

22. Peter van Inwagen, "The Problem of Evil, the Problem of Air, and the Problem of Silence," in *The Evidential Problem from Evil*, ed. Daniel Howard-Snyder (Bloomington, Ind.: Indiana University Press, 1996), 150.

23. Howard-Snyder, *The Evidential Problem from Evil*, xiii.

24. William L. Rowe, "The Problem of Evil and Some Varieties of Atheism," *American Philosophical Quarterly* 16 (October 1979): 41n. This essay is also found in R. Douglas Geivett and Brendan Sweetman, eds., *Contemporary Perspectives on Religious Epistemology* (New York: Oxford University Press, 1996).

25. There is also the *evidential* or *probabilistic* problem of evil, which I address only partially below. This problem grants that God and evil can logically coexist, but given the vast amounts of evil in the world, God's existence seems improbable.

Besides the answers given in the rest of this chapter, one must also keep in mind that the evidential problem of evil depends on the background information under consideration. If we focus only on evils in the world, God's existence will seem less likely, but if we look at the breadth of available evidence for God's existence and his loving revelation and subduing of the powers of evil in the incarnation, death, and resurrection of Christ, God's existence reasserts its high plausibility.

26. Richard Swinburne, "Cacodaemony," in *Contemporary Philosophy of Religion*, ed. S. Cahn and D. Shatz (Oxford: Oxford University Press, 1982), 8.

27. Ibid., 61.

28. Comments that follow are taken from Peter van Inwagen's excellent article, "The Magnitude, Duration, and Distribution of Evil," *Philosophical Topics* 16 (fall 1988): 161–87; reprinted in Peter van Inwagen, *God, Knowledge, and Mystery: Essays in Philosophical Theology* (Ithaca, N.Y.: Cornell University Press, 1995).

29. One could argue that although phenomena such as hurricanes and earthquakes occurred before the fall, human beings were not vulnerable to them (just as they weren't to thorns or harmful microbes). Daniel Howard-Snyder suggests, "The potentially destructive forces of nature became [Adam's and Eve's and their offspring's] foe since a consequence of separating themselves from God was the loss of special intellectual powers to predict where and when natural disasters would occur and to protect themselves from disease and wild beasts, powers dependent upon their union with God. The result is natural evil ("God, Evil, and Suffering," 93).

30. Hugh Ross, "Hurricanes Bring More Than Destruction," *Facts and Faith* 12, no. 4 (1998): 4–5.

31. Hugh Ross, "Tremors Touch Off Questions," *Facts and Faith* 6, no. 3 (1992): 2–3.

32. These and other comments in this section are taken from Howard-Snyder, "God, Evil, and Suffering," 95.

33. Ibid., 96.

CHAPTER 11: WHY WOULD A GOOD GOD SEND PEOPLE TO HELL?

1. Gary Larson, *A Far Side Collection: Last Chapter and Worse* (Kansas City, Mo.: Far-Works, 1996), 78.

2. See Matthew 8:12; 22:13; 25:30; 2 Peter 2:17; Jude 13.

3. William Crockett says that "the precise nature of the resurrected bodies [of the righteous and the wicked] is not always clear" (William V. Crockett, "The Metaphorical View," in *Four Views on Hell*, ed. William V. Crockett [Grand Rapids: Zondervan, 1996], 69). Murray Harris speaks of the "silence of Paul and the other New Testament writers about the nature of that embodiment for the wicked for judgment" ("Resurrection and Immorality in the Pauline Corpus," in *Life in the Face of Death*, ed. Richard N. Longenecker [Grand Rapids: Eerdmans, 1998], 151).

4. Crockett, "Metaphorical View," 61.

5. This emphasis on "worms" and "maggots" in hell is found in the extrabiblical writings of Judith 16:17 and Sirach 7:17.

6. Keith Yandell, "The Doctrine of Hell and Moral Philosophy," *Religious Studies* 28 (1992): 80.

7. Mortimer Adler, "A Philosopher's Religious Faith," in *Philosophers Who Believe,* 222 (my emphasis).

8. John Calvin, *Commentary on a Harmony of the Evangelists, Matthew, Mark, and Luke,* trans. William Pringle (Grand Rapids: Eerdmans, 1949), 200–201.

9. Martin Luther, *Luther's Works: Lectures on the Minor Prophets, II (Jonah, Habakkuk),* trans. Jaroslav Pelikan (St. Louis: Concordia, 1974), 19:75.

10. J. I. Packer, "The Problem of Eternal Punishment," *Crux* 26 (September 1990): 25.

11. Some of my comments are taken from Crockett, "Metaphorical View."

12. Jesus tells the thief on the cross, "I tell you the truth, today you will be with me in paradise" (Luke 23:43); Paul speaks of being either "at home in the body [and] absent from the Lord" *or* "absent from the body and . . . at home with the Lord" (2 Cor. 5:6, 8 NASB). When Paul says, "For to me, to live is Christ and to die is gain" (Phil. 1:21), he means that the alternatives are to be either (1) "in the flesh" of a this-worldly existence or (2) "with Christ," which is "better by far" (1:22–23).

13. In the final state for believers, the new Jerusalem of heaven—that is, the community of God's people—comes down out of heaven "prepared as a bride beautifully dressed for her husband" (Rev. 21:2). When one of the seven angels shows John "the bride, the wife of the Lamb" (21:9), John sees "the Holy City, Jerusalem, coming down out of heaven from God" (21:10). This community of believers is the new Jerusalem— not a literal heavenly city with literal pearly gates and literal streets of gold. (Cp. Heb. 12:22–23, where the "heavenly Jerusalem" is described as being "the church of the first-born [Christ], whose names are written in heaven.")

The gemstone imagery of the new Jerusalem in Revelation 21:10–21 is descriptive of the beauty of the people of God, who reflect the spectacular glory of God himself, whose presence is described with the very same gemstone imagery in Revelation 4:3 (cp. Ezek. 1:28). And this language reflects the building and temple metaphors used to describe God's people in 1 Peter 2—"living stones"of "precious value"—and elsewhere in the New Testament.

14. Or more accurately, the new heavens and the new earth and the lake of fire.

15. As an exception, one might bring up Matthew 7:21–23, where self-proclaimed believers seem surprised that their prophesying, miracle-working, and exorcizing in Jesus' name do not rescue them from damnation. But their lives are described by Jesus as being lawless, and such persons would not ultimately find joy in being united with the Holy One, as their inner lives on earth had run so counter to Christ's purposes. Remember that many religious leaders of Jesus' day appeared fine on the outside ("whitewashed"), but inside they were full of rotting bones and uncleanness ("tombs"). And some of these "sincere, religious people" would actually instigate Jesus' death!

16. Peter Kreeft and Ron Tacelli, *Handbook of Christian Apologetics* (Downers Grove, Ill.: InterVarsity Press, 1994), 300.

17. William Lane Craig, "Politically Incorrect Salvation," in *Christian Apologetics in the Postmodern World,* ed. Timothy R. Phillips and Dennis L. Okholm (Downers Grove, Ill.: InterVarsity Press, 1995), 88.

18. Joel B. Green and Mark D. Baker, *Recovering the Scandal of the Cross* (Downers Grove, Ill.: InterVarsity Press, 2000), 54–55; cp. 95.

19. Adapted from Michael J. Murray, "Heaven and Hell," in *Reason for the Hope Within,* 296.

20. D. A. Carson, *How Long, O Lord?* (Grand Rapids: Baker, 1990), 103.

21. Craig, "Politically Incorrect Salvation," 88.

22. From the album, *The Ancient Faith*, Sparrow Corporation, 1993.

23. Lewis, *The Problem of Pain*, 122.

24. Ibid., 127.

25. Taken from William Lane Craig (debate with Ray Bradley), "Can a Loving God Send People to Hell?" Debate found at http://www.leaderu.com/offices/billcraig/docs/craig bradley0.html.

26. See Paul K. Moser, *Why Isn't God More Obvious?* RZIM Critical Questions Booklet Series (Norcross, Ga.: Ravi Zacharias International Ministries, 2000), 29.

27. Stephen Travis, "The Problem of Judgment," *Themelios* 11 (January 1986): 53.

28. C. S. Lewis, *The Screwtape Letters* (New York: Macmillan, 1982), 38.

29. C. S. Lewis, *George MacDonald: An Anthology* (New York: Macmillan, 1948), 85.

30. Cited in Yandell, "Hell," 90.

31. Lewis, *The Problem of Pain*, 124.

32. Yandell, "Hell," 90.

33. For a brief summary and assessment of this and related issues, see Robert A. Peterson, "Undying Worm, Unquenchable Fire," *Christianity Today*, 23 October 2000, 30–37.

34. C.S. Lewis, *The Great Divorce* (New York: Macmillan, 1946).

35. Carson, *How Long, O Lord?* 102.

36. Stephen Davis, "Universalism, Hell, and the Fate of the Ignorant," *Modern Theology* 6 (January 1990): 179.

37. Carson, *How Long, O Lord?* 102.

38. Lewis, *The Problem of Pain*, 118–19.

39. Some of my comments in alternative 1 are taken from James F. Sennett, "Is There Freedom in Heaven?" *Faith and Philosophy* 16 (January 1999): 69–82; and Murray, "Heaven and Hell," 287–317.

40. "Not to be able to sin," or *non posse peccare.*

41. Sennett, "Is There Freedom in Heaven?" 78. Sennett points out that "the best [sort of] world God could create would contain not a heaven and earth with libertarian freedom, but an earth with libertarian freedom and a heaven with proximate compatibilist freedom [i.e., the fixed nature of the final state is the result of free choices made in a state of affairs in which evil is a genuine possibility]. Thus, God permits libertarian freedom on earth not only to provide a significant good on earth, but also to make a greater good possible in heaven" (82 n).

42. Murray, "Heaven and Hell," 301. Furthermore, God in his omniscience knows which among them would choose to turn to him if they had lived on and which would not. Perhaps God permits certain ones who would have chosen to turn to him had they lived to die in infancy and receive the satisfaction of their inclinations if they had lived. But those who would ultimately reject God's love would grow up to repudiate or reject it and thus be condemned by their deeds. This is simply a logically possible suggestion.

43. Sennett, "Is There Freedom in Heaven?" 76–77. There is a potential objection to this view, however. This view appears to assume that only those who have lived long enough to develop a certain character that fully determines actions for the good will be allowed into heaven. (I am not here dealing with the question of infants and young children.) But what about the thief on the cross who would join Jesus in paradise? The answer is that it is the pattern we establish throughout a life of persistent, intentional character building that is critical—not our actually attaining the desired character in our lifetimes: "By establishing this pattern, we are, in effect, giving God permission to fill in the gap" (77–78).

44. For a similarly argued case regarding apostasy, see William Lane Craig, "'Lest Anyone Should Fall': A Middle Knowledge Perspective on Perseverance and Apostolic Warnings," *International Journal for Philosophy of Religion* 29 (1991): 65–74.

45. Or, more accurately, a "no-minder."

CHAPTER 12: RELIGION IS NOTHING MORE THAN THE HUMAN WISH FOR A FATHER FIGURE

1. *Humanist Manifesto II* (Buffalo: Prometheus Press), 16.

2. Karl Marx and F. Engels, *Collected Works*, vol. 3, *Introduction to a Critique of the Hegelian Philosophy of Right* (London: Lawrence & Wishart, 1975).

3. Sigmund Freud, *Future of an Illusion*, ed. and trans. J. Strachey (New York: Norton, 1961), 30.

4. Ibid., 29.

5. Richard Dawkins, "Viruses of the Mind," *Free Inquiry* (summer 1993): 34–41. Dawkins is speaking against "a conviction that doesn't seem to owe anything to evidence or reason" and a mentality that might seek to kill or harm others out of religious conviction. However, such a mentality should be repudiated by the thinking Christian.

6. Sigmund Freud and Oskar Pfister, *Psychoanalysis and Faith: The Letters of Sigmund Freud and Oskar Pfister*, ed. H. Meng and E. French, trans. E. Mosbacher (New York: Basic Books, 1962), 117.

7. Paul C. Vitz, *Faith of the Fatherless* (Dallas: Spence, 1999), 8–9.

8. Alvin Plantinga makes this point in *Warranted Christian Belief.*

9. See Plantinga's discussion on this and other issues related to this Freudian claim in *Warranted Christian Belief*, 135–63.

10. R. C. Sproul, *If There Is a God, Why Are There Atheists?* (Minneapolis: Bethany Fellowship, 1978), 49.

11. Peter Berger, *A Rumor of Angels*, 2d ed. (New York: Doubleday, 1990), 51. "If the religious projections of man correspond to a reality that is superhuman and supernatural, then it seems logical to look for traces of this reality in the projector himself" (52).

12. See my *"True for You, but Not for Me,"* parts 3–5.

13. James D. G. Dunn writes, "Were [abba] a common prayer idiom of (some) Jews at the time of Jesus, it would not have had this significance of linking the one who said *abba* so distinctively and directly with the sonship of Jesus. . . . The likelihood remains that Jesus was marked out among his fellow Jews at least in the fact that *abba* was his characteristic and regular form of address to God in prayer" ("Prayer," in *Dictionary of Jesus and the Gospels*, ed. I. Howard Marshall et al. [Downers Grove, Ill.: InterVarsity Press, 1992], 619). In conjunction with this, see James Barr, "Abba Isn't Daddy," *Journal of Theological Studies* 39 (1988): 28–47. Barr notes that while *abba* was a term used in Jesus' day by children of their fathers to denote filial warmth, "Daddy" is an inadequate rendering, since *abba* was used by Jews of their fathers throughout their lives, not just as children.

14. Though James Barr points out that *abba* was not used just by children (see "Abba Isn't Daddy," 28–47). The fact that there is such a close connection between Jesus and the use of *abba* indicates something quite significant and distinctive.

15. In the Old Testament, God is sometimes seen as Father but only in a collective sense (i.e., as the Father of Israel), not a personal one (e.g., Exod. 4:22; Deut. 32:5; Isa. 63:15–16; 64:8; Jer. 31:9, 20; Mal. 1:6; 2:10). The only exception to this is when the king is said to have a personal relationship to God as his father (2 Sam. 7:14; Ps. 89:28). New Testament scholar Joachim Jeremias remarks, perhaps to the point of overstatement, "There is as yet no evidence in the literature of ancient Palestinian Judaism that 'my Father' is used as a personal address to God." See *The Prayers of Jesus* (Philadelphia:

Fortress Press, 1978), 21. However, there are hints that some intimacy toward God as Father was expressed in the relevant Jewish literature. Wisdom 14:3 states, "But it is thy providence, O Father, that is [a ship's] pilot, for thou hast given it a pathway through the sea; (see also Sirach 23:1, 4; 51:10; 3 Maccabees 6:3, 8).

16. Jeremias, *Prayers of Jesus*, 62.

17. These descriptions are found in the Fatiha (opening chapter/Sura) of the Qur'an (1:3).

18. Bilquis Sheikh, *I Dared to Call Him Father* (Waco: Word, 1978), 52.

19. Vitz, *Faith of the Fatherless*, 7.

20. Paul C. Vitz, "The Psychology of Atheism," *Truth* 1 (1985): 29–36. See also Vitz's *Faith of the Fatherless*, 17–57.

21. Sartre apparently did become a believer in God before he died, however. See *National Review* (11 June 1982): 677.

22. See Vitz, *Faith of the Fatherless*.

23. See her son William J. Murray's book *My Life without God* (Nashville: Nelson, 1982), 8.

24. Some of this is summarized in Art Moore, "Madalyn Murray O'Hair's Stepchildren Seek Atheist Revival," *Christianity Today*, 1 March 1999.

25. Lewis, *The Problem of Pain*, 147.

CHAPTER 13: HOW CAN GOD BE THREE *AND* ONE?

1. Unitarians affirm that *one* God exists and deny the deity of Jesus Christ and the Holy Spirit.

2. Cited in Keith Yandell, "The Most Brutal and Inexcusable Error in Counting? Trinity and Consistency," *Religious Studies* 30 (1994): 201 (emphasis in original).

3. Watchtower Bible and Tract Society, *Should You Believe in the Trinity?* (Brooklyn, N.Y.: Watchtower Bible and Tract Society, 1989), 31. For a response to this booklet, see Robert Bowman, *Why You Should Believe in the Trinity: An Answer to Jehovah's Witnesses* (Grand Rapids: Baker, 1989).

4. Incidentally, the Western Church (Catholic/Protestant) has historically emphasized the unbreakable oneness of the divine nature (stressing God's Being) whereas the Eastern (Orthodox) Church has emphasized the distinctiveness of the three persons (stressing personhood). Although God is Triune, it seems that Scripture itself begins with the primary emphasis on God's oneness (which favors the Western Church's emphasis). In the Old Testament, Deuteronomy 6:4 emphasizes the oneness of God in this credal formula: "Hear, O Israel: The LORD our God, the LORD is one." This oneness theme is reemphasized in the New Testament in Mark 12:29, 1 Corinthians 8:6, and James 2:19 as the hallmark of biblical religion. Note, however, that in 1 Corinthians 8:6, which echoes Deuteronomy 6:4, the Father *and* the Son ("one Lord") are brought together as *both* being worthy of worship. Thanks to Paul Owen for his comments from an unpublished paper on the oneness and threeness of God.

5. See also 1 Corinthians 12:4–6: "Now there are varieties of gifts, but the same *Spirit*. And there are varieties of service, but the same *Lord* [Jesus]. And there are varieties of effects, but the same *God* [the Father] who works all things in all persons" (NASB, emphasis added).

6. The Athanasian Creed declares, "The Father is God, the Son God, and the Holy Spirit God; and yet not three Gods but one God." On the other hand, "There is one Father not three Fathers, one Son not three Sons, and one Holy Spirit not three Holy Spirits."

7. Cornelius Plantinga, "The Threeness/Oneness Problem of the Trinity," *Calvin Theological Journal* 23 (1988): 51; Cornelius Plantinga, "The Perfect Family," *Christianity Today* 28, 4 March 1988, 27.

8. Plantinga, "The Perfect Family," 27.

9. This relationship within the Trinity is what philosophers call an *internal* relation: If x loses its relationship to y, then x ceases to exist. This relationship is inseparable. On the other hand, in an *external* relation (as with, say, Socrates and Plato), Socrates could cease to exist, but this would not entail that Plato must also cease to exist. Furthermore, internal relations are rooted in the very *nature* of what is being connected and nothing else. See Gustav Bergmann, *Realism* (Madison: University of Wisconsin Press, 1967), 54.

10. For a defense of "substance dualism," see Moreland and Rae, *Body and Soul;* Charles Taliaferro, *Consciousness and the Mind of God* (Cambridge: Cambridge University Press, 1994); and John Cooper, *Body, Soul, and Life Everlasting* (Grand Rapids: Eerdmans, 1989).

11. Taken from Charles Sherlock, *The Doctrine of Humanity* (Downers Grove, Ill.: InterVarsity Press, 1996), 221.

12. For example, the soul is separated from the body in the "intermediate state" (2 Cor. 5:1–9), even if this is an abnormal state of affairs.

13. Richard Swinburne, "Could There Be More Than One God?" *Faith and Philosophy* 5 (1988): 236.

14. Ibid., 235.

15. William Wainwright argues that there are not three distinct creative wills in God, which would be polytheism ("Monotheism," in *Rationality, Religious Belief, and Commitment,* ed., R. Audi and W. Wainwright [Ithaca, N.Y.: Cornell University Press, 1986], 310).

16. Though there appears to be a ranking or degrees of authority within the Godhead (e.g., the Son submits to or does the will of the Father), this is not a distinction of essence. Each person in the Trinity is equally divine: "Yet this very superordination and subordination of wills that distinguish the three persons also unite them. For in fact *only one divine will is expressed*—that of the Father who sends the Son and who, with the Son, sends the Paraclete" (Plantinga, "The Perfect Family," 26, emphasis added).

17. Thomas Morris, *The Logic of God Incarnate* (Ithaca, N.Y.: Cornell, 1986), 215.

18. Roger Nicole rightly emphasizes the proper balancing of three aspects of the Trinity: threeness, oneness, and equality ("The Meaning of the Trinity," in *One God in Trinity,* ed. Peter Toon and James D. Spiceland [Westchester, Ill.: Cornerstone, 1980], 1–4).

• If we overemphasize threeness, this leads to polytheism or tri-theism.

• If we overstress oneness, this leads us to modalism in which there is only one person who is manifested as Father or Son or Spirit.

• If we reject equality, this leads to subordinationism (e.g., such as the Jehovah's Witnesses' distinction between Jehovah God and Jesus as "a god").

In orthodox Christianity, (1) only *one* God exists; (2) this God exists *eternally* in *three* distinct persons (Father, Son, Spirit); (3) these persons are *fully equal* in every divine perfection; they possess alike the fullness of the divine essence.

19. For example, see Colin E. Gunton, *The One, the Three, and the Many: God, Creation, and the Culture of Modernity* (Cambridge: Cambridge University Press, 1993); David S. Cunningham, *These Three Are One: The Practice of Trinitarian Theology* (Malden, Mass.: Blackwell, 1998); and Kevin D. Vanhoozer, ed., *The Trinity in a Pluralistic Age: Theological Essays on Culture and Religion* (Grand Rapids: Eerdmans, 1997).

CHAPTER 14: ISN'T THE IDEA OF GOD BECOMING A MAN INCOHERENT?

1. The Council of Chalcedon (A.D. 451) declared that Jesus Christ is "truly God and truly man, the same of a reasonable soul and body; consubstantial with the Father in

Godhead, and the same consubstantial with us in manhood, like us in all things except sin . . . acknowledged in two natures without confusion, without change, without division, without separation."

The Westminster Catechism states that "the Lord Jesus Christ, who, being the eternal Son of God, became man, and so was, and continueth to be, God and man, in two distinct natures, and one Person, forever" (Q21).

2. John Hick, ed., *The Myth of God Incarnate* (Philadelphia: Westminster, 1977).

3. John Hick, *The Fifth Dimension: An Exploration of the Spiritual Realm* (Oxford: One World, 1999), 234.

4. Ibid., 235.

5. Ibid., 236.

6. In Marcus J. Borg and N. T. Wright, *The Meaning of Jesus: Two Visions* (San Francisco: HarperSanFrancisco, 1999), 149.

7. For a further defense of Jesus' deity and uniqueness, see my previous book, *"True for You, but Not for Me,"* 91–121.

8. Note that here Jesus does not deny this—a marked difference from angels, who forcefully reject any hint of worship (Rev. 19:10; 22:8–9; on the other hand, God and the Lamb [Jesus] accept such worship in Rev. 5:11–14). Rather, Jesus quotes Psalm 82:6, where wicked rulers are called "God" since they as leaders are to *represent God to the people,* a typical Old Testament rendering (e.g., Exod. 21:5–6: ". . . his master shall bring him to God [a judge] . . ." [NASB]). Jesus is saying, in effect, "If these sinful human beings/rulers are called 'god,' then how much more should I be considered God's Son?" In Matthew 26:64, Jesus confesses that he is the Son of God ("Yes, it is as you say"). If Jesus were not God, he had the perfect opportunity to correct the misunderstanding.

Also, after Jesus claimed to exist before Abraham ("Before Abraham was, I am"), Jews picked up stones to throw at him for blasphemy—slandering or demeaning God (John 8:59). Jesus had just claimed to be "one" with the Father. Jehovah's Witnesses claim that Jesus was just affirming his oneness in purpose and will with the Father, not equality in nature. But why would Jews pick up stones to throw at Jesus if he were merely claiming to be one in purpose and outlook as God, which should be true of each one of us?

9. See John 1:1, 18; 20:28; Acts 20:28; Romans 9:5; Titus 2:13; Hebrews 1:8; 2 Peter 1:1; 1 John 5:20. For comments on these passages, see Murray J. Harris, *Jesus as God: The New Testament Use of Theos in Reference to Jesus* (Grand Rapids: Baker, 1992).

10. Aramaic was a Hebrew dialect spoken during Jesus' time. This Aramaism reveals that Gentile Corinthians did not corrupt the Jerusalem church's belief about Jesus but rather followed its lead in holding to Jesus' divinity.

11. I discuss and document reasons for an earlier dating of the Gospels and also for considering the importance of the epistles in *"True for You, but Not for Me,"* 102–3.

12. Paul Barnett, *Jesus and the Logic of History* (Grand Rapids: Eerdmans, 1997), 40. See also his impressive *Jesus and the Rise of Early Christianity: A History of New Testament Times* (Downers Grove, Ill.: InterVarsity Press, 1999).

13. When we read Philippians 2:6–11, we see that Paul is looking back to Isaiah 45:22–23; 52:13; 53; 57:15 (where God is high and lofty but dwells with the contrite and lowly in spirit). Old Testament themes of humiliation and exaltation are brought together and cohere in the New Testament. Paul says that the career of the Servant of the Lord—including his suffering, humiliation, death, and exaltation—is the way in which the sovereignty of the one true God comes to be acknowledged by all the nations. It is in the humiliation of the Servant that God's greatness is most clearly revealed to the world.

In John's Gospel, these words and themes are brought together in such a way that the Servant is exalted and glorified *in* and *through* his humiliation and suffering. The words for "to lift up" *(hypsoô)* and "to glorify" *(doxazô)*, which are found in John 3:14–15; 8:28; 12:32–34, are taken from Isaiah 52:13 of the Greek Old Testament (Septuagint) and applied to Jesus with regard to his passion/death predictions. John offers a double meaning for the word "to lift up": It is used both literally (crucifixion elevated one above the earth [cp. 12:33]) and figuratively (in the humiliation of the crucifixion, we note Jesus' simultaneous elevation to the status of divine sovereignty over the cosmos. The cross is already his exaltation.). For further elaborations on these themes, see Richard Bauckham, *God Crucified: Monotheism and Christology in the New Testament* (Grand Rapids: Eerdmans, 1998).

14. Acts 2:22; Romans 5:15, 17, 19; 1 Corinthians 15:21, 47–49; 1 Timothy 2:5; 3:16; 1 John 4:2–3.

15. Knowing people's thoughts (Luke 6:8; 9:47); the private life of the Samaritan woman (John 4:18); the character of Nathanael (John 1:47–48); the details of various circumstances (Matt. 26:25, 34).

16. John 6:69: "the Holy One of God"; 2 Corinthians 5:21: he "had no sin"; Hebrews 4:15: "was without sin"; 7:26: "blameless, pure"; 9:14: "unblemished"; 1 John 3:5: "in him is no sin"; cp. 1 Peter 2:22). Christ himself acknowledged his perfect obedience to the Father (John 8:29; 15:10).

17. This comes from the Greek word *kenos* ("empty") and its cognate verb *kenoô* ("to empty"). Cp. Philippians 2:7, where Jesus "empties" himself. For an excellent discussion, see Paul D. Feinberg, "The Kenosis and Christology: An Exegetical-Theological Analysis of Philippians 2:6–11," *Trinity Journal* NS 1 (spring 1980): 21–46. See also P. T. O'Brien, *Commentary on Philippians,* New International Greek Testament Commentary (Grand Rapids: Eerdmans, 1991), 202–62.

18. In the next chapter, I will return to this point in greater detail.

19. Anselm, *Why God Became Man*: "Man the sinner owes to God, on account of sin, what he cannot repay, and unless he repays it he cannot be saved" (1.25).

20. See J. I. Packer, "What Did the Cross Achieve? The Logic of Penal Substitution," *Tyndale Bulletin* 25 (1974): 3–45.

21. "[T]here is no one . . . who *can* make this satisfaction except God himself. . . . But no one ought to make it except man; otherwise man does not make satisfaction. [Therefore,] it is necessary that one who is God-man should make it" (ibid., 2.6).

22. See John Stott's exposition on this theme: *The Cross of Christ* (Downers Grove, Ill.: InterVarsity Press, 1986), 87–163.

23. For a fascinating discussion of Anselm's influence on Bach's *St. Matthew Passion,* see Jaroslav Pelikan, *Bach among the Theologians* (Philadelphia: Fortress Press, 1986), 89–101.

24. Water is H_2O—two atoms of hydrogen and one of oxygen. Without these two components you cannot have water. But what happens if the water in the glass from which you are drinking is dirty? Is dirt part of the essence of water? No. Water can exist without dirt, but it cannot exist without hydrogen or oxygen.

25. Technically speaking, the mind is the reasoning faculty/aspect of the soul. For a fuller discussion, see Moreland and Rae, *Body and Soul.*

26. Alvin Plantinga, "Essence and Essentialism," in *A Companion to Metaphysics,* ed. Jaegwon Kim and Ernest Sosa (Malden, Mass.: Blackwell, 1995), 138. Regarding essences and essentialism, see Plantinga, *The Nature of Necessity.*

27. Notice that we are talking specifically about *capacities,* not *functions,* such as solving intricate math problems or having a certain level of rationality or degree of social skills. Whether a person is sleeping or, for that matter, is a child still in a mother's

womb, one has certain *capacities* that are not presently being exercised. And even mentally handicapped persons still have the *capacity* to know multiple languages or solve math problems, and those capacities could be realized *if* certain physical problems were not blocking them.

28. For further reading on this topic, see Plantinga, *Does God Have a Nature?*

29. Thomas V. Morris puts it this way: "There are properties which happen to be *common* to members of a natural kind, and which may even be *universal* to all members of that kind, without being *essential* to membership in the kind" (*Our Idea of God*, 164).

30. In this way, the term "sinful nature" can be misleading. A phrase such as "sinful condition" or "sinful state" better captures our deep fallenness (Alister McGrath, personal conversation on 22 June 2000 in Atlanta, Ga.). Also, British theologian Colin E. Gunton writes that because creation—which includes the image of God—is the work and gift of God, which is good, "it is necessary to conclude that evil . . . is not intrinsic to the creation, but some corruption of, or invasion into, that which is essentially good" (*The Triune Creator: A Historical and Systematic Study* [Grand Rapids: Eerdmans, 1998], 203). German theologian Wolfhart Pannenberg says something similar: "The perverting of the glory of God by human sin, and especially by idolatry, does not alter the fact that ordination to be in the image of God characterizes human beings as creatures" (*Systematic Theology*, vol. 2, trans. Geoffrey W. Bromiley [Grand Rapids: Eerdmans, 1994], 215).

31. According to Scripture, human beings even have the capacity to exist in an "intermediate state" (between earthly life and the final state) *without* a body, even if this state is not an optimal one for believers (2 Cor. 5:1–9). So *always possessing a body* is not necessary for us to be human.

32. Revelation 21:4 states that there will be no more tears, death, or pain.

33. It appears that the predominant characteristic of the divine image in Genesis 1:26–27 is *relationality*, but this does not exclude the secondary aspects of personality, rationality, morality, volition, and the like. Also, the image of God—though it sets humans apart from animals as unique creations (cp. Psalm 8)—is being transformed into that of Christ, who *is* the image of God (2 Cor. 4:4). There will be an eschatological realization of the fullness of this image.

34. John S. Feinberg, "The Incarnation of Jesus Christ," in *In Defense of Miracles*, ed. R. Douglas Geivett and Gary R. Habermas (Downers Grove, Ill.: InterVarsity Press, 1997), 238.

35. In E. K. Simpson and F. F. Bruce, *The Epistles of Paul to the Ephesians and to the Colossians*, New International Commentary on the New Testament (Grand Rapids: Eerdmans, 1957), 194.

36. Gerald O'Collins, *Christology* (Oxford: Oxford University Press, 1995), 233. O'Collins cites Thomas V. Morris's *Logic of God Incarnate* (Ithaca, N.Y.: Cornell University Press, 1986) as being such a model. Other endorsers of Thomas Morris's model ("two minds") of the incarnation are evangelicals such as Ronald Nash (*Faith and Reason* [Grand Rapids: Zondervan, 1988], 262); and John S. Feinberg ("The Incarnation of Jesus Christ," 239). Feinberg writes: "I do not see how Christ could be fully human and fully divine and not have two minds. If he lacks either mind, he is either not fully human or not fully divine" (239). However, because of the potential confusion that may come from using "two minds" (which may hint of Nestorianism—the idea that there were two selves or egos in Jesus), I speak of two *consciousnesses* or *awarenesses*.

37. Here is a related question: Wasn't Jesus Christ *created*, or didn't he become *finite*? How can a creature be God? This is incompatible. However, the Christian denies that God the Creator became a creature. Jesus was not created nor is he finite. Rather, God the Son took on a human nature and a human body. (Even though human nature and

a human body are God's creations and are connected with finite human beings, the fact that God's Son took on these does not imply that he therefore became a creature.) "But aren't human beings *necessarily* created or *necessarily* finite?" The Christian can respond, "I deny that being created or being finite is part of the *essence* of being human. Otherwise, how could God become something essentially contrary to his nature?" (Thomas Senor, "The Incarnation and the Trinity," in *Reason for the Hope Within*, 247).

38. This analogy is taken from Morris, *The Logic of God Incarnate*, 91.

39. J. I. Packer, *Knowing God* (London: Hodder & Stoughton, 1973), 63.

40. Gerald Hawthorne, *The Presence and the Power* (Dallas: Word, 1991), 218.

41. Weakness of will *(akrasia)* or multiple personalities might also serve as analogies to this point.

42. Gerald O'Collins speaks of "a clear distinction between his two consciousnesses"—namely, his "real human consciousness (which he had individually as a man) was neither replaced by nor interfered with his divine consciousness (which as Logos he shared/shares with the Father and the Spirit)" (*Interpreting Jesus* [Ramsey, N.J.: Paulist Press, 1983], 190).

Thomas Morris adds:

The two minds of Christ should be thought of as standing in something like an asymmetric accessing relation: The human mind was contained by, but did not itself contain, the divine mind; or, to portray it from the other side, the divine mind contained, but was not contained by, the human mind. Everything present to the human mind of Christ was thereby present to the divine mind as well, but not vice versa. There was immediate direct access from the human mind to the divine mind, but no such converse immediacy of access.

See Morris, *Our Idea of God*, 171.

43. Thus, even while Jesus slept during his earthly life, his divine awareness/omniscience would have been fully operative (as he necessarily *continued* in this awareness and sustained the universe in being, which is required in trinitarian doctrine). Jesus' inter-Trinitarian communion with Father and Spirit *necessarily* continued; this *perichôrêsis* did not cease while Jesus was on earth.

The incarnation appears to entail that there were two wills in Christ (dyotheletism), not one will (monotheletism). However, see Hawthorne's discussion in *The Presence and the Power*, 212–14.

John Feinberg points out that analogies, while helpful, are limited. For example, we do not have analogies of two consciousnesses in dreams or self-deception, only two levels or ranges of one consciousness or mentality. This, however, does not show that the idea of two consciousnesses is incoherent. After all, the incarnation confronts us with a unique situation—two natures in one person ("The Incarnation of Jesus," 241). Thomas Morris writes, "In the case of Jesus, there would then be a very important extra depth he had in virtue of his being divine" (*The Logic of God Incarnate*, 105).

Such a distinction is supported by the Council of Chalcedon's declaration (no confusion between the two natures). On the other hand, we must resist the doctrine of Nestorianism in which there are two egos or two selves in Christ. O'Collins notes, "What we meet in Jesus Christ is one (divine) person acting under the conditions of human consciousness, human feelings, and the rest. Through the incarnation the eternal Son became humanly conscious of himself in his relationship to his Father. He now perceived his divine 'I' or Self in a human way. Thus in this unique case a human consciousness was able to 'seize' a divine Self, albeit in a human way" (*Christology*, 233).

44. Morris, *The Logic of God Incarnate*, 103.

45. R. T. France, "The Uniqueness of Jesus," *Evangelical Review of Theology* 17 (January 1993): 13.

46. Hawthorne, *The Presence and the Power*, 212, 216.

47. Thomas Morris writes, "God the Son Incarnate had two minds and chose to live out the life of the body on this earth normally through the resources of the human mind alone. That was the primary font of most of his earthly behavior and speech" ("The Metaphysics of God Incarnate," in *Trinity, Incarnation, and Atonement,* ed. Ronald J. Feenstra and Cornelius Plantinga Jr. [Notre Dame: University of Notre Dame Press, 1989], 125; cp. 123).

48. Gerald Hawthorne argues that it was the presence of the Spirit in Jesus' life that enabled him to see who he was by nature and what his true relationship was with the Father. This places proper emphasis on the reality of Jesus' humanity. Furthermore, we must not overlook the genuine freedom that Jesus possessed to make choices, but he did so by depending on the Spirit. We see this when comparing Mark's emphasis (Mark 1:12) on the role of the Spirit, who *drove* (using the verb *ekballein*) him into the wilderness (perhaps by means of a powerful ecstatic vision or possibly something more subtle), with Matthew (Matt. 4:1) and Luke (Luke 4:1–2), who balance this divine influence by emphasizing Jesus' free choice as a human being, stressing that Jesus *was being led* (using the verb *[an-]agein)* rather than being overpowered in his will and consciousness. Jesus' victory over sin, therefore, was not the result of some necessity of his nature but of his freely choosing to obey in dependence on the Spirit (*The Presence and the Power*, 137–38, 217).

49. Hawthorne, *The Presence and the Power*, 210–11.

50. The soul is able to survive the death of the body, but this is not because it is naturally or intrinsically immortal (as only God is); it is graciously sustained by God. Murray Harris notes that immortality for humans is a divine gift gained through bodily resurrection (1 Cor. 15:52): "According to Paul and the New Testament, what is immortal when one uses that term with regard to humanity is the resurrected believer" ("Resurrection and Immortality in the Pauline Corpus," in *Life in the Face of Death: The Resurrection Message of the New Testament,* ed. Richard N. Longenecker [Grand Rapids: Eerdmans, 1998], 160).

51. Cp. Genesis 6:6; Psalm 78:40–41; Jeremiah 31:20; Hosea 11:8–9. The fact that God is unchanging has to do with his faithfulness to his character and his covenant promises; this more personal view of God rightly opposes God as some static principle. Contrary to what some assume, suffering does not necessitate alteration of a good state to a bad one (or vice versa). One can change within a range of good states without one being inferior or superior to the other. Yale church historian Jaroslav Pelikan notes, "It is significant that Christian theologians customarily set down the doctrine of the impassibility of God, without bothering to provide very much biblical support or theological proof. . . . The concept of an entirely static God, with eminent reality, in relation to an entirely fluent world, with deficient reality" is a concept that came into Christian doctrine from Greek philosophy (*The Emergence of the Catholic Tradition, 100–600,* vol. 1 of *The Christian Tradition* [Chicago: University of Chicago Press, 1971], 52–53).

52. Carson, *How Long, O Lord?* 186.

53. Ibid., 187–88.

54. Richard Creel, "Immutability and Impassibility," in *A Companion to Philosophy of Religion,* ed. Philip L. Quinn and Charles Taliaferro (Malden, Mass.: Blackwell, 1997), 313–19. Creel does stress, however, that "God in himself is perfectly, imperturbably happy through enjoyment of his own perfection, through knowledge of the goodness of his creation, through enjoyment of his creation, and through knowledge of his ultimate control over history" (318).

55. Plantinga, "A Christian Life Partly Lived," 71.

56. See Bauckham, *God Crucified.*

CHAPTER 15: IF JESUS IS GOD, HOW COULD HE REALLY BE TEMPTED?

1. Nelson Pike claims that we seem to have "a logical conflict in the claim that God is both omnipotent and perfectly good" ("Omnipotence and God's Ability to Sin," in *Readings in the Philosophy of Religion,* ed. Baruch Brody [Englewood Cliffs, N.J.: Prentice-Hall, 1974], 352).

2. *Proslogion,* 7; Taken from Eugene R. Fairweather, ed., *A Scholastic Miscellany: Anselm to Ockham* (Philadelphia: Westminster Press, n.d.).

3. Anselm, *Why God Became Man,* 2.10; cited in Fairweather, *A Scholastic Miscellany.* Thomas Aquinas said, "To sin is to fall short of a perfect action; hence to be able to sin is to be able to fall short in action, which is repugnant to omnipotence" (*Summa Theologiae,* 1.25.3 ad 2, in *The Basic Writings of St. Thomas Aquinas,* ed. Anton Pegis [New York: Random House, 1945]). Thomas V. Morris writes, "To say of God that he cannot sin, should not be taken to imply on God's part any lack of power. It only indicates a necessarily firm directedness in the way in which God will *use* his unlimited power" (*Our Idea of God,* 80).

4. On the other hand, it could be argued, in the name of incompatibilist freedom, that it is possible for redeemed human beings to sin, but God in his foreknowledge knows that they won't. I discussed this in chapter 11.

5. Graham H. Twelftree, *Jesus the Miracle Worker* (Downers Grove, Ill.: InterVarsity Press, 1999), 288. Incidentally, the mention of such potentially "embarrassing" details indicates that the Gospel writers were not *inventing* such things but *reporting* them. This potential for embarrassment indicates authenticity.

6. Let me briefly explain what I mean by "Israel's sins" and "exile." I am following N. T. Wright, who has labored to place Jesus squarely in his first-century, second-temple, monotheistic Jewish context and belief system. Wright argues that the prevailing belief among Jews was that when Yahweh becomes king, (1) Israel will return from exile, (2) evil will be defeated, and (3) Yahweh himself will return to Zion. This view was steadfastly believed by the Jews of Jesus' day. In his self-replacement of the temple, Jesus the reformer called people to abandon their hope in political revolution and to join him in his vision.

In this thoroughly Jewish context, Jesus sought to bring about a true Israel that would be a light to the nations, and thus Israel's redemption would come through suffering. Once Israel's exile had been dealt with on the cross, forgiveness could be granted. Jesus' death as a self-conscious suffering servant—taking on Israel's death, on Israel's behalf—was the supreme exile. Thus, salvation for individuals through Christ's work on the cross, while truly obtained, is not the whole story. But given the fact that Jesus dealt with Israel's exile, it is not a giant step to think he has thus dealt with the whole world's exile and its enslavement to principalities and powers. See Wright's essays in his book with Borg, *The Meaning of Jesus;* and N. T. Wright, *The Challenge of Jesus* (Downers Grove, Ill.: InterVarsity Press, 1999). For a more detailed elaboration, see his *Jesus and the Victory of God* (Minneapolis: Fortress Press, 1996).

7. O'Collins, *Interpreting Jesus,* 186.

8. Ibid., 185.

9. Morris, *The Logic of God Incarnate,* 148–49.

10. For example, John S. Feinberg wonders how Jesus could think of himself as divine yet be ignorant of his inability to sin. While this may have been true of Jesus early in life, this could not have been the case when he was a man ("The Incarnation of Jesus

Christ," 241). I would disagree. We could use the same line of reasoning about Jesus' ignorance about the timing of his return (Matt. 24:36). According to Feinberg's assumption, wouldn't Jesus, who was aware of his divine identity, have known that it is unthinkable that God be *ignorant?* Rather, just as Jesus temporarily surrendered access to knowledge of certain things (e.g., the time of his return), so he also surrendered access to the awareness that he could not sin. Apparently Jesus could be ignorant of both yet exhibit a profound awareness of his standing in the place of God.

Furthermore, the question of Jesus' divine self-awareness must be discussed in Jesus' first-century context rather than asking the question, Did Jesus know he was God? Jesus obviously did not go around saying, "I am God," but he assumed prerogatives that were restricted to Yahweh alone. Jesus forgave sins (thus displacing the temple); he said, "But *I* say to you" (Matt. 5:22, etc.); he had authority over the Sabbath; and he declared all foods clean (thus speaking with greater authority than Moses and as the revealer of divine truth). On this, see Wright, *The Challenge of Jesus.*

11. Morris, *The Logic of God Incarnate,* 149–50.

12. O'Collins, *Christology,* 271.

13. Hawthorne, *The Presence and the Power,* 139.

CHAPTER 16: THE GENESIS CREATION ACCOUNT CONTRADICTS CONTEMPORARY SCIENCE (PART 1)

1. Stanley Jaki, *The Savior of Science* (Washington: Regnery Gateway, 1988), 11–45.

2. Ibid., 202.

3. For instance, God *creates* Israel (Isa. 43:1) and future generations of people (Ps. 102:18), actions that are not instantaneous. Nothing precludes the possibility of God utilizing ordinary processes and means to accomplish his ends. Evangelical theologian Carl Henry indicates, "God's method is surely that of divine fiat—that is, Elohim creates by the instrumentality of his powerful word. . . . A fiat need not entail a *how.* The *how* of God's creation is his authoritative word or command. Whatever duration the term day may signify, the days of Genesis are time periods identifiable sequentially as first, second, third, and so on. The created universe, in short, does not appear as a single completed act" (*God, Revelation, and Authority,* vol. 6 [Waco: Word, 1983], 114).

4. See John Gribbin, *In the Beginning* (Boston: Little, Brown, 1993). Note that belief in stellar and planetary evolution hardly demands belief in biological evolution.

5. On 23 February 1987, astronomer Ian Shelton photographed a supernova (an exploding star); its light was 160,000–170,000 light years away. That is, the explosion actually took place 160,000–170,000 years ago, but its light only reached the earth in 1987. For more details on this phenomenon, see the 23 March 1987 *Time* cover story, "Supernova!" as well as James E. Peebles et al., "The Evolution of the Universe," *Scientific American* 271, no. 4 (October 1994): 53–64, in which studies of the rate of velocity and emission of energy of the explosions of various supernovae have shown that the universe is 12 to 16 billion years old. Furthermore, the appearance of celestial bodies millions or billions of light years away has been noted during recorded human history (e.g., beginning back in 1572, when Tycho Brahe observed a distant starburst). Such observations make it difficult to believe that God created the universe with the appearance of age. For further examples, see Hugh Ross, *Creation and Time: A Biblical and Scientific Perspective on the Creation-Date Controversy* (Colorado Springs: Navpress, 1994).

6. Ross, *Creation and Time,* 43. Ross says this in response to a statement by John Morris of the Creation Research Institute. Morris said, "I still am uncertain about young-earth creationism being a requirement for church membership; perhaps it would be proper to give new members time to grow and mature under good teaching. But I do

know one thing: [young earth] creationism *should be* made a requirement for Christian leadership!" (43).

7. Victor Hamilton, *The Book of Genesis: Chapters 1–17,* New International Commentary on the Old Testament (Grand Rapids: Eerdmans, 1990), 53.

8. I am grateful to Berry Driver for introducing this term to me.

9. See, for example, J. P. Moreland, ed., *The Creation Hypothesis* (Downers Grove, Ill.: InterVarsity Press, 1994); and William A. Dembski, ed., *Mere Creation: Science, Faith, and Intelligent Design* (Downers Grove, Ill.: InterVarsity Press, 1998).

10. John Sailhamer, *The Pentateuch as Narrative* (Grand Rapids: Zondervan, 1993), 4. For example, note, "these are [the books of] the generations" (listed in Gen. 2:4, author's rendering; etc.); Numbers 21:14 refers to "the Book of the Wars of the Lord."

11. Charles Hummel, *The Galileo Connection* (Downers Grove, Ill.: InterVarsity Press, 1986), 214.

12. Derek Kidner, *Genesis,* Tyndale Old Testament Commentary (Downers Grove, Ill.: InterVarsity Press; Grand Rapids: Eerdmans, 1967), 54. For example, this passage has poetic features such as parallelism (1:27; 2:2).

13. Meredith Kline, "Because It Had Not Rained," *Westminster Theological Journal* 20 (May 1958): 155. For example, this passage has poetic features such as parallelism (1:27; 2:2). Also, its structure is arranged in the form of strophes, which contain "echo" and "re-echo" (155).

14. Gordon J. Wenham, *Genesis 1–15,* Word Biblical Commentary, vol. 1 (Dallas: Word, 1987), 55.

15. Bruce Waltke, "The Literary Genre of Genesis, Chapter One," *Crux* 27 (December 1991): 2–10.

16. Kline, "Because It Had Not Rained," 156. See also Meredith G. Kline, "Space and Time in the Genesis Cosmogony," *Perspectives on Science and the Christian Faith* 48 (1996): 2–15.

17. Vern S. Poythress, "Response to Paul Nelson and John Mark Reynolds," in *Three Views on Creation and Evolution,* ed. J. P. Moreland and John Mark Reynolds (Grand Rapids: Zondervan, 1999), 91.

18. C. Cassuto, *A Commentary on the Book of Genesis,* vol. 1 (Jerusalem: Magnes Press, 1992), 13.

19. Davis Young, *Creation and the Flood: An Alternative to Flood Geology and Theistic Evolution* (Grand Rapids: Baker, 1977), 116.

20. Article XIII of the Chicago Statement on Biblical Inerrancy (formulated by evangelicals in 1978) states, "We further deny that inerrancy is negated by biblical phenomena such as a lack of modern technical precision, irregularities of grammar or spelling, observational descriptions of nature."

21. For documentation on these, see Ross, *Creation and Time.*

22. John Calvin, *Genesis,* trans. John King (Grand Rapids: Baker, 1984), 86–87.

23. Francis Schaeffer, *Genesis in Space and Time* (Downers Grove, Ill: InterVarsity Press, 1972), 36.

24. E. A. Speiser, *Genesis,* Anchor Bible Commentary, vol. 1 (Garden City, N.J.: Doubleday, 1964), 10.

25. Ibid., 11; see also Kenneth Kitchen, *Ancient Orient and the Old Testament* (Downers Grove, Ill.: InterVarsity Press, 1966), 89.

26. Gordon J. Wenham, "Genesis," in the *New Bible Commentary,* ed. Gordon Wenham et al. (Downers Grove, Ill.: InterVarsity Press, 1994), 57.

27. Richard Clifford, "Creation in the Bible," in *Physics, Philosophy, and Theology,* ed. Robert Russell et al. (The Vatican: Vatican Observatory, 1988), 155.

28. Cassuto, *Genesis,* 1:7.

29. Ibid.

30. Kitchen, *Ancient Orient and the Old Testament,* 89 (and note).

31. John Sailhamer, "Genesis," in the *Expositor's Bible Commentary,* vol. 2, ed. Frank Gaebelein (Grand Rapids: Zondervan, 1990), 19–20.

32. Davis Young, "Scripture in the Hands of Geologists," *Westminster Theological Journal* 49 (1987): 291 n.

33. Young, *Creation and the Flood,* 175. Biologist Pattle Pun argues that "the fossil record of life seems to suggest the presence of carnivorosity long before man's appearance. Therefore, it seems necessary to postulate the existence of physical death in the non-human world to account for the food chain before the human fall" ("First Response," in *Evangelical Affirmations,* ed. Kenneth Kantzer and Carl Henry [Grand Rapids: Zondervan, 1990], 429).

34. Some may disagree with this analysis, appealing to Isaiah 11:7 and 65:25 (where the wolf and lamb feed together and the lion will eat straw like an ox) to justify the belief that carnivores were originally created to be herbivores. But we must be cautious about literalizing a poetic and highly symbolic text (that animals will inevitably be part of the new heavens and the new earth, although they may be). For instance, another passage that talks about the final state of the Messiah's reign is Isaiah 65:20 (in the same context as one of the verses mentioned above): "He who dies at a hundred will be thought a mere youth; he who fails to reach a hundred will be considered accursed." Surely the text does not urge literalism here! It uses understatement to stress the longevity of life during the Messiah's reign. As commentator John Oswalt argues, the text of Isaiah 11:7 makes an overarching point that during the the the Messiah's reign, "the fears associated with insecurity, danger, and evil will be removed" (*Isaiah 1–39,* New International Commentary on the Old Testament [Grand Rapids: Eerdmans, 1986], 283).

Moreover, I would add that the emphasis in these allegedly vegetarian texts is not the nature of the lion's *diet* but his *domestication,* his being tamed so that he is no longer a threat. To eat straw like an ox is to be tamed and not to be a danger. (It may also be the case that during the Messiah's reign this will be an advance on Eden rather than a return to it. The idealized situation in these prophetic passages should not necessarily be taken as a complete return to the way things were in Eden. For example, there will be no need for the sun and moon any longer, for there will be no night (Rev. 21:23; 22:5); humans will no longer marry (Mark 12:24–25). See Young, *Creation and the Flood,* 167–68.

35. Ibid., 161. Romans 8:20–22 does not necessarily imply that Adam's sin ushered into creation cell death, animal death, all manner of natural decay, or pain (e.g., Gen. 3:16: "I will greatly increase your pains [not introduce pains] in childbearing"). Regarding cell death, large organisms grow because of the continual sequence of cell multiplication and death (Randy Isaac, "Chronology of the Fall," *Perspectives on Science and the Christian Faith* 48 [March 1996]: 37).

36. Gordon J. Wenham, *Genesis 1–15,* Word Biblical Commentary, vol. 1 (Dallas: Word, 1987), 34.

37. Gordon J. Wenham, "Genesis," in the *New Bible Commentary,* ed. Gordon Wenham et al. (Downers Grove, Ill.: InterVarsity Press, 1994), 61.

38. Henri Blocher, *In the Beginning: The Opening Chapters of Genesis* (Downers Grove, Ill.: InterVarsity Press, 1984), 209 n.

39. Augustine, *The Literal Meaning of Genesis,* 1.42–43.

CHAPTER 17: THE GENESIS ACCOUNT CONTRADICTS CONTEMPORARY SCIENCE (PART 2)

1. Mark Noll, *Scandal of the Evangelical Mind* (Grand Rapids: Eerdmans, 1994), 193–95. See some of Noll's comments in chapter 7, "Thinking about Science."

2. A fine example of this genre-sensitive approach is Gordon Fee and Douglas Stuart, *How to Read the Bible for All Its Worth* (Grand Rapids: Zondervan, 1993).

3. Craig L. Blomberg, "The Diversity of Literary Genres in the New Testament," in *New Testament Criticism and Interpretation*, ed. David Alan Black and David S. Dockery (Grand Rapids: Zondervan, 1991), 524. For some discussion of this phenomenon in America, see Timothy Weber, "'Happily at the Edge of the Abyss': Popular Premillennialism in America," *Ex Auditu* 6 (1990): 87–100.

4. As I noted in chapter 16, our modern approach to the text must be distinguished from the more phenomenalistic or observational approach fitting for agrarian Hebrews in the Ancient Near East—not a technical, scientifically precise one.

5. This, despite the claim by Gordon Wenham: "There can be little doubt that here [in Genesis 1] 'day' has its basic sense of a 24-hour period" (*Genesis 1–15*, 19).

6. Augustine, *The City of God*, XI, vi; *The Literal Meaning of Genesis*, 4.43.

7. Schaeffer, *Genesis in Space and Time*, 57; Francis Schaeffer, *No Final Conflict* (Downers Grove, Ill.: InterVarsity Press, 1976), 30.

8. John Sailhamer, *Genesis Unbound: A Provocative New Look at the Creation Account* (Sisters, Ore.: Multnomah, 1996). See my review of this book in the American Scientific Affiliation (ASA) journal, *Perspectives on Science and the Christian Faith* 49, no. 1 (March 1997): 64–65.

9. Sailhamer, *Genesis Unbound*, 15.

10. One of Eden's rivers, the Gihon (Gen. 2:13), ran through the land of Cush (Ethiopia).

11. For detailed commentary, see Sailhamer, *The Pentateuch as Narrative*; John Sailhamer, "Genesis," in the *Expositor's Bible Commentary*, vol. 2, ed. Frank Gaebelein (Grand Rapids: Zondervan, 1990).

12. Arthur Custance, *Time and Eternity* (Grand Rapids: Zondervan, 1977), 115.

13. Cp. Amos 1–3, where a similar figurative use of sequenced numbers ("three . . . four") is used: "for three transgressions . . . and for four," which connotes an abundance of transgressions.

14. For example, Isaac was delivered from death on the third day (Gen. 22:4; cp. 34:25; 40:20); Joseph released his brothers on the third day (Gen. 42:18); Israelites are given water after traveling for three days (Exod. 15:22ff.); Hezekiah is delivered from death on the third day (2 Kings 20:5); see also Exod. 19:11; Esther 5:1; Jonah 1:17–2:2.

15. David Aune makes a case for this breakdown in *Revelation 1–5*, Word Biblical Commentary, vol. 52A (Dallas: Word, 1997). For a couple examples of effective analysis of Revelation, see G. K. Beale, *The Book of Revelation*, New International Greek Testament Commentary (Grand Rapids: Eerdmans, 1999); and Richard Bauckham, *The Theology of the Book of Revelation* (Cambridge: Cambridge University Press, 1993).

16. Gleason Archer, *A Survey of Old Testament Introduction* (Chicago: Moody Press, 1974), 186.

17. Some may point to the reference to the Sabbath day in Exodus 20, but there the emphasis is on the number seven, not on the duration of days (Thomas Key, "How Long Were the Days of Genesis?" *Journal of the American Scientific Affiliation* 35 [September 1984]: 160).

18. Wenham, *Genesis 1–15*, 40. If the recent-creation interpretation of Genesis 1 is correct, the light on day one is *prior* to the sun's creation on the fourth day. Pattle Pun states that the "sun's visible function of defining days and years did not begin until the fourth day, when the sun was revealed. Therefore, the first four days were definitely not 24-hour solar days as we have" (*Evolution*, 255). The earth's light comes from the sun, and we have quite a logistical problem if literalism is pushed too far.

19. See Genesis 19:33–34; Judges 6:38; 21:4; 1 Samuel 19:11; 28:19.

20. Cp. Exodus 12:18 (Passover); Leviticus 23:32 (Day of Atonement). See Cassuto, *Commentary on the Book of Genesis,* 1:28–29.

21. Kline, "Because It Had Not Rained," 156.

22. Poythress, "Response to Paul Nelson and John Mark Reynolds," in *Three Views on Creation and Evolution,* 93.

23. Key, "How Long Were the Days of Genesis?" 106. While some argue that Adam named only the animals in the Garden of Eden, if they are to be consistent with the way in which they interpret the rest of the early chapters of Genesis, they would have to say he named *all* species. Furthermore, it is unconvincing to argue that Adam (who was not yet suffering from the effects of sin) could have accomplished far more work than we can today because he worked at Superman-like speed. After all, Jesus himself, the second Adam, did not churn out more wooden oxen yokes or farming implements than Joseph did in the woodworking shop just because Jesus was not born with original sin!

24. Archer, *Old Testament Introduction,* 186.

25. This word is translated "now" or "this time" in the Old Testament (NIV, NASB), and the implication of waiting or the elapsing of time is apparent (cp. Gen. 46:30; Judg. 15:3).

CHAPTER 18: HOW COULD A LOVING GOD COMMAND GENOCIDE?

1. Gerd Lüdemann, *The Unholy in the Holy Scripture,* trans. John Bowden (Louisville: John Knox Westminster, 1997), 54.

2. Ibid., 74.

3. Acts 13:19 speaks of "seven nations" that were singled out to be destroyed. Numbers 13:29 includes the Amalekites as one of the nations of this region (cp. Gen. 10:15–17). The terms *Canaanite* (in their language, *Kinahu* or *Kinanu*) and *Amorite* or *Hittite* often overlap in Scripture (cp. Gen. 36:2–3; Ezek. 16:3). For further reading on these and other peoples of the ancient Near East, see Alfred J. Hoerth, Gerald L. Mattingly, and Edwin M. Yamauchi, eds., *Peoples of the Old Testament World* (Grand Rapids: Baker, 1994).

4. In the Old Testament, we see that from God's point of view war is at least in principle justifiable. God commanded the Israelites to destroy the Canaanites. Not that it was a neat, clean task: "It was a ghastly business; one shrinks from it in horror. Nevertheless, the biblical text plainly attributes it to the specific command of God" (David Edwards and John Stott, *Evangelical Essentials* [Downers Grove, Ill.: InterVarsity Press, 1988], 263).

Furthermore, the fighting of Israel should not be considered a "holy war" (as comparable to the Muslim concept of *jihad,* in which war serves as an instrument to spread the faith). It was a war commanded by God and thus religiously motivated, but its purpose was the serving of divine judgment on Canaan, which also contributed to the preparation of the land for the Israelites to use. The Old Testament is clear that *God* is the initiator of the idea of war, not human beings. Yahweh himself is declared to be "a warrior" (Exod. 15:3), "a victorious warrior" (Zeph. 3:17 NASB), going forth "like a mighty man, like a warrior" (Isa. 42:13), who is "mighty in battle" (Ps. 24:8). If the biblical record is to be trusted, then these battles are not part of a "holy war" but of a "Yahweh war."

5. Deuteronomy 7:1 includes the Girgashites, listing all "seven nations"; cp. Acts 13:19 ("seven nations").

6. John L. McKenzie, *Dictionary of the Bible* (Milwaukee: Bruce Publishing, 1965), 919.

7. Peter Craigie, "Yahweh Is a Man of Wars," *Scottish Journal of Theology* 22 (1969): 185.

8. William F. Albright, *From the Stone Age to Christianity* (Baltimore: Johns Hopkins, 1940), 219.

9. Roland de Vaux, *Ancient Israel: Its Life and Institutions,* 2d ed., trans. J. McHugh (London: DLT, 1968), 258.

10. J. Gary Millar, *Now Choose Life* (Grand Rapids: Eerdmans, 1998), 147. This book is now being published by InterVarsity Press.

11. Edwards and Stott, *Evangelical Essentials,* 263.

12. For the historical plausibility of the exodus event, see Kevin Miller, "Did the Exodus Never Happen?" *Christianity Today,* 7 September 1998, 44–51.

13. Albright, *From the Stone Age to Christianity,* 214.

14. J. P. U. Lilley, "The Judgment of God: The Problem of the Canaanites," *Themelios* 22 (January 1997): 7.

15. Kaiser, *Toward Old Testament Ethics,* 178.

16. Millar, *Now Choose Life,* 148.

17. More technically, Judah entered the Babylonian captivity. After Solomon, the kingdom of Israel had been split in two—Judah (in the south) and Israel (in the north). Israel was subdued and utterly scattered by the Assyrians in 722 B.C.

18. Peter C. Craigie, *The Book of Deuteronomy,* New International Commentary on the Old Testament (Grand Rapids: Eerdmans, 1976), 276.

19. Deuteronomy 7:2: "Make no treaty with them, and show them no mercy."

20. Charles Taliaferro, *Contemporary Philosophy of Religion* (Malden, Mass.: Blackwell, 1998), 317.

21. For a fuller discussion on Yahweh wars, see Charles Sherlock, *The God Who Fights,* Rutherford Studies in Contemporary Theology, vol. 6 (Lewiston, N.Y.: Edwin Mellen Press, 1993).

22. He was pope from 1088 to 1099.

23. Cited in Thomas H. Greer, *A Brief History of Western Man,* 3d ed. (New York: Harcourt Brace Jovanovich, 1977), 223.

24. William Henry Greene, "The Ethics of the Old Testament," in *Classical Evangelical Essays,* ed. Walter Kaiser (Grand Rapids: Baker, 1972), 222.

25. Regarding the alleged permissibility of rape that some have foisted on the Old Testament, see Paul Copan, "Is Michael Martin a Moral Realist? *Sic et Non,*" *Philosophia Christi,* series 2, 1, no. 2 (1999): 67–72.

26. The Book of Deuteronomy was written in the form of an ancient Near Eastern suzerainty treaty: A "great king" and a "vassal" would enter into an alliance with certain stipulations and conditions. For a discussion, see Craigie, *The Book of Deuteronomy,* 36–45.

27. Christopher Wright, *Deuteronomy,* New International Bible Commentary, vol. 4 (Peabody, Mass.: Hendrickson, 1996), 110.

28. Tremper Longman III and Daniel G. Reid, *God Is a Warrior* (Grand Rapids: Zondervan, 1995), 33.

29. Jericho had opportunity to repent since it knew of God's greatness (Josh. 2:8–14), but only Rahab and her family did so (6:25).

30. Millar, *Now Choose Life,* 153.

31. Ideas in this section are taken from John A. Wood, *Perspectives on War in the Bible* (Macon, Ga.: Mercer University Press, 1998), 97–103.

32. Wright, *Deuteronomy,* 114.

CHAPTER 19: DOESN'T THE BIBLE CONDONE SLAVERY?

1. This account is taken from John Carey, ed., *Eyewitness to History* (Cambridge: Harvard University Press, 1988), 318–19.

2. See, for example, Frederick Douglass, *Narrative of the Life of Frederick Douglass: An American Slave,* ed. Deborah E. McDowell (Oxford: Oxford University Press, 1999);

or Harriet Beecher Stowe, *Uncle Tom's Cabin,* ed. Jean Fagan Yellin (New York: Oxford University Press, 1998).

3. Walter Kaiser, *Toward Old Testament Ethics* (Grand Rapids: Zondervan, 1983), 98.

4. Ibid.

5. A. A. Ruprecht, "Slave, Slavery," in *Dictionary of Paul and His Letters,* ed. Gerald Hawthorne et al. (Downers Grove, Ill.: InterVarsity Press, 1993), 881–83.

6. D. B. Martin, *Slavery as Salvation: The Metaphor of Slavery in Pauline Christianity* (New Haven: Yale University, 1990), 1–49.

7. Ben Witherington III, *Conflict and Community in Corinth: A Socio-Rhetorical Commentary on 1 and 2 Corinthians* (Grand Rapids: Eerdmans, 1995), 182. Some of my comments in this section are taken from Witherington, 181–85.

8. Ibid., 183–84.

9. Simply because there were many brutalities toward slaves in the South does not mean that *every* slave was treated with such extreme cruelty.

10. Richard Bauckham, *The Bible in Politics: How to Read the Bible Politically* (Louisville: Westminster John Knox, 1989), 36.

11. Ibid., 108.

12. Ibid., 36.

13. See John Goldingay, *Theological Diversity and the Authority of the Old Testament* (Grand Rapids: Eerdmans, 1987), chap. 5.

14. Bauckham, *The Bible in Politics,* 36.

15. Cp. Malachi 2:14–16.

16. Harriet Beecher Stowe, *A Key to Uncle Tom's Cabin; Presenting the Facts and Documents upon Which the Story Is Founded, Together with Corroborative Statements Verifying the Truth of the Work* (Boston: John P. Jewett, 1853), I.10, 139.

17. Ibid.

18. Kaiser, *Toward Old Testament Ethics,* 289.

19. Exodus 21:20–21 reads, "If a man beats his male or female slave with a rod and the slave dies as a direct result, he must be punished, but he is not to be punished if the slave gets up after a day or two, since the slave is his property." Although some maintain that the slave here is mere property and can be mishandled, this passage actually endorses the personhood and dignity of human slaves. If the master struck a slave so severely that he died immediately, the master was tried for capital punishment (Walter Kaiser, "Exodus," in *Expositor's Bible Commentary,* ed. Frank C. Gaebelein [Grand Rapids: Zondervan, 1990], 433). This capital punishment ("life for life" [20:23]) confirms that the slave was considered a human being with dignity. On the other hand, if the slave did not die immediately as a result of this act of using the rod—not a lethal weapon but an instrument of discipline—then "the master was given the benefit of the doubt; he was judged to have struck the slave with disciplinary and not homicidal intentions" (ibid.). This would prove that the master's intent was not murderous; if the slave died immediately, no further proof was needed. Later on we read that even the slightest injury to a slave would entitle the slave to freedom and exemption from any further debt (26–27).

When the passage says that the slave is the master's "property," the point is not that slaves are mere chattel but that "the owner has an investment in this slave that he stands to lose either by death (not to mention capital punishment as well) or by emancipation (vv. 27–28)" (ibid., 435). To kill a slave would harm the master's pocketbook (his "money"). Kaiser comments, "This law is unprecedented in the ancient world where a master could treat his slave as he pleased" (ibid., 433). So we see here that the intent of the passage upholds rather than tears down the dignity of the slave.

20. Christopher J. H. Wright, *Walking in the Ways of the Lord* (Downers Grove, Ill.: InterVarsity Press, 1995), 124.

21. Muhammad A. Dandamayev, "Slavery (OT)," in *Anchor Bible Dictionary*, vol. 6, ed. David Noel Freedman (New York: Doubleday, 1992), 65.

22. P. T. O'Brien, *The Letter to the Ephesians* (Grand Rapids: Eerdmans, 1999), 454.

23. See Gordon D. Fee, *1 and 2 Timothy, Titus* NIBC, vol. 13 (Peabody, Mass.: Hendrickson, 1988), 45–46, 49n.

24. Ibid., 455.

25. Bauckham, *The Bible in Politics*, 109.

26. R. T. France, "God and Mammon," *Evangelical Quarterly* 51 (1979): 16. For a superb discussion of a biblical theology of material possessions, see Craig L. Blomberg, *Neither Poverty nor Riches* (Grand Rapids: Eerdmans, 1999).

27. N. T. Wright, *Colossians and Philemon*, Tyndale New Testament Commentary, vol. 12 (Downers Grove, Ill.: InterVarsity Press, 1986), 150, 169.

28. See Ruprecht, "Slave, Slavery," 882.

29. Ibid.

30. James Tunstead Burtchaell, *Philemon's Problem: A Theology of Grace* (Grand Rapids: Eerdmans, 1998), 21.

31. John Stott, "The Bible and Behavior/Response," *Evangelical Essentials*, 269.

32. Witherington, *Conflict and Community in Corinth*, 185.

33. Burtchaell, *Philemon's Problem*, 16.

34. Thanks to Travis Poortinga for this point.

CHAPTER 20: THE GOSPELS CONTRADICT EACH OTHER

1. Thanks to Craig A. Evans for suggesting this term to me.

2. I am adapting what satirist H. L. Mencken wrongly attributed to the Puritans, many of whom were actually so preoccupied with finding their greatest joy in God that they avoided anything that might diminish that enjoyment.

3. Remsburg's work has been relatively recently resurrected: *The Christ: A Critical Review and Analysis of the Evidence of His Existence* (Amherst, N.Y.: Prometheus, 1994), 190.

4. For a helpful introduction to understanding these differences, see Robert Stein, *The Synoptic Problem* (Grand Rapids: Baker, 1987).

5. Remsberg, *The Christ*, 81.

6. "You are the Christ, the Son of the living God" (Matt. 16:16); "You are the Christ" (Mark 8:29); "The Christ of God" (Luke 9:20).

7. "This is Jesus the King of the Jews" (Matt. 27:37); "The King of the Jews" (Mark 15:26); "This is the King of the Jews" (Luke 23:38); "Jesus of Nazareth, the King of the Jews" (John 19:19).

8. This point is made in Twelftree, *Jesus the Miracle Worker*, 243–44. Twelftree points out another category of "doing history"—phenomenalism: All we can know is what appears to us (phenomena), what we sense and perceive. This approach denies that we can have any objective knowledge about history. Of course, this skeptical method cannot be sustained, since it claims that phenomenalism itself is *really* or *factually* true, that it describes how studying history *really* operates, that it is not simply a matter of perception.

9. In addition to work of Arthur Jeffery, *The Qur'an as Scripture* (New York: Russell Moore, 1952); and Arthur Jeffery, ed., *Materials for the History of the Text of the Qur'an: The Old Codices* (Leiden: Brill, 1937), see the more popular-level essay by Toby Lester, "What Is the Koran?" *Atlantic Monthly* (January 1999): 43–56.

10. See especially the meticulously documented work by Colin J. Hemer, *The Book of Acts in the Setting of Hellenistic History* (Tübingen: Mohr, 1989), which confirms the credibility of Luke as a first-rate ancient historian.

11. For a presentation of the reliability of Luke's Gospel, see I. Howard Marshall, *Luke: Historian and Theologian,* 3d ed. (Downers Grove, Ill.: InterVarsity Press, 1998). It should be noted that the Book of Luke is technically the first part in the single story of Luke-Acts, as many of its themes are anticipated in Acts (such as the gospel's coming to the Gentiles, as promised in Luke 2:32). By itself, Luke is incomplete. See Joel B. Green, *The Gospel of Luke,* New International Commentary on the New Testament (Grand Rapids: Eerdmans, 1997), 6–10.

12. Luke 22:7–15 indicates that on the evening that the Passover lamb was sacrificed, Jesus celebrated the Passover with his disciples (see also Matt. 26:17–20). (The Passover, of course, was the commemoration of God's deliverance of Israel from Egypt, especially when the angel of death "passed over" the houses that were marked with lamb's blood on the doorposts [Exod. 12:13ff.].) John 18:28 seems to contradict this: "Then the Jews led Jesus from Caiaphas to the palace of the Roman governor. By now it was early morning, and to avoid ceremonial uncleanness the Jews did not enter the palace; they wanted to be able to eat the Passover."

John 19:14 (also 19:31) speaks of the "day of Preparation." But preparation for what? If it is the preparation for the Passover, then John suggests Jesus was sent to execution about the same time the Passover lambs were being slaughtered. If this is the case, then the meal Jesus and his disciples enjoyed the night before was not the Passover supper, which would contradict what the Synoptic Gospels indicate—that they did eat the Passover. (See Mark 14:12, where preparations were made for the Passover; the Passover lamb was slaughtered between 3:00 and 5:00 P.M. on the fourteenth day of Nisan, which happened to be Thursday during this particular year [D. A. Carson, *The Gospel according to John* (Grand Rapids: Baker, 1991), 456]). However, the Synoptics seem correct in implying that the disciples ate the Passover meal with Jesus. So when Judas allegedly went out, after having eaten this last supper, "to buy what was needed for the Feast" (John 13:28–29), he was not going to get something for the Feast of the Passover, which had already been celebrated and which began the week-long Feast of Unleavened Bread. He was getting what was needed for the next meal during the Feast of Unleavened Bread (i.e., for Friday evening).

Thus, when John refers to the Jewish leaders' desire to "eat the Passover," it should be taken to mean "eat the meal that fell on the day of the passover festival" (i.e., during the week-long Feast of Unleavened Bread), not the Passover meal in which the slaughtered lamb was eaten (David Wenham, *Easter Enigma,* 2d ed. [Grand Rapids: Baker, 1992], 151 n). The four Gospels agree, therefore, that the Passover supper was eaten on Thursday evening (the onset of Friday, according to Jewish reckoning) and not an ordinary meal (Carson, *The Gospel according to John,* 604):

• Day 1 (Passover)—*Thursday* (14 Nisan/2 April, A.D. 33—although many historians believe it was A.D. 30): Beginning of Passover Week/Feast of Unleavened Bread. Passover celebrated.

• Day 2 (Day of Preparation)—Good *Friday* (15 Nisan/3 April): The "day of Preparation" (for the Sabbath [John 19:14]); disciples believed Judas was going to buy something for this meal (John 13:28–29).

• Day 3 (Sabbath)—*Saturday* (16 Nisan/4 April).

• Day 4 (First Easter)—*Sunday* (17 Nisan/5 April).

13. Luke 2:1–2 indicates that a census went out from Caesar Augustus that the civilized world should be taxed—a census during the time of Quirinius, governor of Syria. From A.D. 6–9, Publius Sulpicius Quirinius was a legate or assigned ruler over Syria and

died in A.D. 21. A couple of problems emerge: (1) Jesus was probably born in 4 B.C. (just before Herod the Great died; how long Jesus was in Egypt with Mary and Joseph is not clear); so this would have been *before* Quirinius was governor or ruler of Syria. (2) There is no trace of a decree at this time in existing historical research.

There was no doubt a decree under Augustus, issued in 10–9 B.C., and this was repeated every fourteen years. Augustus decreed censuses several times; we just do not have access to all of them. And sometimes what one governor began was completed by the next one, who then received the credit for it. A decreed census would no doubt have taken a long time to complete. But what about this census taking place during the time of Quirinius's rule? First, keep in mind that Quirinius may have governed Syria during two separate periods, one between 12 and 2 B.C. Although most English translations state that the census was *during* his rule, the text could be translated, "This census took place *before* [*prôtos* is used in a comparative sense here] Quirinius was governor of Syria." John 5:36 and 1 Corinthians 1:25 carry the same meaning (Marshall, *Commentary on Luke*, New International Greek Testament Commentary [Grand Rapids: Eerdmans, 1978], 99, 104). So perhaps with all these factors in mind, the biblical account should not be judged as historically inaccurate. (For more detailed discussion, see Darrell L. Bock, *Luke 1:1–9:50*, Baker Exegetical Commentary on the New Testament, vol. 1 [Grand Rapids: Baker, 1994], 903–9.)

14. A. A. Trites, *The New Testament Concept of Witness*, Studies in the New Testament Series, Monograph 31 (New York: Cambridge University Press, 1977), 128.

15. John Gray, *Men Are from Mars, Women Are from Venus* (New York: HarperCollins, 1992).

16. Paul *does* give the impression that he is familiar with the circumstances surrounding the birth of Jesus. Paul notes that Jesus is born "under the law" (Gal. 4:4), which hints at his circumcision and presentation at the temple (Luke 2:23–24). Jesus is also "born of a woman" (Gal. 4:4); his *mother* (rather than his father) is highlighted, which reinforces the virgin birth theme in Matthew and Luke. Also, Matthew and Luke were taking a risk by mentioning the virgin birth because it could be misconstrued by critics as an attempted cover-up of an illegitimate birth. Paul says that Jesus was born "when the time had fully come" (Gal. 4:4), which is what Luke 1–2 especially notes regarding Jesus' arrival being the fulfillment of what the Old Testament anticipated. Paul is working within the same kind of framework as Matthew and Luke. For a discussion of Paul's assumption regarding the virgin birth, see David Wenham, *Paul: Follower of Jesus or Founder of Christianity?* (Grand Rapids: Eerdmans, 1995), 338–43.

17. Atheist Michael Martin makes this charge in *The Case against Christianity* (Philadelphia: Temple University Press, 1991), 109.

18. Michael Martin applies the argument from silence to Mark and John: "Neither Mark nor John give [sic] any account of Jesus' birth. . . . This is remarkable" (*The Case against Christianity*, 108).

19. See my *"True for You, but Not for Me,"* 100–106.

20. Ibid.

21. For a brilliant biblical defense of the necessary suffering of the Messiah—and a defense of Jesus' identity as God—see Richard Bauckham's concise and readable book, *God Crucified;* see also Larry W. Hurtado, *One God, One Lord: Early Christian Devotion and Ancient Jewish Monotheism* (Philadelphia: Fortress Press, 1988).

22. Another such example is Mark 3:17, where the list of apostles includes the not-so-complimentary name for James and John—Boanerges, or "Sons of Thunder." This title is omitted in Matthew's and Luke's list of disciples.

23. See Robert Stein, *The Synoptic Problem: An Introduction* (Grand Rapids: Baker, 1987).

24. Note also that *just after* Peter's confession that Jesus is the Christ, Jesus rebukes Peter for rejecting the necessity of his going to the cross (Matt. 16:16–23); see also Mark 4:35–41.

25. Borg and Wright, *The Meaning of Jesus,* 173.

26. Then the line jumps to Joseph by default. See D. A. Carson, "Matthew," in *Expositor's Bible Commentary,* vol. 8, ed. Frank E. Gaebelein (Grand Rapids: Zondervan, 1984), 60–65. Also, the number fourteen in Matthew's genealogy (broken up into three sets of fourteen) in all likelihood is Matthew's literary attempt to show that Jesus is the rightful heir to the Davidic throne, using *gematria:* the name David *(dvd)* has the numerical value of fourteen in Hebrew (d=4, v=6, d=4) (Carson, "Matthew," 68–69).

27. See J. Gresham Machen, *The Virgin Birth of Christ* (New York: Harper & Row, 1930), 202–9.

28. Wright and Borg, *The Meaning of Jesus,* 180.

29. R. T. France, *The Evidence for Jesus* (Downers Grove, Ill.: InterVarsity Press, 1986), 159.

30. In Palestine, a manger was not normally found in a separate stable; rather, it was "in the main living room of a peasant house, where animals are brought in at night" (France, *The Evidence for Jesus,* 159). For a fuller explanation of the cultural context of the Christmas story, see Kenneth E. Bailey, "The Cultural Background of Luke 2:7," *Evangelical Review of Theology* 4 (1980): 201–17. Bailey notes that the manger Christ was laid in was "built into the floor of the raised terrace of the peasant home" (207).

31. I make this point here: Mark (as does John) uses the title Rabbi ("teacher") for Jesus, and he is called Rabbi by believers. Matthew, however, frequently uses the authoritative title Lord *(kyrios),* and those who do not fully or truly believe in Jesus call him teacher in Matthew (8:19; 12:38; 19:16; 22:16, 24, 36). Interestingly, in Matthew, among the disciples only Judas calls Jesus Rabbi. The rest of the disciples call him Lord.

32. Matthew 5:1–7:29; 10:5–11:1; 13:1–53; 18:1–19:2; 24:1–25:46.

33. Matthew's bracketing of two passages (called an *inclusio*) intends to make a particular point. In 4:23, Matthew writes, "Jesus went throughout Galilee, teaching in their synagogues, preaching the good news of the kingdom, and healing every disease and sickness among the people." Then the same phrasing is used in 9:35: "Jesus went through all the towns and villages, teaching in their synagogues, preaching the good news of the kingdom and healing every disease and sickness."

Between these two verses, we see two large sections that exemplify these two primary areas of Jesus' ministry: (1) Jesus' preaching and teaching (in the Sermon on the Mount in Matthew 5–7) and then (2) his healing and exorcisms (Matthew 8–9). Then in chapter 10 the disciples are sent on a mission to "preach" (10:7) and "cure every kind of disease and sickness" (10:1; cp. 10:8). What we have here is Jesus exemplifying the ministry that he wants his disciples to participate in later. He is showing them how to minister effectively before he sends them out on their internship.

CHAPTER 21: OLD TESTAMENT "PROPHECIES" ARE TAKEN OUT OF CONTEXT IN THE NEW TESTAMENT

1. Craig A. Evans notes that the context of Hosea 11:1 "makes quite clear" that it "is looking back to the exodus, not to a future deliverance" ("The Function of the Old Testament in the New," in *Introducing New Testament Interpretation,* ed. Scot McKnight [Grand Rapids: Baker, 1989], 174); see also Craig A. Evans, "From Language to Exegesis," in *The Interpretation of Scripture in Early Judaism and Christianity: Studies in Language and Tradition,* ed. Craig A. Evans, JSP Supplement 33/Studies in Scripture in Early Judaism and Christianity 7 (Sheffield: Sheffield Academic Press, 2000), 19.

2. Craig L. Blomberg, *Jesus and the Gospels* (Nashville: Broadman & Holman, 1997), 200. Blomberg adds, "Probably 'virgin' . . . meant simply 'a young woman of marriageable age,' while the promised son was Maher-Shalal-Hash-Baz (8:3)." Yet in the larger context of Isaiah 7–9, the son born in Ahaz's day *points forward* to a greater "Son" who will be "Mighty God" (9:6).

John N. Oswalt says that "the most attractive option is that Immanuel and Maher-shalal-hash-baz were one and the same" (*Isaiah 1–39*, New International Commentary on the Old Testament [Grand Rapids: Eerdmans, 1986], 213). Craig A. Evans notes that Isaiah's own children fit best into the context of Isaiah 7–8—Shearjashub (7:3), Maher-shalal-hash-baz (8:3), and possibly Immanuel (7:14) ("The Function of the Old Testament in the New," 192). See also Herbert M. Wolf, "A Solution to the Immanuel Prophecy in Isaiah 7:14–8:22," *Journal of Biblical Literature* 91 (1972): 449–56. Wolf suggests that Shear-jashub's mother (Isaiah's first wife) may have died—perhaps in childbirth; thus, Isaiah took on another maiden *('almah)* as his wife (called "the prophetess" in 8:3, who later "conceived and gave birth to a son" [8:3; cp. 7:14]). The son they have is called "Maher-Shalal-Hash-Baz" (which means "hasty to the plunder, swift to the prey")—a sign of God's protective presence with the people of Judah and Jerusalem ("Immanuel"—"God with us"). In fact, both (or three) of these children are "signs and symbols in Israel from the LORD Almighty" (8:18).

Regarding the "messianic exegesis" and an exploration of the constellation of verses such as 2 Samuel 7:12–16; Isaiah 7:14, 9:5–6; and Micah 5:2–4; see Rudolf Pesch, "'He Will Be Called a Nazarean': Messianic Exegesis in Matthew 1–2," in *The Gospels and the Scriptures of Israel*, ed. Craig A. Evans and James A. Sanders, JSOT Supplement 104/Studies in Scripture in Early Judaism and Christianity 3 (Sheffield: Sheffield Academic Press, 1994), 129–78.

3. Primarily, Matthew is saying that Herod's cruelty, which brought sorrow, perfectly embodies what Jeremiah was talking about when Judah was going into exile. Perhaps secondarily, Matthew is going deeper. The context of Jeremiah 31:15 is one of hope: The exiles will return. Now Matthew, echoing Jeremiah, says that "despite the tears of the Bethlehem mothers, there is hope because Messiah has escaped Herod and will ultimately reign." Just as the tears associated with the exile will end, so this Messiah will bring an end to the tears through his reign (D. A. Carson, "Matthew," in *Expositor's Bible Commentary*, vol. 8, ed. Frank Gaebelein [Grand Rapids: Zondervan, 1984], 95).

4. In addition to these four, we could add a fifth category—targum. The Old Testament (once it was canonized) came to be paraphrased; such paraphrasing is called targum. The Targum is an Aramaic paraphrase of Scripture. Even the Septuagint, the Greek translation of the Old Testament, is a kind of paraphrase and could thus be considered targum (Evans, "The Function of the Old Testament in the New," 166).

5. Taken from Richard Longenecker, *Biblical Exegesis in the Apostolic Period* (Grand Rapids: Eerdmans, 1975), which has been recently reprinted by InterVarsity Press.

6. Paul's use of the allegorical approach in responding to Judaizers (who argued that Christianity must be Torah-centered with circumcision and food laws as "boundary markers" for God's people) beats them at their own game. Paul gives a Christocentric interpretation of this favorite allegorized prooftext of the Judaizers. See Richard N. Longenecker, *Galatians*, Word Biblical Commentary, vol. 41 (Dallas: Word, 1990), 197–219.

7. Moisés Silva writes, "If we compare the bulk of quotations in the New Testament with the bulk of quotations in rabbinic literature, we cannot but be struck by the greater sensitivity of New Testament writers to the original context. . . . A sympathetic study of the relevant New Testament passages reveals a notably sane, unfanciful method ("The New Testament Use of the Old Testament," in *Scripture and Truth*, ed. D. A. Carson and John Woodbridge [Grand Rapids: Zondervan, 1983], 159).

8. In Borg and Wright, *The Meaning of Jesus,* 174.

9. Herbert Lockyer, *All the Messianic Prophecies of the Bible* (Grand Rapids: Zondervan, 1973).

10. Much of my discussion is taken from C. F. D. Moule, "Fulfillment-Words in the New Testament: Use and Abuse," *New Testament Studies* 14 (1967–68): 293–320.

11. R. T. France, *Matthew: Evangelist and Teacher* (Grand Rapids: Zondervan, 1989), 168. This book has been reprinted with InterVarsity Press.

12. For instance, see Genesis 3:15; 49:8–12; Numbers 24:17; Deuteronomy 18:18; 30:6; 34:10–12.

13. Moule, "Fulfillment-Words," 314.

14. John W. Wenham, *Christ and the Bible,* 3d ed. (Downers Grove, Ill: InterVarsity Press, 1994), 106.

15. Douglas Moo, "The Problem of *Sensus Plenior,*" in *Scripture and Truth,* ed. D. A. Carson and John Woodbridge (Grand Rapids: Zondervan, 1983), 197.

What we see in Psalm 22 describes the kinds of afflictions that the psalmists and other godly Old Testament writers experienced:

• v. 1: "My God, why have you forsaken me?" (cp. Ps. 42:9: "Why have you forgotten me?"; cp. Ps. 43:2).

• v. 2: "I cry out by day ... [and] by night" (cp. Ps. 42:3: "My tears have been my food day and night").

• vv. 6–8: "I am ... scorned by men and despised by people. All who see me mock me.... 'He trusts in the LORD; let the LORD rescue him'" (cp. Ps. 42:3: "while men say to me all day long, 'Where is your God?'").

• vv. 12–13: "Many bulls surround me.... Roaring lions tearing their prey open their mouths wide against me" (cp. Pss. 35:11, 17; 58:4; 69:34).

• v. 14: "I am poured out like water, and all my bones are out of joint" (cp. Job 30:16–17: "And now my life ebbs away.... Night pierces my bones"; Ps. 31:10: "My bones grow weak"; cp. Job 23:16; Pss. 38:3–8; 55:4; 73:26).

• v. 16: "Dogs have surrounded me; a band of evil men has encircled me (cp. Ps. 59:3, 6: "Fierce men conspire against me ... snarling like dogs").

• v. 16: "They have pierced my hands and my feet" (cp. Job 30:17: "Night pierces my bones"; Prov. 7:23; cp. Isa. 36:6: "pierced hand").

• v. 18: "They divide my garments among them and cast lots for my clothing" (Job 27:17: "What he lays up the righteous will wear, and the innocent will divide his silver").

However, the remarkable clustering of phrases that are perfectly embodied or completed in the suffering of Jesus—the ultimate instance of the suffering of the innocent—can hardly be accidental.

16. Ibid., 104.

17. Sometimes New Testament writers will combine allusions to the Old Testament. For example, Matthew 27:3–8 refers to Zechariah 11:12–13 and (loosely) Jeremiah 18:1–3; 19:11; 32:6–15. These Old Testament passages are not *predictions* about the purchasing of a potter's field with blood money. Zechariah is referring to the prophet's action of casting thirty pieces of silver into the temple treasury (or to the potter—the Hebrew text is unclear), while Jeremiah mentions the potter, place of burial, and purchase of the potter's field. Matthew is drawing on more than one Scripture passage and is resignifying them in 27:3–8, understanding these actions typologically (or as pesher ["this is that"]). What we see in the New Testament is a reenactment of the scriptural story. In this sense, prophecy has been fulfilled.

18. On the other hand, symbols, in which something material represents something immaterial (such as gold, bread, blood, or salt) are *transhistorical* ("timeless"); their meaning cuts across the testaments.

19. R. T. France, *Jesus and the Old Testament* (Downers Grove, Ill.: InterVarsity Press, 1977), 38–39.

20. Ibid., 75 (my emphasis).

• Though national Israel was a "vine" taken from Egypt (Ps. 80:8) or "vineyard" (Isa. 5:1–7), which bore only worthless grapes, Jesus sees himself as "the true/genuine vine" (John 15:1), and those who remain dependent on him "bear much fruit" (John 15:7–8).

• Though Israel was to be a light to the nations (Isa. 42:6), Jesus proclaims himself to be the "light of the world" (John 8:12), and, by virtue of their relationship to him, his new community of disciples participates in this role (Matt. 5:16).

• Alluding to the manna that came to Israel under Moses, Jesus calls himself "the living bread"—unlike the manna that spoiled—and "the bread of life" (John 6:48–51). He was the perfect completion of what the manna could not do: give eternal life.

• Not only is Jesus identified as the new and true Israel in the New Testament, he is also the divine Savior who will rescue his people from the exile of sin. See Wright, *The Challenge of Jesus,* and his comments in *The Meaning of Jesus.*

• Yahweh is the bridegroom of his covenant people Israel (Isa. 62:5), whereas Jesus is the bridegroom for his people (Mark 2:19).

• Yahweh was the shepherd of his people (Ps. 23:1; Ezek. 34:15), whereas Jesus describes himself as the "good shepherd" (John 10:11–16; cp. Mark 14:27).

21. Ibid., 59.

22. Evans, "Function of the Old Testament in the New," 169.

23. Klyne Snodgrass, "The Use of the Old Testament in the New," in *New Testament Criticism and Interpretation,* ed. David Alan Black and David S. Dockery (Grand Rapids: Zondervan, 1991), 416.

24. See Craig A. Evans, "Old Testament in the Gospels," in *Dictionary of Jesus and the Gospels,* ed. I. Howard Marshall et al. (Downers Grove, Ill.: InterVarsity Press, 1992), 570–90; and Robert Banks, *Jesus and the Law in Synoptic Tradition* (Cambridge: Cambridge University Press, 1975). Another piece worth noting is F. F. Bruce, *The Time Is Fulfilled* (Grand Rapids: Eerdmans, 1978).

25. N. T. Wright speaks of the *fluidity* of thought between Israel as the servant and a divine figure in Isaiah 42–53 (*Jesus and the Victory of God* [Minneapolis: Fortress Press, 1996], 602). In Jesus, we see the combining of these referents—the divine figure and true Israel.

26. See Richard Longenecker, "'Who [sic] Is the Prophet Talking About?' Some Reflections on the New Testament's Use of the Old," *Themelios* 13 (October–November 1987): 4–8.

27. Snodgrass, "The Use of the Old Testament," 427. We must be careful of imposing contemporary interpretive standards upon the New Testament writers (which liberal scholars tend to do) and imposing unnatural interpretations on a "prophecy" (as fulfillment of prediction) when prediction was not in view by the Old Testament or New Testament writer (which conservatives tend to do). Cp. Evans, "Function," 193.

CONCLUSION

1. *Richard III,* act I, scene 4.